FOOTBALL'S QUICK PASSING GAME

VOLUME 3:

IMPLEMENTING THE PACKAGE

Andrew Coverdale
Dan Robinson

COACHES CHOICE

ISBN: 1-57167-192-7
Library of Congress Catalog Card Number: 97-69611

Book Design: Michelle A. Summers
Cover Design: Deborah M. Bellaire
Develomental Editor: Joanna Wright
Front Cover Photo: © David Gonzales

Coaches Choice Books is a division of: Sagamore Publishing, Inc.
                                                P.O. Box 647
                                                Champaign, IL 61824-0647
                                                Web Site: http//www.sagamorepub.com

DEDICATION

This book is dedicated to A.J. Rickard, who several years ago gave an impetuous young coach his first opportunity in the profession, and who is among the finest coaches I have ever known in any sport, at any level. My deepest thanks for everything you've done.

—A.C.

This book is dedicated to Coach Ken Kaufman, my mentor, my friend, a first-class gentleman, and one of the finest judges of young football talent in the game of football. Although Coach Kaufman is retired, he taught me most of what I know about coaching young people. I shall always cherish the years he spent on my staff at Northwestern High School.

—D.R.

CONTENTS

"The quick passing game? Oh yeah, you mean like the Slant and the Hitch and the Fade. Sure we've got that. Everybody's got that. What else is there to it?" This type of reaction is probably not uncommon among coaches in America, and logically leads to the question, "why write a whole book on something everybody already does?" The reasons are numerous. First, the simple fact is that, to our knowledge, no such authoritative, comprehensive book exists that details this mode of attack. Secondly, the number of ways to attack with the quick passing game have grown vastly over the past several years, and many of these new ideas are on the very cutting edge of how offenses are dealing with defenses' evolution. Third, and perhaps most importantly, the quick passing game, as a quotation like the one above would indicate, is, in our opinion, a widely underutilized, "taken for granted" way of moving the football that has vast potential to move the chains, increase offensive efficiency on a play-to-play basis, and create numerous opportunities for the best athletes on the field to do what they do best in the open field. Having a full understanding of what it can do within an offense and how to best teach and implement it can be a real plus for any team, for reasons that will be thoroughly spelled out throughout the text. Some coaches will find use for this book as a reference tool; some will find an entire, untapped resource that they can use to make substantial improvements in their scheme.

We would, of course, be remiss in writing any book if we did not acknowledge all the men who have gone before us in advancing offensive football in general, and the quick passing game in particular. As with our previous work, we owe large debts to coaches such as Sid Gillman, Don Coryell, Bill Walsh, and a whole host of contemporary colleagues for their innovations in this area of football. Ideas incorporated into this work have come from a diverse array of sources, ranging from Hanover College to the Green Bay Packers to Wayne State University. A large percentage of the material in this book is not original, and so its strength lies not in being revolutionary, but in the quality of those sources from whom it is drawn and the comprehensiveness and detail with which it breaks down concepts into teachable, useful blocks that can result in very tangible benefits for the reader. It is our sincere hope as fellow coaches that you reap a whole host of those benefits from the pages that follow.

Andrew Coverdale
Dan Robinson

DIAGRAM KEY

B	General symbol for any type of linebacker
C	Cornerback
D	"Dime" player—6th defensive back substituted for a LB
	Also a general symbol refering to defenders in a controlled drill
E	Defensive End
F	Free safety
J	"Joker"—combination rush/drop player in a nickel defense
M	Middle linebacker, either "Mike" or "Mac"
N	Nose tackle, or "Nickel" player—substituted 5th defensive back
R	Symbol for a receiver in a controlled drill situation
S	"Sam," or strongside outside linebacker
SS	Strong safety
T	Defensive tackle
V	General symbol refering to any defensive player
W	"Will," or weakside outside linebacker

Ⓥ   Circle indicates a defender who is the quarterback's primary read or whose movement is key to our thought process in the play design

V̄   Box indicates either a "danger player" to the read or some sort of secondary or pre-snap key for the quarterback.

————o   Indicates a defender's *pre-snap* movements/adjustments

————   Indicates a defender's *post-snap* movements/adjustments

— — —   Shows possible *alternate post-snap* movements and how an offensive player would adjust to such movement.

· · · · ·   Indicates the path of a thrown pass.

- - - - -   Shows a defender matched up in man-to-man coverage with the receiver to whom the line connects him.

●———x   Shows an offensive player going in motion prior to the snap; "x" marks the point where he should be at the snap of the ball.

⊘   Shows original position of an offensive player who has shifted.

↑   ↓   Indicates one person stepping *on* to the line of scrimmage as another steps *off*, possibly as a precursor to pre-snap motion.

CHAPTER 1

Using Play Action with the Quick Passing Game

Play action, when it is carefully taught, and the right actions are matched with the right routes, can be a tremendous way to attack defenses within the quick passing game. *Timing* is the key to its effectiveness, so a premium is placed on the quarterback's footwork, as well as the use of run actions that enable him to fake, get his body in position to make the throw, make a read, and deliver in the correct rhythm. Receivers must often help this process by adjusting the depth of their route.

Systematics of Play Action
Before dealing with the actual actions and routes themselves, we would be remiss if we did not deal with the basics of how a play action pass is assembled in our system. Our basic play action protection is "300" protection, which we will describe in more detail later. "3," then, is always the first of three digits in our play action calls, indicating to our line that 300 is the protection we'll use. This number can be preceded by our other basic protection adjustment calls, such as "Y," "Max," and "Stay."

The next two digits correspond with numbers in our running game and tell the backs what run action we will fake. This number also indicates to the line and receivers the direction of protection and frontside: an even last digit takes the protection and frontside to the right, an odd last digit means both go to the left. Generally, we favor actions that take us to the right, because it helps the quarterback's footwork, vision, and timing a great deal. A summary of the runs we will use for "quick" play action routes and their corresponding numbers is listed below:

06 (right) & **07** (left)	Inside Zone
10 (right) & **11** (left)	Midline "Gut"
20 (right) & **21** (left)	"Slice" Trap
24 (right) & **25** (left)	Veer
36 (right) & **37** (left)	Off-tackle "Blast"

The route package we want to run is indicated with a word or words after the three-digit number. "Stop," for example, indicates that the #1 receiver runs a Stop, the #2 runs a Seam, and #3 runs a "Get Open." Tag words may be added to the route call, just as in basic 90-190 routes.

The full "assembly" of a play action call is illustrated below:

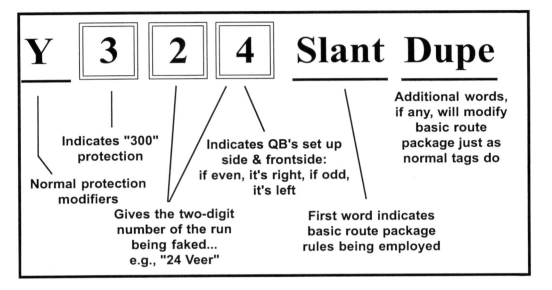

Play Action Protection

As noted, we call our basic play action protection "300." The basic idea of the protection is for our offensive linemen to account for all down people by stepping to the playside gap, with any back or backs accounting for linebackers. Any tight end releasing into his pattern must "slam" release to help his tackle reach the end over him.

Our emphasis, particularly with the linemen, is to take an aggressive, low step. By keeping their head and shoulders low as they come out of their stance, they prevent linebackers and secondary people from keying pass, creating the hesitation we need. Everyone involved must also understand the difference between five-step play action and three-step play action. Three-step play action means that shutting off penetration is vital, especially up the middle.

Structurally, the place that the protection is most likely to run into trouble is from the backside. We use "One" and "Two" calls by our backside tackle to communicate how many potential backside rushers exist that we may not be able to account for with our basic "gap" protection. These players are usually ends or outside linebackers. This call communicates to frontside players how many and which people need to "peel back" to try to handle these people if their initial gap or assignment shows no rushers.

Obviously, this approach isn't always an ideal way to protect, but it is a starting point in the teaching progression. Our next answer, which we use a large percentage of the time, is to keep a backside tight end in to block, which can account for the player who would normally be identified by a "One" call. "Stay" and "Max" calls can give us even more blockers and put extra bodies on either the front or backside. Using these calls means that frontside interior protectors do not have to peel back, leaving them available to hang on double teams and shut down interior penetration, which we noted is vital to running "quick" play action. Since many of the routes we emphasize from our quick play action package are very simple and don't involve backside reads, we will use these types of restrictive protections more with the quick routes than we normally would with our five-step game.

Finally, we will teach our quarterback to identify particular problem fronts, especially eight-man fronts, and have him check out of 300 when he sees them. Usually he can stay with the same base route and just change to 90 protection, because the fronts that would chase us out of 300 usually dictate coverage that simple 90s can be successful against.

Illustrations of our basic 300 protection, along with individual assignments and calls, follow.

DIAGRAM 1-1
BASIC 300 PROTECTION FROM ONE AND TWO BACK SETS

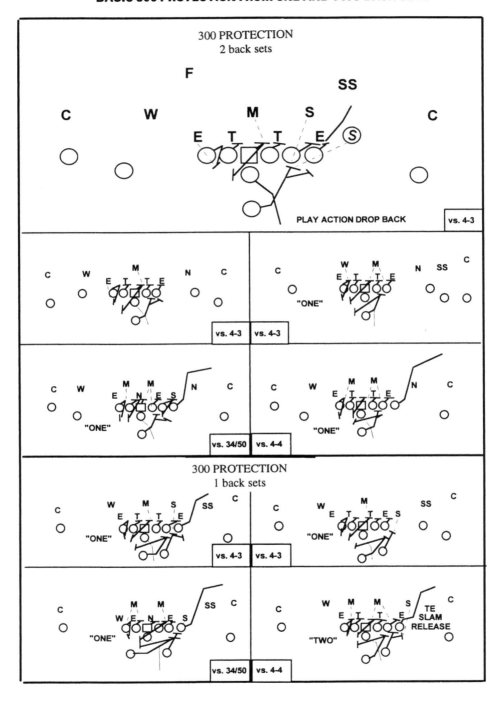

300 Protection Rules

Fundamental Keys: Linemen keep their helmets and pads low, which communicates "run" to linebackers and secondary. Covered linemen drive their man one yard off the line of scrimmage.

Backside Tackle: He is responsible for the "One" and "Two" calls identifying extra backside rushers. He steps to seal the playside gap. If he is uncovered, he looks for stunts from linebacker or defensive linemen; if no one is there, he turns backside for the end man on the line of scrimmage. If he is covered, he seals the playside gap from a slant. He does not hang on double teams.

Backside Guard: He steps to seal the playside gap. If he is covered, he looks for a stunt; if there is none, he turns backside for the end man on the line of scrimmage. If he is covered, he seals the playside gap from a slant. If no one is there to block, he turns to help backside unless we have a "Y," "Stay" or "Max" call on and have no "One" or "Two" call. In those cases, he can look to double to prevent inside penetration.

Center: He steps to seal the playside gap. If he is covered, he looks for a stunt; if there is none, he turns backside for the end man on the line of scrimmage. If he is covered, he seals the playside gap from a slant. If no one is there to block, he turns to help backside unless we have a "Y", "Stay" or "Max" call on and have no "One" or "Two" call. In those cases, he can look to double to prevent inside penetration.

Frontside Guard: He steps to seal the playside gap. If he is covered, he looks for a stunt; if there is none, he turns backside for the end man on the line of scrimmage. If he is covered, he seals the playside gap from slant. If no one is there to block, he turns to help backside unless we have a "Y", "Stay" or "Max" call on and have no "One" or "Two" call. In those cases, he can look to double to prevent inside penetration.

Frontside Tackle: He reminds the tight end to "slam" release into the pattern. His cardinal rule is to *never* allow an inside rush. He steps to seal his playside gap, looking for a stunt from the end man on the line of scrimmage, if he is uncovered. If he is covered, he forces the end man on the line of scrimmage playside.

Frontside Tight End: If he is in the pattern, he "Slam" releases, keeping his outside shoulder free and forcing the end man on the line of scrimmage to inside rush to the offensive tackle. If he is blocking ("Max" or "Y" call), he uses frontside tackle rules.

Backside Tight End: If he is in the pattern, he "Slam" releases, forcing the end man on the line of scrimmage *outside*. If he is kept in to block, he uses Backside Tackle rules.

Running Back: He fakes the run called, rolling over the ball to make a good fake while keeping his head up. He eyes the playside linebacker to the end man on the line of scrimmage. If no rush or stunt shows, he seals the backside from the inside out.

Quarterback: He is responsible for the blitz. He should be aware of rush numbers and stunt problems, checking out or adding protection. He steps to the run fake called, makes a good fake and sets up normally behind the Guard/Tackle gap. He quickly gets his eyes to his read and his body in throwing position.

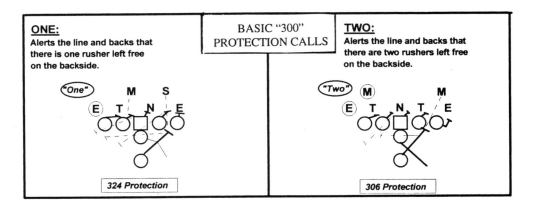

DIAGRAM 1-2
BASIC "ONE" AND "TWO" CALLS FOR 300 PROTECTION

Run Actions

The run actions we use with our "quick" play action routes fall into two categories: "quick flow" and "full flow" actions. Because they simulate runs that hit quickly, our "quick flow" actions enable us to create a brief "mesh point" between quarterback and ball carrier on the way to a quick drop, with the quarterback using a quick, two-handed "jab fake." The general formula for the quarterback's footwork on "quick flow" actions is to take two steps to the mesh point, a "reach step" after the mesh in which he tries to gain depth, and then a "hippity hop," which gathers his feet together in position to drive off the back foot. It is critical on this hippity hop that his front shoulder be down and his body lean forward so that all his momentum is moving forward toward the throw. We reinforce this idea by using the phrase "get your chin over your front knee."

Our two main "quick flow" actions come off our "Veer" play (324-325) and our midline "Gut" (310-311).

In "full flow" run actions, we are employing runs that develop at a slower pace. This slower pace means that the quarterback can not make a full fake at a "mesh point" and still be able to take his drop and make a throw on the right timing. On full flow fakes, we give the running back full responsibility for selling the fake by taking a full-speed course identical to the corresponding run, opening his arms and rolling over an imaginary fake, and attacking into the line. The quarterback's first two steps simulate the run exactly, facing the back. An actual "mesh point" won't have occurred by his second step, though, and he must immediately go from his second step to get his eyes to the read, gaining depth and executing his "hippity hop."

Basic "full flow" run actions include the Inside Zone (306-307), the "Slice Trap" (320-321), and the off-tackle "Blast" (336-337).

One of 300 protection's real strengths is that it gives us the ability to use a variety of different faking actions without changing protection. This ability creates great versatility on game day and in week-to-week preparation without requiring new teaching. These "quick" and "full" flow actions are illustrated and detailed below:

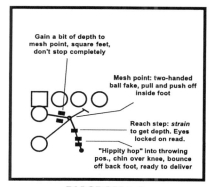

DIAGRAM 1-3
324-325 "VEER" ACTION MECHANICS

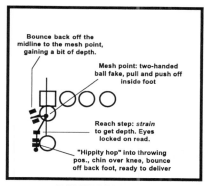

DIAGRAM 1-4
310-311 "GUT" ACTION MECHANICS

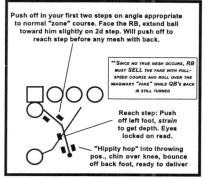

DIAGRAM 1-5
306-307 "ZONE" ACTION MECHANICS

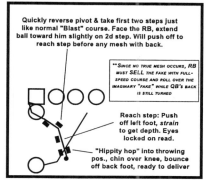

DIAGRAM 1-6
336-337 "BLAST" ACTION MECHANICS

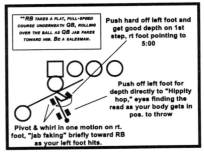

DIAGRAM 1-7
320-321 "SLICE" ACTION MECHANICS

The Routes

The Slant

The Slant is the quick route that may have the best application to play action, because the run fake can attack and help account for players that cause the Slant the most problems: inside linebackers. A good play fake forces them to take one to two steps forward; in doing so, they lose any chance of getting into the Slant's throwing lane. At times on the straight dropback Slant, the flat coverage will run with the Shoot, leading the quarterback to think he should throw the Slant, only to have it taken away from an active inside linebacker who has worked from the inside out. Play action can neutralize this problem.

When Slants are called with play action, it is important that receivers lengthen their route by about one yard or one step, and spend "quality time" on any misdirection moves. If they do not, they will get through the open lane too quickly and have become almost a "skinny post" by the time the quarterback is ready to throw. This action brings the free safety into the picture, makes the quarterback's throw difficult, and in general creates all sorts of problems. Widening their split 1-2 yards also helps maintain the right timing.

The first example we will look at is a combination Bill Walsh developed successfully many years ago, using a full-flow, Slice trap fake from split backs:

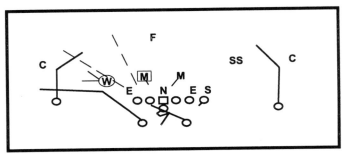

DIAGRAM 1-8
SPLIT RIP Y321 SLANT
Trap fake to hold M and isolate W on two receivers

The read is the same as a normal Slant, W being the flat defender that is read, and M the inside backer that we have held, widening the throwing lane considerably. The Shoot coming from the backfield helps the Slant come open in the timing that the quarterback needs. If he was lined up wide, the Slant would have a tendency to come open far too early.

Another formation concept that lends itself well to play action Slants is our "Ram," or two tight end, two receiver package. It is a staple running set, it allows for good protection backside, and it often creates defensive adjustments that are based on crowding interior run lanes. The "Veer" action, or "324/325" is one we like to use with this type of set, because its wide track gives us a chance to hold two linebackers on the fake side.

The first "Ram" package illustration uses a trips rule Slant off this Veer fake. Most times, a maximum of two short defenders (often fewer) will be able to effectively get into coverage on the Slant side because of the play action. The read for the quarterback is not much more complicated than "throw to the one they don't cover" (see Diagrams 9 to 11 in Vol. 1 Chap 7), giving the Shoot his first attention since it is the one that will potentially be open first. Because of protection and timing concerns, the tight end will slam the outside shoulder of the end as he releases, which slows this defender's progress, gets the receiver into the flat area in the right timing, and most important, helps sell the run. It is important that he step to the outside shoulder of the defender, because he will have a tendency to get held up and not get cleanly into the pattern if he does not keep moving and keep his outside shoulder free.

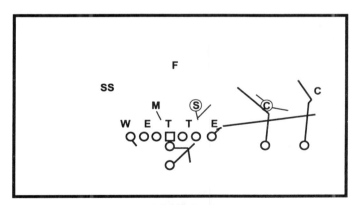

DIAGRAM 1-9
RAM X F324 SLANT
3 on 2 situation vs. S & C—throw to the one they don't cover

In the second "Ram" illustration, we take advantage of a front that has become a very common "adjustment front" against two tight ends: the 6-1 with both outside linebackers locked down over the tight ends. By faking the Veer directly at the outside linebacker and aggressively blocking him with the tight end, we force this defender to play run. This action opens the Slant lane outside him.

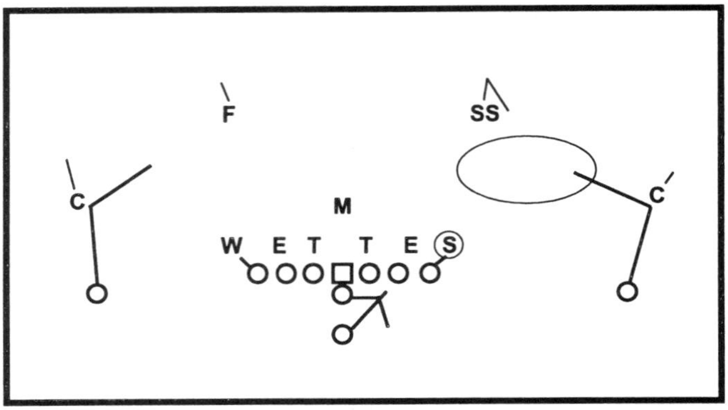

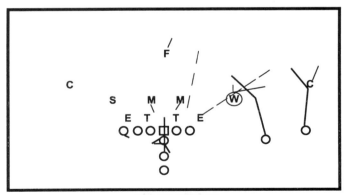

DIAGRAM 1-10
RAM MAX 324 SLANT
Taking advantage of 6-1 adjustment, faking right at S. Slant
must flatten route slightly to avoid SS

Slants are also proven as a solid complement to the Freeze Option series. Faking the midline "Gut" portion of this series holds the inside linebackers and isolates two Slants on one short defender.

DIAGRAM 1-11
RAY Y310 SLANT DUPE VS. 4-4 COVER 3

The Hitch

In much the same fashion as the previous illustration, the Hitch route can be "Duped" to attack and isolate a short defender off the Gut Freeze action. While a play action Hitch done this way may not have the same explosive run after catch potential of the Slant, something is gained because it is a stationary, more high-percentage throw. Again, the outside Hitch needs to deepen his break from six to seven yards. The inside Hitch will break at six yards as he normally would, but he has the added freedom to maneuver between the first and second short defenders to be certain he is in an open window. Again, the inside linebacker must honor the Gut fake, allowing the quarterback to throw to the Hitch that the first short defender inside the cornerback doesn't cover.

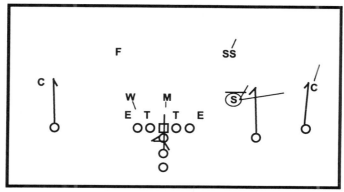

DIAGRAM 1-12
ROY 310 HITCH DUPE VS. 4-3 COVER 4

The Stop

Because of the depth of the Stop, the rhythm of the throw for the quarterback is often more natural from play action than from a normal three-step drop. Either "quick flow" or "full flow" fakes can be adapted for effective use with the Stop.

When using play action with this route, our purpose is to create just enough hesitation by a run force-conscious flat defender to hinder him from working underneath the Stop on the outside. Often, formations will be used in conjunction with this idea to dictate coverage to this flat player.

In the first illustration, two receivers are placed to the left to set the strong safety in underneath coverage on that side, while two tackles are placed in an unbalanced set to the right to force the flat player on that side to lock down tightly to keep from being outflanked for the run. Many times a 50 defense will have a "drop" end who is more of a cover player that normally lines up weak to drop to the flat opposite the strong safety, and a "strong" end who is a thicker player normally set over the tight end who rarely, if ever, drops into coverage. This formation has forced a strong end into a position where he does not have the strong safety or anyone else outside him to cover the flat, yet is still locked down over a third body to his side. We then fake right at him, and if he *is* assigned to the flat, where he is not used to going, he will have a tough time getting there.

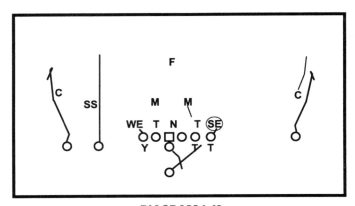

DIAGRAM 1-13
BEAR 9 Y306 STOP VS. 50 DEFENSE
Locking down a strongside end with unbalanced—no one underneath the Stop

The second "Stop" example shows the use of the "Ram" package again, trying to take advantage of a 6-1 adjustment. Again, the Veer is faked and the outside linebacker aggressively blocked, isolating the cornerback. Motion is used in this case to create a coverage check that will create a bit of pre-snap movement by the cornerbacks, hopefully "loosening" them.

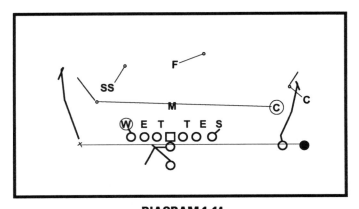

DIAGRAM 1-14
RAM X X11 MAX 325 STOP
Holding 6-1 flat coverage with fake directly at him. Motion used to soften cornerback

The Quick Smash

Within the past several years, defenses have begun to use their safeties in run support much more than previously. Often, this support comes in the form of "Cover 4" and "Double Invert" packages in which safeties on either side read the tight end or tackle over them and move quickly into a run support position if their key blocks aggressively (see Vol. 1 Chap 5). Against these types of defenses, a play action "Quick Smash" can be effective because the fake can gain at least a moment's hesitation by a run conscious hash safety, which in turn really helps open up the Quick Smash by #2. In throwing the Quick Smash off play action, we will tell the Hitch not to deepen, but to hesitate a count before releasing to help the timing. His final depth remains at six yards because we don't want the spacing between the Hitch and Quick Smash to change, for fear that it could allow the cornerback to cover them both.

Two examples of how a play action Quick Smash could be used follow; again, the quarterback is reading the cornerback, and will never try to throw the Quick Smash over his head if his read is retreating.

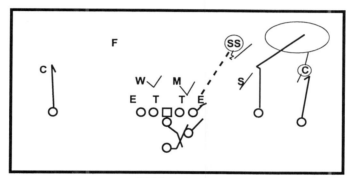

DIAGRAM 1-15
STRONG REX 336 QUICK SMASH VS. 4-3 COVER 4
SS keying right tackle steps up briefly when he sees
aggressive block—hole opened for Quick Smash

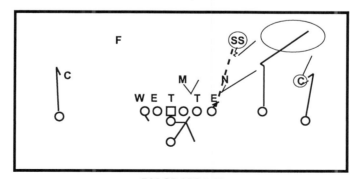

DIAGRAM 1-16
BEAR 8 Y324 QUICK SMASH VS. COVER 2 INVERT
SS keying right tackle steps up briefly when he sees
aggressive block—hole opened for Quick Smash

The Fade

Play-action Fades can be used to attack in two basic ways. First, play action at times can function in a similar fashion as with the Quick Smash, holding a hash safety to enlarge the hole on the deep outside portion of coverages in the "Cover 2" and "Cover 4" families. Secondly, play action Fades can be employed to gain a step on the short defender responsible for the Break Out (who is reading the offensive tackle), either to a two- or three-receiver side.

Because we have two different "Fade" packages, it is important systematically to distinguish for our players that if we call, for example, "324 Fade," we will use the "Fade/Out" rules rather than the "Fade/Seam" rules (see Vol. 1 Chap 8). If we wanted the latter, we would call "324 Fade/Seam." For us, the Fade/Out is the more useful because it provides both of the dimensions noted above, and is thus used as the "default."

Several examples of both the "doubles" and "trips" rule play-action Fades are depicted below. In each, you can see that we are accounting for the short defender nearest the Break Out through the fake, and reading the cornerback. The quarterback should remember that through his fake and footwork, we are still operating off of three-step timing. In other words, he still has to be able to get his body in a position to drive the Fade in between a Cover 2 corner and safety at 18 yards if his read tells him to; this pass is not to be a 35 yard throw down the field. Timing is vital.

The Break Out is told to get a *full* 6 to 6 1/2 yards of depth before breaking, pushing inside a bit at the short defender he is defeating. The Fade, likewise, spends a bit longer on his release technique—either ensuring a clean, outside escape versus a hard cornerback, or turning a soft corner's hips inside—so he does not run past the open void behind the cornerback too early or outrun the quarterback's arm.

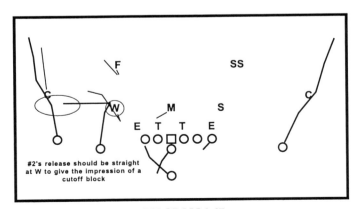

DIAGRAM 1-17
RIP 9 Y307 FADE VS. COVER 4
Using play action to gain a step on W for Break Out

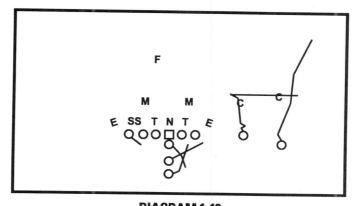

DIAGRAM 1-18
RAY Y336 FADE VS. COVER 1
Play action gives #2 more time to develop his route and
gain separation from C. QB can peek at deep throw to Fade

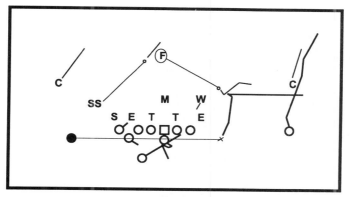

DIAGRAM 1-19
BLUE LIZ MINUS Z8 STAY 320 FADE VS. COVER 3

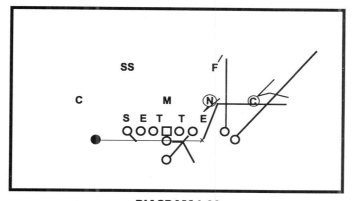

DIAGRAM 1-20
SQUEEZE RAY 9 H6 Y324 FADE VS. COVER 2
Holding N while putting C in a bind with a lot of field to cover

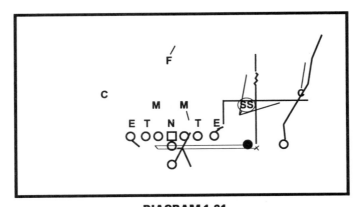

DIAGRAM 1-21
RAM X Z RETURN F324 FADE VS. COVER 3
Motion loosens SS & helps time up Seam; QB reads Out to
Seam off SS after fake

"Short" Variations

The "Short" route and its variations can be emphasized in two basic ways. First, the basic "Short" combination can be helped by a "quick flow" fake that holds the inside linebacker who is often a "danger" to the basic combination. The ability to hold this player with the fake and thus isolate the next defender outside him allows you to run the "Short" against more coverages and from different field widths. The fake must, however, be a "quick flow" fake, or the timing will be a real problem. The Short helps timing by pushing up one yard before coming inside, and the Slant helps timing by lining up off the ball and stretching his route 1/2 yard deeper.

Next, the "Plant" tag to the Short can be effectively used off play action, since the deeper "Plant" naturally lends itself to play action rhythm. Again, an inside linebacker is held to isolate the next short defender outside him on the Plant and the Short. The Plant needs no depth adjustment except to ensure that he gets a full 8 to 9 yards, and the Short once again pushes up a yard before breaking.

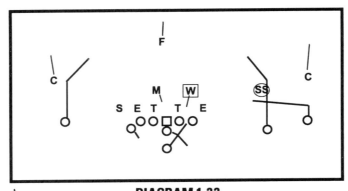

DIAGRAM 1-22
L 8 Y324 SHORT VS. COVER 3
Holding the "danger" LB with the fake, Short & Slant isolated on SS

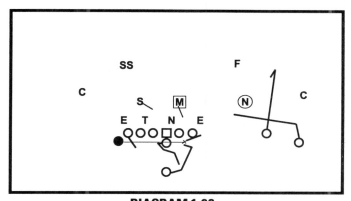

DIAGRAM 1-23
RAY PLUS F4 Y336 SHORT Z PLANT VS. COVER 4
Blast fake to hold M inside, isolate N on Plant/Short combination

The Turn

Very quick play action can help the Turn by forcing hesitation on the part of the man that the Turn route is assigned to beat: The second short defender inside the cornerback, usually an inside linebacker. Freezing this man creates a clean two-on-one isolation on the *first* short defender inside the corner, which enables the play to function optimally.

The Turn will push to six or seven yards before making his break, and the Shoot will push up a step deeper than he normally would before accelerating flat to the outside. The quarterback's fake will be very fast paced, since we only need *hesitation* on the part of the linebacker we're attacking, and this hesitation can largely be created by the low, aggressive steps of the line and the action of the back. It is more important for the quarterback to get his eyes quickly to the read and his hips immediately into throwing position than it is for him to make the great fake.

Following are examples of play action "Turn" adaptations.

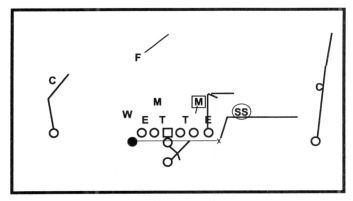

DIAGRAM 1-24
RIP HIP F6 324 TURN VS. COVER 3
M held by fake, SS isolated on Shoot and Turn

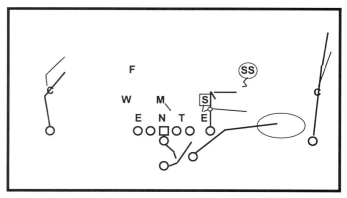

DIAGRAM 1-25
NASTY BROWN RIP 306 TURN SWITCH VS. COVER 2 INVERT
Good chance to hit the Shoot in open space, since **SS** will likely jump the tight end upon seeing his release; **S**, responsible for near back, will be held by fake and have to negotiate a course around the Turn; **C** will be run off by Go outside.

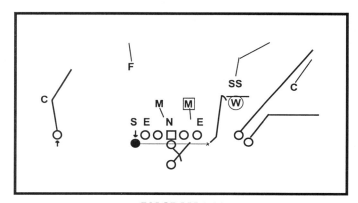

DIAGRAM 1-26
BUNCH LIZ 8 Y6 324 TURN TRADE VS. QUARTERS
Fade by #2 draws bracket coverage by **SS & C**, isolating **W** on the Turn and the Shoot after Veer fake holds **M**.

CHAPTER 2

Creating and Using "Packaged Calls" within the Quick Passing Game

One of the recent additions to our offense that has really helped our development and improved our good play/bad play ratio is the use of "packaged" calls and sides. By packaging two or more plays together in a huddle call (the quarterback choosing from among them at the line and using an appropriate cadence to alert the team of his choice), or packaging different sides of a route to do different jobs within a single play call, we take much of the guesswork out of our own playcalling and eliminate some of the "surprise element" that the defense can wield by building answers for a number of different defenses into our package. For the quick passing game, we have a number of reasons for wanting to package a call; we are accounting for specific factors in our quick passing packaged calls:

1. **Man or Zone?** Obviously, some of our routes are built to function much better against man coverage than others, while we have certain things that we really like better against zones. Because we can often make this distinction through a pre-snap read of the defense or through motion, packaged calls that give us the best of both help us get the best play regardless of which we see.

2. **Cover 2 or Cover 3? Hard Corner or Soft Corner?** Some teams on our schedule do a good job of mixing different coverages from down to down. If we don't have a really good line on what they might be playing on a given down, we will create a packaged call that includes good options versus both possibilities rather than guess. Having a Cover 2 package and a Cover 3 option is the most common form of this, though teams who play different types of basic coverage demand different multiple-coverage package calls. We can also create more generalized packages, based simply on whether the cornerbacks are aligned tight or loose rather than a specific coverage.

3. **Underneath Coverage Structure.** The nature of our offense is to use a wide variety of formations, many of which are used by no one else in our league. As a result, we may have no idea from game to game how our opponent will defend given sets because we have not seen them face it on film. We have to account not only for different, generalized forms of coverage, as discussed above, but

also for structural adjustments with linebackers and underneath people that occur within those coverages against our formations.

For example, we might face a team that plays Cover 3 the whole game, but against certain forms of Trips they slide their linebackers in such a way that the Trips side is overloaded, opening the Slant lane on the backside. Other forms of Trips might not warrant the same adjustment, making the Trips side more workable. Rather than wasting a play to find out what's what to the defense, we will teach and call packages that give us a chance no matter what the underneath adjustment.

4. **Techniques Within Coverages**. Different teams and players within teams have different idiosyncracies and techniques within coverages and calls. For example, safeties play different widths and with different emphases within Cover 2. Packaging helps us work against all these variations.

5. **Boundary and Field Considerations**. Some of our quick passes are much better to the wide field, while some of them do quite well into the boundary. Instead of wasting an entire side of a route on a field width situation that doesn't make use of it, we can package that other side with a route that makes the best use of the width (or lack of width) provided.

6. **QB "Feel."** At times, especially with a veteran quarterback who has become a master of the system, our packaging is less scientific. Sometimes we can provide a package from which, all other major factors being equal, the quarterback can just choose the one he has the best *feeling* about on the field. We believe we are much better off when our field general has great confidence in what is being called, and this type of flexibility lends itself to him having something to run that he can have great faith in. It is also true that players can sometimes see and understand certain things from the trenches that we cannot from the sideline or press box; packaged calls can help account for that as well. Obviously, giving the quarterback this kind of license is not a starting point and is not done haphazardly. It can only happen after all the other fundamental training is already in place and ingrained in his mind; he must already have complete command of the system.

A number of categories fall within the broad idea of "packaging" that we will use, all of which will be discussed throughout this chapter. The first category is to create different packages within a certain call, which we do with what we call a "B" tag. The next general category encompasses those packages that depend on a "check with me" situation where the quarterback determines the part of the package that will actually be run at the line of scrimmage. The two basic ways we do this are: a) with "Run/Quick" checks where the quarterback chooses between a running play and one or more quick passes, and b) with "Quick/Quick" checks that give the quarterback a choice between two quick passes.

Packaged Sides and the "B" Tag

The "B" tag is a very specific type of Backside tag that expands our capabilities in creating combinations away from our call side. In short, the "B" tag enables us to take any combination of routes that we normally use on the frontside and apply it to our backside receivers, further enabling us to "mix and match" route combinations on either side of the ball, giving us a virtually unlimited toolbox full of ways that we can construct the best possible route package for any given situation. "B" is short for "Backside," and is followed by the name of one of our conventional route combinations, telling the backside receivers that they take on the assignments of that route package.

For example, "91 B Slant" means "91 (frontside "Hitch" rules), with the backside receivers running a Slant combination." In this example we would get a Hitch and a Seam on the right, or front, side, and a Slant and Shoot on the left, or "B" side. "194 B Quick Smash" indicates that receivers on the left side execute "Stop" route rules, while the backside to the right will run Quick Smash.

This tag is a very potent tool we have at our disposal, and will begin employing very early on to ensure that we have answers to anything the defense can show us, and to give our quarterback a number of options.

"Short" with "Turn": 97 B Turn

Because the "Short" route is dependent on wide field space to operate correctly, we need a tag to use on the boundary side that complements it when we are on a hash. The "Turn" fits this description well because it does not need a wide field to be successful with a two receiver rule. The two things that can take the Turn away would be a) a hard corner rolled up to the Turn side playing with outside leverage, or b) an underneath coverage structure that overadjusts to the Turn side. Either of these adjustments should provide leverage for the Short. This package is a solid, high-percentage combination to gain four to six yards.

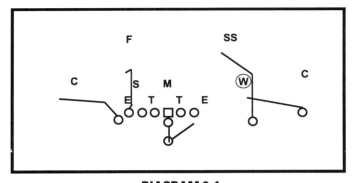

DIAGRAM 2-1
RAY OUT 97 B TURN
Hard corner takes away Turn; W isolated 2 on 1 on W

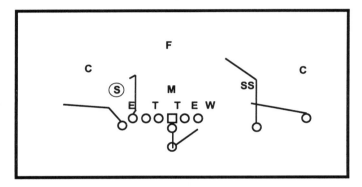

DIAGRAM 2-2
RAY OUT 97 B TURN
Soft corner to Turn side, underneath coverage allows clean
2 on 1 vs. S backer—throw the Turn

Short with "In": 97 B In

While the Short route, with the right separation technique, is adequate against man coverage, it is really at its optimum against zone defenses. The exact opposite is true of the "In." While adequate against zone, it is one of the two or three best things we do against man. These two routes naturally work, then, as a zone/man package. The pairing of such a distinct zone-beater and a strong man-beater is a very effective concept as you approach the Red Zone, because defenses are often in a transition period as you cross their 30 and then their 25. Teams who rely mostly on zone coverage in the regular operating field begin to play more and more man, but you're not sure exactly when they will and exactly how much man you will get. "97 B In" is an example of a tool that can deal with this problem.

In the example below, we use motion to define and reveal things for our quarterback prior to the snap. If he sees a man running with the motioning halfback, he knows there is man coverage and he'll work the "In" side. If he only sees sliding/adjusting by linebackers, or no movement at all, it's zone to him and he works the "Short" side.

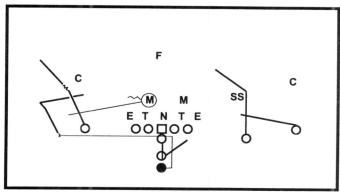

DIAGRAM 2-3
ROY H11 97 B IN
If M runs with motion (MAN), throw In;
if M bumps (ZONE), throw Short

Short with Fade: 97 B Fade/Seam

Against two-deep coverages, the Fade/Seam can also be used as a companion to the Short, providing an insurance policy into the boundary for the quarterback if he feels the safeties tightening down to squeeze the inside Slant (which can happen through a planned defensive disguise coverage or simply an individual defender's habits/technique) *or* if the wide field underneath coverage isn't to his liking.

One of the complementary, disguised coverages many defenses that employ a two-deep look use is a "double invert" principle in which man is played by the corners on the outside, and the two deep safeties play tighter and read to either support the run quickly or employ a tight man coverage on #2 to their side. This coverage could cause problems for 97 if the hash safety crept up and took the Slant away, and the Short couldn't shake free of the inside leverage corner playing man against him. In this particular case, the backside Fade package saves us from such treachery, because we have a good vertical combination away from the Short working against this tightened coverage. The quarterback knows to go there immediately when he sees the safeties tightened before the snap.

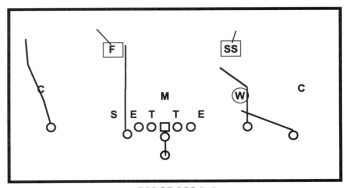

DIAGRAM 2-4
L 10 97 B FADE/SEAM VS. BASIC COVER 2
Safeties at normal depth, nothing taking away "Short"

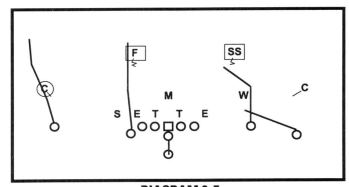

DIAGRAM 2-5
L 10 97 B FADE/SEAM VS. COVER 2 INVERT
Work Fade/Seam when safeties jump into low,
aggressive coverage

"Stop" with "Turn": Stretching underneath coverage

The Stop and Turn work very well together because it is very difficult for underneath coverage to stretch themselves to the extent that they can get someone underneath the Stop on one side and have two short defenders in a position to deal with the Turn on the other, while being gap sound against the run. In using this package, we will simply prioritize one route or the other by calling it as the main route, and then tagging the other as the "B" tag to let the quarterback know where he goes if the underneath structure takes away the first choice. In other words, "94 B Turn" means we are throwing the Stop unless underneath coverage slides to take it away and leaves the Turn open opposite it; "95 B Stop" is a call in which the Turn is to be thrown unless two short defenders are in close proximity and Stop will not be threatened from underneath.

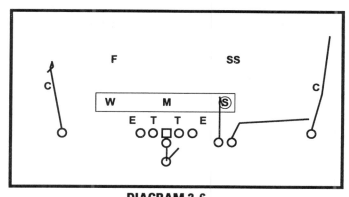

DIAGRAM 2-6
RON PAIR 95 B STOP
Underneath coverage can't take away 95—go ahead with Turn

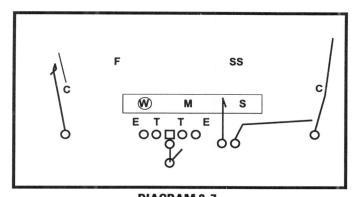

DIAGRAM 2-7
RON PAIR 95 B STOP
Two short defenders within reach of Turn; no one to get under Stop

Packaged Fade Combinations: 98 B Fade/Seam

The Fade/Seam can also work well as an "insurance" boundary tag paired with a "Fade/Out" to the wide field. Here, we make use of field width with our Fade and Out. Both of these routes, employed in this kind of space, can cause problems for defenders' angles. The room that the wide field creates to run in also creates good run after catch possibilities. Using "Bunched" alignments can enhance both of these benefits, creating a more unfamiliar angle for breaking defenders, and additional leeway to run outside.

Regardless of coverage or our sets, we can work this Fade/Out combination by throwing off the cornerback if he is lined up tight, or emphasizing the Out if he is soft. The only situation that frustrates this plan is if, in Cover 2, the safeties are aligned wide in position to stop the Fade, leaving the corners free to squat in the flat and sit on the inside Breakout. When the quarterback sees this type of width by the safeties, he knows to go backside, since he has two vertical routes to control that safety.

Summarized, the thought process is: "Go wide side Fade/Out, and key flat coverage. Fade or Out off the cornerback if he is tight, hit the Out running into space against a soft corner. If Cover 2 with wide safeties shows, go backside and work off the safety deep, Fade to Seam."

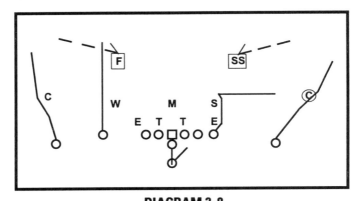

DIAGRAM 2-8
RIP 9 98 B FADE/SEAM VS. COVER 2 SHELL
Work Fade/Out unless safeties gain drastic width through alignment or movement

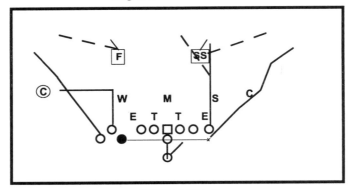

DIAGRAM 2-9
SQUEEZE LARRY 7 H6 198 B FADE/SEAM
Packaged Fade concepts in a squeezed environment to cause difficult angles for the safeties; quick motion and "stacked" effect of H's Fade off TE's hip can create an effective "wall" for him vs. man coverage.

Trips Fade/Out with Slant: 98 B Slant

Another concept applicable to "Bunch" packages is a pairing of a Trips rule Fade/Out with a single Slant backside. With a Fade, a Seam, and an Out all popping out of a bunched environment to create potential picks and two-on-one situations both deep (with the Fade and Seam) and short (with the Fade and Out or Seam and Out), the only thing that can take away our frontside leverage is an over-rotation by either a safety or the linebackers to our trips side. Either of these adjustments is easily recognizable before the snap, and they both create an open lane for the backside Slant.

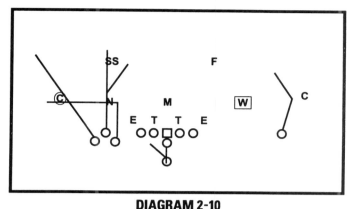

DIAGRAM 2-10
SQUEEZE LEX 7 198 B SLANT VS. BASIC COVER 2
**W in a position to take away Slant; lack of LB slide to trips
leaves leverage for 3 receiver Fade**

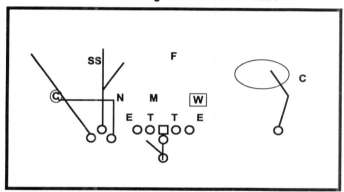

DIAGRAM 2-11
SQUEEZE LEX 7 198 B SLANT VS. COVER 3 CLOUD
Slant left open by linebacker slide to trips

Other "B" Tag Applications

The "B" tag can be used in limitless ways, from all kinds of formations, depending on the coverages you face and the quick passes you want to emphasize. Some other examples of "B" tags follow, including packages from "Empty" no-back formations as well as basic two-back looks.

No-back sets, when equipped with sound protection principles, can be an ideal way to use the "B" tag because they provide a trips side and a doubles side, enabling good route leverage to be gained on either. The stretch created in the defense, especially horizontally, can help open seams as well, and matchups are improved. This stretch also tends to make coverage identification clearer and easier for the quarterback, since it is much harder for defenses to disguise effectively with so much width to cover.

The two-back versions show sound ways that "B" tag packaging can be very effective even without the use of wider, multiple receiver sets. These sets provide the opportunity to use seven- and eight-man protection schemes, increasing the number of double-teams that can be utilized up front.

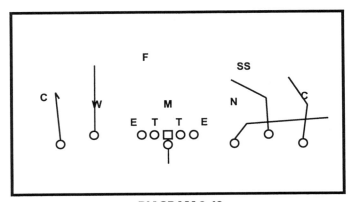

DIAGRAM 2-12
EMPTY 93 B HITCH
Throw the Slant vs. Man, Hitch vs. Zone

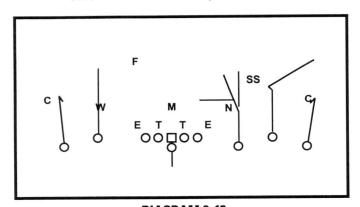

DIAGRAM 2-13
EMPTY 96 B HITCH
Throw the Quick Smash vs. Cover 2, the Hitch vs. Cover 3

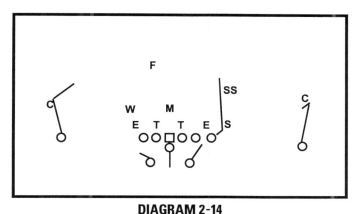

DIAGRAM 2-14
SPLIT RIP 91 B SLANT
Hitch is thrown against ZONE coverages, Slant against MAN

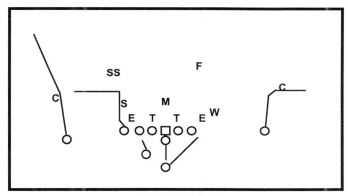

DIAGRAM 2-15
STRONG LIZ 198 B QUICK OUT
Throw Fade vs. Cover 2, Quick Out vs. Cover 3

"Run/Quick" Checks

In packaging a quick pass with a run in a "check with me" situation, we are trying to account for the number of defenders a defense leaves in the "box," and/or the width of edge players who could serve as run supporters or pass defenders. In doing so, we hope to provide ourselves with a numerical edge.

This type of check can be a great first-down concept, because it provides a guarantee of a high-percentage play to gain solid yards, which is often vital to the success of second and third down. Depending on the strength of your running game, "run/quick checks" may have similar use on third and three to six.

If the number of defenders that can be involved in immediately defending the run is no greater than the number of blockers we have available, we feel that it is to our advantage to run, because we can create angles for blocking and leverage to run with those numbers.

If there is one more defender than blocker, it is in our best interests to throw, because the extra defender who has been committed to the run can not easily defend quick routes, and the extra numbers in the box often mean specific voids have been left in the coverage.

Should there be two more defenders than blockers, it is indicative of a either a blitz coverage or an uncovered receiver, either of which requires a special blocking check or uncovered call.

Translated, in our one-back sets we usually run against five in the box, throw versus six in the box, and check when there are seven. In two-back looks, we'll run against six, throw versus seven, and check against eight. In our case, our philosophy commits us to the former of these two more often, but the principle holds true for either type of formation.

When using this check, it is important to use sets and alignment that force outside linebackers and strong safeties to clearly distinguish whether they are going to be part of the secondary covering the pass, or in the front defending the run. If they try to play in between, the uncovered throws discussed in chapter three must become an equalizer, or this whole "run/quick check" concept breaks down.

Following are some examples of check packages we might typically use.

Counter or 91 Hitch
In this case, we are operating from a basic "Flex" set, placing two pairs of split receivers on either side of the ball. Against a five-man front like the one shown in Diagram 2-16, we have a terrific angle to double team the tackle back to the middle linebacker and kick out the frontside end on our Counter Trap. Our numbers also mean we can shut down backside penetration by having a tackle available to block the end, which sometimes does not happen in traditional counter schemes. The quarterback will always check the counter to be run away from the defensive tackle with the tightest technique, making the center's job easier in blocking back.

Teams that put six in the box against this formation are generally confined to some form of Cover 3, assuming all receivers are covered down. If they are, we have a tailor-made Hitch/Seam combination in which we can work off the flat defender, most often hitting the Hitch. Diagram 2-17 illustrates this scenario.

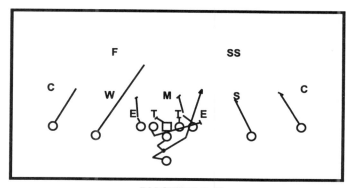

DIAGRAM 2-16
FLEX CHECK 91 OR COUNTER VS. 4-1 COVER 2
Check to Counter vs. 5 in the box—excellent blocking angles

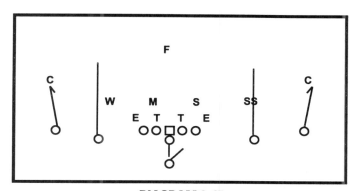

DIAGRAM 2-17
FLEX CHECK 91 OR COUNTER VS. 4-1 COVER 3
Check to Hitch vs. 6 in the box—soft corner for Hitch

Isolation or 92 Quick Out

The next two examples illustrate the same principle with a lead blocker added.
Now, we look to run against six in the box to get good angles for the isolation, while
checking to the throw if we see seven in the box, in this case the Quick Out. Again,
the split of the #2 receiver is vital; he must force the outside linebacker or safety
over him to either distinctly widen and play pass or leave him definitively uncovered.
The defender can not be allowed to play both.

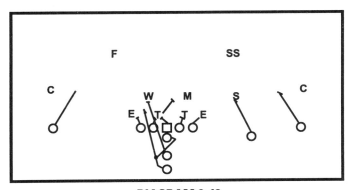

DIAGRAM 2-18
REX CHECK 92 OR ISOLATION VS. 4-2 COVER 2
2-back check vs. 6 men in the box—good blocking angles

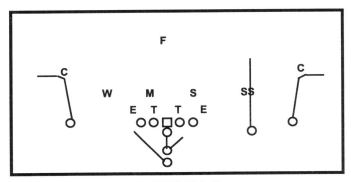

DIAGRAM 2-19
REX CHECK 92 OR ISOLATION VS. 4-3 COVER 3
Check to Quick Out vs. 7 in the box

Checks off the width of a single defender

Many times we will have a good idea of the general type of structure a team will use throughout a game, but will not always know how specific players will align within this structure. To account for this player, we will pair a run that can get "under" him should he align wide with a quick pass that will cause problems for him if he lines up tight. Examples of this type of call are on the following page.

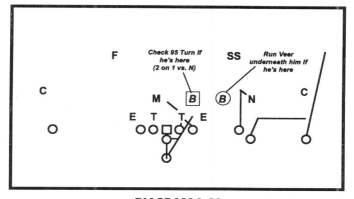

DIAGRAM 2-20
REX OUT CHECK 95 OR VEER OFF WIDTH OF B BACKER
2 on 1 vs. N for Turn if he's tight, good angles for Veer
underneath if he's wide

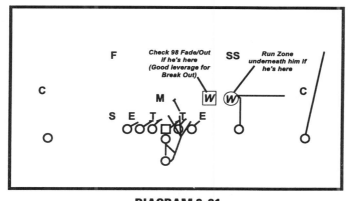

DIAGRAM 2-21
LIZ 8 CHECK 98 OR ZONE VS. 4-3 COVER 4
Breakout to #2 if W is tight; Zone to bubble if W is wide

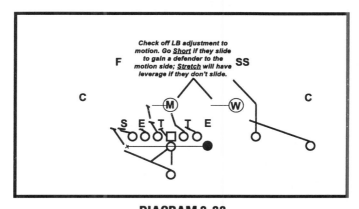

DIAGRAM 2-22
RAY HIP F7 CHECK STRETCH OR 97 SHORT VS. COVER 2
Stretch with leverage if LBs don't adjust with motion;
Short into a void if they slide to the motion side.

"Quick/Quick" Checks

The last type of "packaged call" for the quick passing game is something we refer to as a "quick/quick" check. We send in a formation and give the quarterback two quick passes from which he can choose at the line of scrimmage based on coverage. Generally we will use this type of check instead of a "B" tag in situations where we are certain that we can get a distinct pre-snap read on the defense and/or we feel it important to have mirrored sides of the same route available for the quarterback to choose from. We will use the "quick/quick" check to account for all the same types of situations that the other checks accounted for: basic coverage, underneath structure, man/zone, etc. Shown below are a few examples of common types of "quick/quick" checks.

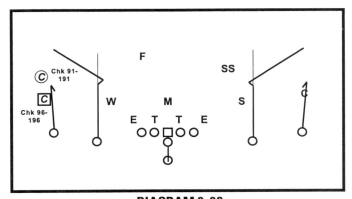

DIAGRAM 2-23
FLEX 91 OR 96 OFF CORNERBACK DEPTH
Check 91 vs. a soft corner, 96 vs. a hard corner—
guarantees the best percentage "Hitch" package

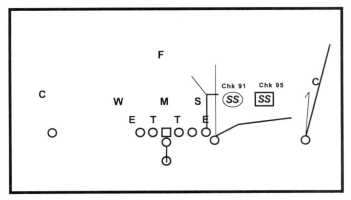

DIAGRAM 2-24
RIP PLUS CHECK 91 OR 95 OFF SS WIDTH
Tight safety can't get under Hitch (Check 91);
Wide safety opens up lane for Turn (Check 95)

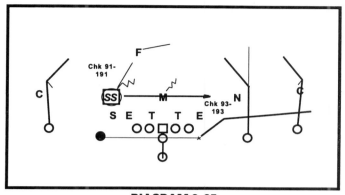

DIAGRAM 2-25
FLEX H6 CHECK 91 OR 93 OFF MAN OR ZONE
SS chases (MAN), check Slant;
SS & others bump (ZONE), check Hitch

CHAPTER 3

Applying the Quick Passing Game to Situational Football

The success that Bill Walsh has had throughout his career with Stanford, the Cincinnati Bengals, and the San Francisco 49ers has served to heighten the awareness of coaches everywhere as to the importance of *situational football* over the past two decades. The situational approach extends not only to preparing certain plays for certain down, distance, and field situations, but also has implications for practice, installations, and the "big picture" planning of our offense (Brian Billick of the Minnesota Vikings does an excellent, in depth job of spelling out this idea in his recent book, *Developing an Offensive Game Plan*).

Stated differently, situational work is what gives offensive theory and the daily grind of practice real, focused relevance and purpose. When players can see definite, realistic application of the things they're learning and being drilled on, focus and improvement levels increase. The other obvious benefit is that when these situations come up in vital parts of games, a sense of confidence has been instilled in your team because they know what to do and they have been there before.

It is for those reasons that every play in our playbook, when introduced, includes a discussion of specific places and times we might call it (see playbook page samples in Appendix A). It is for those same reasons that the teaching and practicing of these situations, what they entail, and what must be done to be successful within them begins very early in pre-season camp. We consider this educating process very important. This process is further reinforced by "situation sheets" that are given to the players which, as they are filled out in meetings, will preview and then reinforce the "situational education" they are receiving on the field. Samples of these follow.

TAYLOR FOOTBALL
SITUATION SHEET

Situation	What we must do as a team:	Things I Must DO:	Things I Must AVOID:	Favored Plays
"BACKED UP"				
RED ZONE: +25				
RED ZONE: +10				
RED ZONE: +5				
1ST AND 10				
2ND AND LONG				
3RD AND 2 OR LESS				
3RD AND 3				

TAYLOR FOOTBALL
SITUATION SHEET

Situation	What we must do as a team:	Things I Must DO:	Things I Must AVOID:	Favored Plays
3RD AND 4 TO 6				
3RD AND 7 TO 11				
3RD AND 12 TO 16				
3RD AND 17 OR MORE				
FALL BEHIND EARLY				
4-MINUTE OFFENSE				
2-MINUTE OFFENSE				
LAST 3 PLAYS				

The rest of this chapter is devoted to discussions of different situations we feel we must account for. Among the things covered in those discussions are typical defensive adjustments to each situation, the types of things within each that we must do to succeed, and illustrations of a few quick route combinations that typify how we will approach that situation. Important to note about the illustrations is that they make use of some of the more advanced tools in our offense to give us the best combination in certain situations, building one level beyond the basic reads of a route. Obviously, we cannot utilize these kinds of calls until the quarterback thoroughly understands why each call is being put together, and how pre-snap decisions are made. For each route's basic reads, refer to the individual route chapters.

Appendix L contains summary capsules of each of the points made about these situations, as well as an expanded menu of route possibilities drawn from the three volumes.

"Coming Out"
To us, "coming out" offense is used any time we are backed up within our own 15 yard line. Obviously, we face different degrees of being backed up, and the very first priority must be to get outside the five so the punter, if we need him, has normal operating room on fourth down. Aside from that basic issue, we concern ourselves with making a minimum of two first downs, which roughly translates into moving past our own 30 yard line. Accomplishing this goal enables our punter to push the opponent back inside the 50, should we be forced to kick. This goal is key to the all-important "battle for field position" throughout the course of a game.

Different defenses have different philosophies here—ranging from base defense to goal line defense to "pressure" mode—but regardless of which of them we are facing, we are going to favor throws to the "edge" of the defense. Why? On the outside edge, there is less defensive traffic to potentially cause disaster, and we are often working single up against a cornerback because underneath defenders tend to be stacked in tighter in "the box," and are less able to work for width underneath outside routes.

The flexibility and timing of our quick passing game reduces many of the usual reservations a coach would normally have about throwing out of this area. We can use formations that widen the edge around which rushers have to come and enable us to use maximum protection. Tightened splits by interior linemen limit penetration, helping the quarterback get the ball out in time.

Within the edge philosophy, we want to ensure that the throws we make will either be caught by our player or fall incomplete. We do not want to be making a throw that can be intercepted and go back the other way if our timing is off or if the corner gets a great break. Therefore, we are generally either throwing deep takeoff routes, where we can take advantage of corners who creep up too tight in their technique throwing the ball deep and outside, or, if we want to throw an out-breaking route to get the first down, use something where the quarterback is holding the ball a bit longer and bringing the ball back downhill, directly away from the defender. The receiver must be able to get his body between the defender and the ball.

Two quicks that fit into this description are "91 Go" to fulfill the former category, in which we want to go up top, and "94 Stop," fulfilling the latter with a downhill-breaking outside cut on the edge. A play action "Fade" combination, fully protected, also provides the ability to keep possession on third and four to six from deep in our own end, holding a tightened flat defender with a fake and throwing a safe Break Out outside of him. Again, a deep shot up the sideline is built into this route, fulfilling the other major criteria we have for "Coming Out" passes.

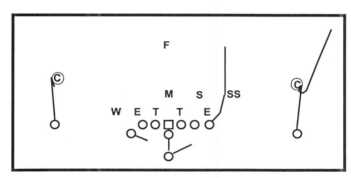

DIAGRAM 3-1
RIP HIP F91 GO
Deep shot on the edge of the field—ball is thrown so that Z catches it or
no one. Hitch backside provides a safe, high-percentage "guarantee"
if QB sees the corners soft pre-snap. "Hip" call helps pass
blocking on the edge, widens rush course for W.

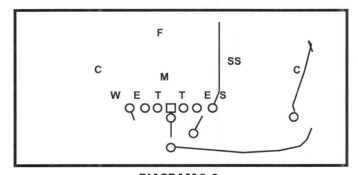

DIAGRAM 3-2
WEAK RAY TIGHT Y94 H SWING
Two tights again used to widen W & S rush angles & provide 7 man
protection. "Stop" a safe edge throw with Swing outlet if C clamps it.

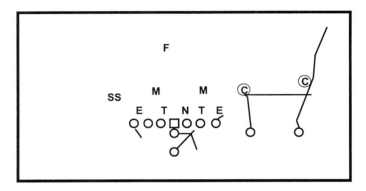

DIAGRAM 3-3
RAM X MAX 324 FADE
Play action gives us a good chance to hold flat coverage,
opening up the Break Out. Can also be used as a potential deep
shot to X as well. Maximum, eight-man protection used.

"Four-Minute Offense"

"Four-Minute Offense" is the term that has grown to be associated with trying to run out the clock when ahead late in a game. Obviously, if we can run the football every play in this situation and continue to make first downs, that's the preferred way to operate. However, there are invariably times when throwing becomes a necessity in this kind of scenario.

Our number-one priority when we are forced to throw is to get a *completion*. If we complete this pass, the clock continues to run, and we are accomplishing what we want in four-minute offense. Throws from our quick passing game, then, are at a premium during this time, especially those containing the highest-percentage breaks.

A type of call that we will favor to get the best of all worlds in our four-minute offense will be a "run/quick" check from power formations. This package is an excellent first-down tactic. The quarterback is trained to identify certain keys within the linebacker structure that tell him if we have the best leverage to run or throw. By pairing a high-percentage throw with a solid run, we know we can always get to a good play.

Play action is also a good option on early four-minute offense downs, taking advantage of defenses that pull in tight to try and stop the run. In the illustration below, the Shoot/Slant combination off play action gives us a high-percentage chance.

Lastly, for situations where we have third and five or more yards to make in a four-minute situation, we can package different sides of a pass with different high-percentage routes. This combination gives the quarterback more pre-snap options and the ability to choose the route that he has the best "feel" about. Diagram 3-6 shows this idea.

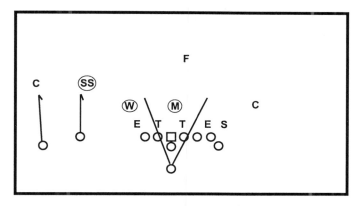

DIAGRAM 3-4
LARRY PLUS CHECK ZONE OR 191 DUPE
"Check with me" allows us to gain leverage for one of two solid, high-percentage plays. Alignment of W, M, and SS tell QB where best bubble is: either zone left, zone right, or dupe Hitch. #2 on the left must get a wide split to force W & SS to clearly define their alignment.

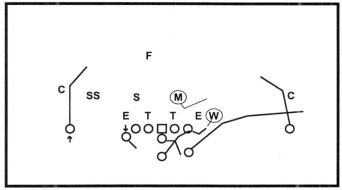

DIAGRAM 3-5
BROWN L Y324 SLANT H SHOOT
Taking advantage of defenses that try to get heat by rushing off the weakside edge in four-minute situations. Slant or Shoot are both viable options. "L" positioning of tight end makes his protection one step easier.

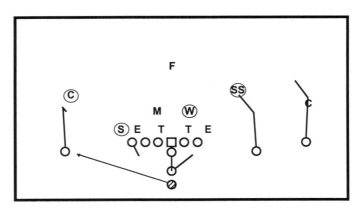

DIAGRAM 3-6
SHIFT TO RAY 11 Y93 DUPE B HITCH
Gives the QB the option of safe throws on either side of him
that can make key first downs off quick rhythm, spreading
the field while maintaining 7-man protection. Circled
defenders indicate pre-snap keys that tell QB who's best
isolated, and therefore where to throw. Shift may get us an
easy isolation to the H.

Red Zone: Plus 25

Our basic philosophy once we reach the 25 yard line is to take at least one shot at the end zone from this point on the field. Were we a more powerful, dominant running team, this philosophy might be different, but we feel like we can create matchups and situations from this area that give us a better chance to score in one strike than if we grind it out on the ground.

The basic thought process from the 25 in generally starts with expecting man coverage and having a safe place to go if we see zone. Many times this anticipation of man coverage will also mean having someone down the middle for the quick score in case the free safety leaves. We also train our players to expect the blitz, understanding the checks and break-offs we will use in that event.

The three illustrations that follow typify our Red Zone approach in the quick passing game, each having a deep shot that can take advantage of a man-to-man mismatch (the Fade, Quick Smash, and Split, respectively) while having a safe place for the quarterback to get a completion if the defense drops off into a zone (the Break Out, Hitch, and Wheel). In two of the cases, we're using backfield motion to try to create a wide mismatch or possibly bring the free safety out of the middle.

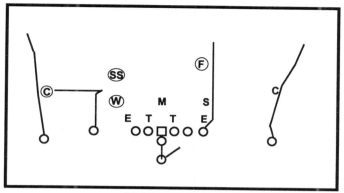

DIAGRAM 3-7
RIP 11 99 B FADE/OUT
Packaged sides give QB the chance to pick the best Fade based
on coverage and/or matchup. Any of the three cuts—Fade, Seam,
or Break Out, have a good chance to succeed in the Red Zone.

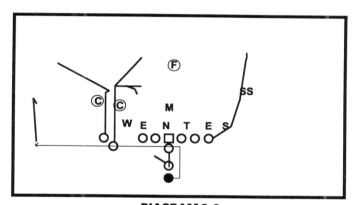

DIAGRAM 3-8
SQUEEZE LARRY H11 196 QUICK SMASH
Backfield motion and how a compacted +25 defense
adjusts to it creates interesting possibilities: Get Open
can score if FS leaves the middle with motion, Quick
Smash is an excellent all-purpose deep shot, especially
against man coverage with no help, and wide Hitch is a
safe guarantee if everyone softens. Backside Y can be
called in to protect if needed.

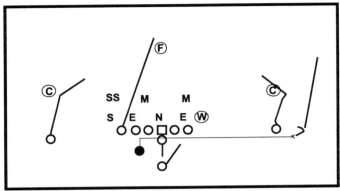

DIAGRAM 3-9
STRONG LIZ F10 90 WHEEL
Wheel route gives us a chance at the deep Split down the
middle to score, along with two potential man-beating Slants
on either side, and a 2 on 1 weakside read vs. basic zones.

Red Zone: Plus 15

As we get closer and closer to the goal line, we're aware that coverage, whether man or zone, becomes tighter and the holes smaller. It used to be that you could count on almost exclusively man coverage in this area, but with the growth of goal line zone concepts and "lanes" coverage (fully "banjoed" man that plays much like a zone to deal with picks and crosses), this is no longer necessarily the case.

Again, we train our people to anticipate blitz, and receivers must put an extra premium on distinct breaks and separation/misdirection techniques because of the tighter coverage.

Our route concepts most often try to do one of two things in the plus 15 area: get someone to a spot in the corner of the end zone in which we can drop the ball out of the reach of defenders (usually some type of Fade route or "Corner" type route), *or* give the receiver a break where he can gain separation on a Slanting or Crossing type route. Within both of these attack ideas, we'll try to have answers for "lanes" coverages, banjos, and so forth. One particularly attractive benefit of both of these general types of routes is that they can normally be thrown off quick rhythm, which is really helpful in dealing with the blitz.

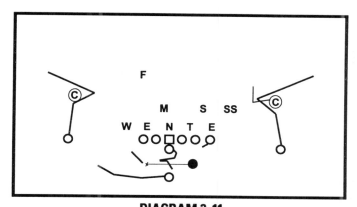

DIAGRAM 3-11
STRONG RIP F SHUFFLE Y329 DOUBLE DOG
"Dog" can look like the beginning of a backside cut-off block for
fake toss away from it; a corner who gets lazy and lets up when
he sees wide run action away from him will get caught flat-
footed. A good example of a Plus 15 throw in which we throw to
the back corner of the end zone out of reach of man defenders
playing with underneath, inside leverage.

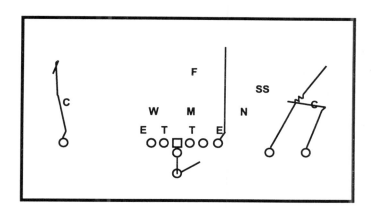

DIAGRAM 3-10
RIP 8 90 Z IN B STOP
"In" is an excellent Red Zone combination against man coverage,
having the ability to make big plays after the catch. #3 up the
Seam aids in controlling inside-out help on #1 from different
types of strongside man combinations. Two outside releases
force man coverage over #2 to turn hips and run with him,
making it hard to "banjo" to the In when it breaks inside. If
single coverage exists weak, the QB has a good place to go in
the Stop if something doesn't feel right about the In as he goes
through his pre-snap scan.

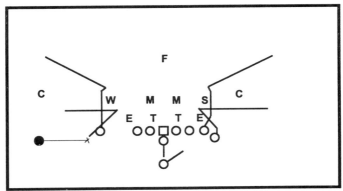

DIAGRAM 3-12
LARRY OUT X SNUG 96 DOUBLE WHIP
Two compressed Whip/Corner combinations allow QB to pick a
side that gives him best matchup/field width. Vs. single LB or SS
coverage, Quick Smash has a good chance to be a deep strike to
back corner of end zone; Whips are solid R.A.C. yard gainers if
nothing is deep. Defensive backs that "Banjo" and switch responsibilities when Whip pushes to the cross will find the Whip
separating away from them back to the outside, since the person
that switched to him was playing with hard inside leverage.

Red Zone: Plus 8 and Plus 4

Once we reach the eight yard line, we are almost assured of the defense making
some sort of substantial adjustment to their front, coverage, and blitz percentage,
possibly with a personnel substitution as well. Now the field is really compressed,
the coverage really tightened, but a few things are on our side as well.

We now know that there are a number of routes that, if we can create isolations for
them, can score for us off quick rhythm without needing a run after catch. Fades,
Stops, and Slants are among the routes that fall into this category at the eight yard
line, Break Outs fit that bill at the five, and Shoots, Turns, and Short routes from the
three yard line in. These routes are important since not as much room exists to
make big run after catch yardage.

Many of the same points we emphasize to our players from the fifteen are
emphasized down in this closer area as well, including distinct receiver breaks and
misdirection moves, anticipating the blitz, and finding ways to beat man coverage,
with or without "lanes" techniques. We add to this list the fact that the
quarterback must not take a sack under any circumstances, and must not miss
short, out-breaking routes to the inside or late. Obviously, avoiding those types of
mistakes can prevent the disastrous plays that turn games around.

Diagrams 3-13, 14, and 15 show three routes that have been effective for us from the ten to the eight yard line; Diagrams 3-16, 17, and 18 are three examples of good plus four plays. Note that play action can be very effective in this area with the quick passing game. Also note that each combination has built into it at least one route that gets into the end zone.

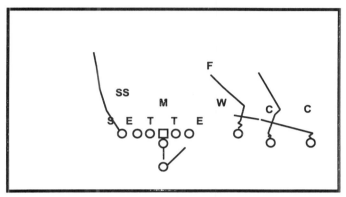

DIAGRAM 3-13
RAY 10 97 SHORT
Two possibilities of hitting an inside Slant in a crease, with a Short running outside-in through two possible picks. Three in-breaking routes causes problems for "lanes," forms of goal line man coverage

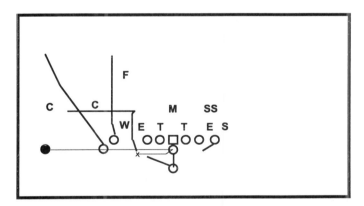

DIAGRAM 3-14
LARRY PAIR X RETURN Y198 FADE
Motioned Out has a good chance of gaining a step & forcing his man to "bubble" because of squeezed environment; squeezed Fade also good because it creates a footrace to corner of the end zone. The depth, timing, and releases make "switching" techniques ineffective.

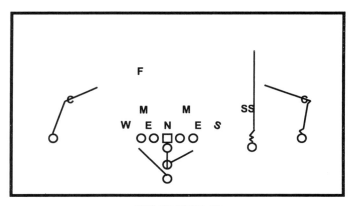

DIAGRAM 3-15
REX 93 SEAM
Seam helps clear out the Slant area, either vs. zone or man, Slant can break in right off his hip. If QB sees a threatening 3rd defender in the Slant/Seam area pre-snap, he can work the singled up Slant backside.

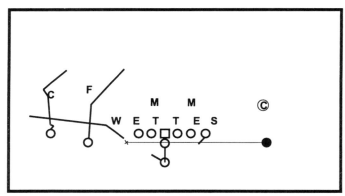

DIAGRAM 3-16
RIP 9 Z7 Y193
Fast motion gives us the chance to throw the Shoot off two rubs with the C trailing. Skinny Slants have a good chance to pop into an open Seam vs. lanes coverage.

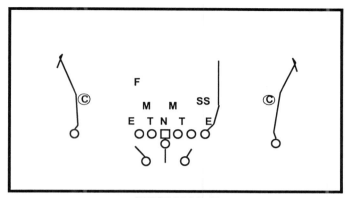

DIAGRAM 3-17
SPLIT RIP 194 STOP
Basic Fade/Stop a goal line staple if properly executed;
corner **must** look back when WR looks back as if to catch
Fade, making it impossible for him to recover and find the
Stop in time.

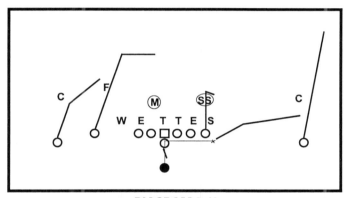

DIAGRAM 3-18
RIP 9 F6 HOT 95 TURN
Fast motion vs. bumped man adjustments and goal line zones
open a quick hole just outside the tight end position that's
hard for the next inside defender to cover up in time; the ball
is thrown FAST.

Second and Long

Second and long is a distinct down and distance that we deal specifically with in practice for a number of reasons. First of all, statistics show that, percentage-wise, whether or not drives are sustained depends in large part on staying out of third- and long-situations. Our players must understand the importance of getting from second and long to third and a manageable distance. Second, most defensive teams have distinct defensive tendencies on this down as well: to some, it is a definite blitz and pressure down, while to others it is a definite "soft" coverage down.

Understanding that the goal is to, above all, get us a completion that enables us to operate from third and six or less, we want to attack with routes that have at least one high-percentage option. Many of our quick passes fit very naturally into our second- and long-game plan slots. We also like to build into our second- and long-calls opportunities for the high-percentage throws to make yards after the catch, which is often done by either spreading the set out or using special sets that can create problem matchups. Finally, we like to have at our disposal at least one route that, if the defense hands it to us, can get the whole chunk back. This route may also be a designated "blitz beater."

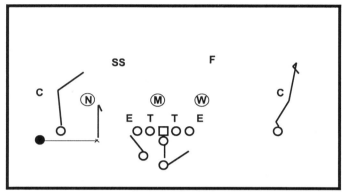

DIAGRAM 3-19
STRONG LOU Y9 193 STICK B STOP
Opportunity to make high-percentage yards with the Stick to get back to third and medium, or take bigger chunks with either the Slant or the Stop. QB goes to left if he can cleanly isolate the flat defender on Stick & Slant, right otherwise. In other words, he picks the side to which the underneath structure is weakest.

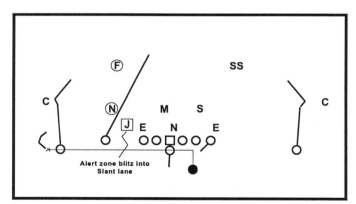

DIAGRAM 3-20
GREEN LARRY 10 F11 Y190 WHEEL
Provides 2nd and long possibilities on three levels: the "Wheel" can catch and make ball-control yards up the sideline if the flat coverage works under the Slant, the Slant is available for a middle range gain if flat coverage widens to the Wheel, and we can get the whole chunk back if coverage opens the deep middle.

3rd and Short: 1 to 2

We will use two different categories of passes on third- and short-situations: one category is to create a sure, short high-percentage throw that gets us the first down, and the second is to take a deep shot, preferably from a formation that looks like a running set and pulls the defense up.

When we want a sure first down and feel like, because of the defensive scheme or personnel we're facing, our percentages of picking it up with a quick pass are as good or better than mashing the ball inside with a run, we'll generally think in terms of getting leverage for "Shoot" routes, either within the 93 Slant or 95 Turn packages. By "gaining leverage," we mean that we are using formations, motion, and/or complementary routes to do two things: match it up with a linebacker who also has run responsibility and may be playing with inside leverage, and create possible rub/pick situations. The throw is gone very quickly, which minimizes our protection problems. This timing also helps with the route itself, because a defender who gets a step behind or takes any kind of steps for depth won't have time to recover enough to stop the completion. He may make the tackle immediately after the completion, but we will have our first down.

The advantage of 93 is that it can create better situations against man coverage, specifically in impeding the man covering the Shoot. It is also more conducive to being run out of sets where we can use two tight ends, which gives us more of a run look and enables us to keep seven or eight in to protect if we need to without compromising the route. The upside to the Turn is that it gives the quarterback a more sure, high-percentage receiver to throw to in the stationary "Turn" route if the Shoot does not open up.

Diagram 3-21 shows the 93 as it might be used on third and short, the quarterback being specifically told to take a miniature, two- to three-step "half roll" drop to get himself closer to the Shoot receiver to make it a higher percentage throw.

Diagram 3-22 illustrates an example of a third- and -short "deep shot" from a tightened set that normally alerts the defense to a power run. Note that we have provided an insurance policy of sort with the "Sit," a stationary player who can work into a void right in front of the quarterback should the deep throw not materialize.

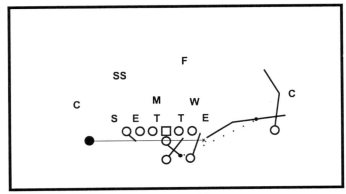

DIAGRAM 3-21
BROWN LIZ Z6 Y93
No read—QB drills Shoot as soon as his head snaps around,
regardless of coverage. Full-speed motion should gain the half-
step needed on any coverage adjustment. QB may use 2- to 3-step
half-roll technique to get closer to throw. Bang-bang timing vital.

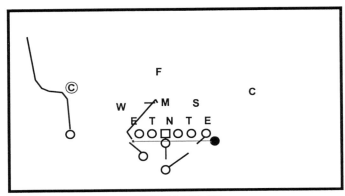

DIAGRAM 3-22
WEAK RIP WING Z7 Y192 GO Z SIT
Deep shot on third and short when defenses pull up to stop the
run vs. a tightened running set, isolating X outside. Z chips the
end and releases to a "Sit," getting in a void in the QB's vision
so we can get the first even if the deep throw doesn't open up.

Third and Three

Third and three can be approached many different ways, depending on the
comparative talent levels of the offense and defense involved, defensive
tendencies, and overall offensive philosophy. Certainly any offense would like to be
able to run the football for the first down a certain percentage of the time, but
many times other types of answers are also needed.

In applying the quick passing game to third and three, we must be able to account for a wide variety of approaches on the defense's part. Since this down sees a lot of coverage "variety" by defensive teams, we must have routes that can account for both man and zone as well as both hard corner and soft corner, blitzes, and so forth. The fact that we need only three yards, however, leaves us a lot of options because almost any individual cut from any of our quick routes can get that for us.

To account for the greatest number of situations, we will often use different types of "packaged calls" as described in Chapter 2, including the "B tag" and "run/quick checks." We will also employ our highest percentage throws (often from a wide set for the sake of clarity), knowing that there is little sense in throwing lower-percentage routes since anything in our arsenal can move the chains for us.

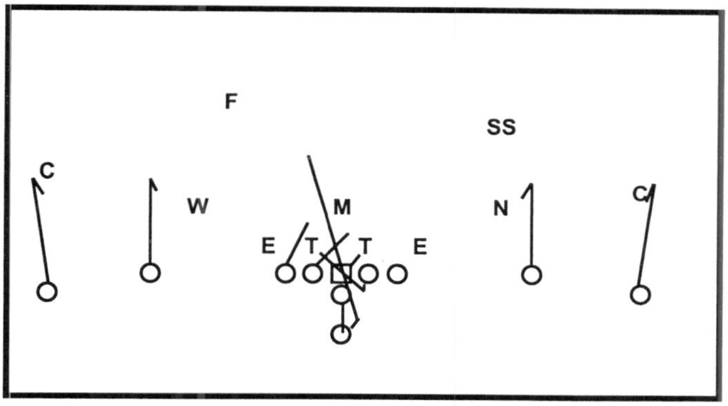

DIAGRAM 3-23
FLEX CHECK TRAP OR 91 DOUBLE DUPE
Check based on number of men in the box: Trap vs. 5, 91 vs. 6.
Trap has excellent angles vs. a 4-1 or 3-2 front; Dupe Hitch vs. 6
means at least one corner is likely to be soft, and QB has four
high-percentage, stationary throws spread across the field.

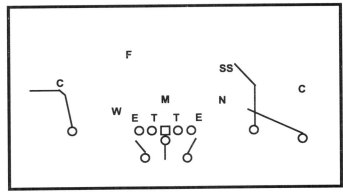

DIAGRAM 3-24
SPLIT REX 97 B QUICK OUT
Packaged call gives a good answer for either a soft corner or hard
corner defenses: "Short" to the right side is a high-percentage
combination vs. a hard corner, Quick Out to left should be open vs.
soft corner. Also a good field width fit with Short to wide field
and Quick Out into boundary.

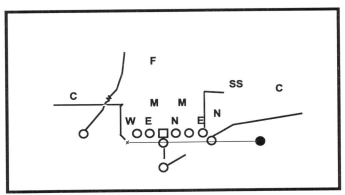

DIAGRAM 3-25
SQUEEZE RIP OUT Z7 190 OUT B TURN
Packaging high-percentage out-breaking routes. QB should throw
the "Out" if he sees a man adjustment to motion _or_ if defense
leaves two short defenders over the wing to the right; will work
the basic "Turn" combination against any zone with a softened
corner or SS to the wing side.

Third and 4 to 6

Third and four to six is another down and distance in which we can and will see a lot
of different defensive styles. Any number of coverages is possible, as well as stunt
and blitz combinations. One particular item we must be especially aware of here is
the "zone blitz." As offenses become proficient at hitting ball-control routes and
hot adjustments for first downs in these situations, defenses have evolved in an
attempt to get defenders in some of the offense's traditional throwing lanes. This
adjustment is often a lineman dropping into a short crossing area or Slant lane while
a linebacker rushes.

Third and four to six may or may not be a heavy blitz down for defenses. Some will stay away from heavy pressure on this down for the better part of a game, coming with it only as a "surprise" element in a key spot. In third- and four-situations at key points in a drive or in the game, we are likely to see the coverage or scheme our opponent plays the very best; they will not fool around.

We also tell our quarterback that if they are going to play Cover 3 or some other soft corner defense we will not get fancy. We check to a Hitch to our best receiver and get the first down. In fact, we feel so strongly about that particular route that we will tell him from day one, "You have the right to throw a Hitch at any time. If down and distance warrant, no matter what our formation, regardless of our call, get us into a Hitch and get us positive yardage if they're giving it to us." In this way, we try to avoid "outsmarting" ourselves.

Following are three other quick route concepts that have had proven success in converting third and four to six situations.

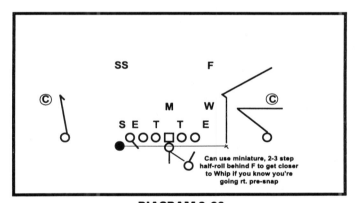

DIAGRAM 3-26
GREEN LIZ OUT H8 Y96 WHIP
Whip combination sound against most defenses to the
motion side; backside Hitch available as a "gimme" if
defense softens with motion.

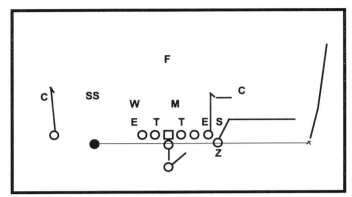

DIAGRAM 3-27
RIP 9 WING H10 95 B HITCH
H's simple clearing route allows this to be run from base
personnel, making a nickel substitution less likely, helping
matchups. "Turn" is a high-percentage 5-6 yard throw, and
placing Z in the position to run the Shoot enhances the
chances of that route getting the first down on R.A.C. yardage.
Backside Hitch is placed on the route to give it a solid guarantee if the underneath defenders overreact to the motion.

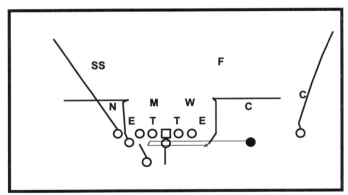

DIAGRAM 3-28
BLUE RAY IN Z RETURN 98 FADE/OUT
QB can pick Break Out that has the best chance to get open,
based on matchup, field width, or coverage structure. "Return" motion helps Z on right gain a step on a man defender, or
catch flat coverage to that side in the middle of a coverage
check. Squeezed effect of the Break Out on the left may
create a rub or bubble and/or cause problems for defenders'
angles because of the space it creates outside.

Long-Distance Downs: Third and 7 to 11 and Third and 12 Plus

All the practice and preparation we do for these longer distance downs fall into two basic categories: plays we're using with the idea that we are going to gain the yardage with the throw and catch itself, and plays where we will throw short and try to create an opportunity to make the yardage by running after the catch. Our players must understand which category a given call falls into. For a game, we will make a decision during the week on what percentage of the time we want to do each, largely based on how much heat our opponent brings on these downs.

In general, going to the "throw-for-the-distance approach" too often can get offenses into trouble, because they begin to find themselves throwing into the teeth of nickel and dime zone defenses, or, worse yet, getting their quarterback hit because he is holding the ball longer. Both of these problems can lead to the types of disastrous plays that lose ballgames.

We are happy many times to throw quickly to a receiver short of the first down, trying to shake him loose to gain the needed yards once he has made the catch. Even if he does not, we've positively affected field position and kept ourselves out of a bad play. In tight contests, this type of patience and game management can make the difference. Diagram 3-29 shows a packaged combination that is an example of this type of third-and-long approach.

On the occasions where we are going to try and make the first down strictly on the distance of the route, we try to do a few things to help ourselves stay out of trouble. First of all, we like routes where we can keep people on the edges of the field, out of the clutches of different robbers, zone blitzes, and so forth. Along the same lines, we will try our best to use sets, shifts, and anything else at our disposal to create a one-on-one isolation for this route we are throwing. Finally, we will often commit to a seven-man protection to ensure that we are solid if they blitz and to create a maximum number of double teams if they do not. Diagrams 3-30 and 3-31 illustrate some ways that a "throw-for-the-yardage" call could be constructed.

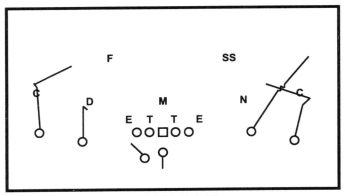

DIAGRAM 3-29
GUN FLEX 193 STICK B IN
Packaging two throws that have a good chance to make yards
on the run—basic rule of thumb is to throw "Stick" vs. zones,
"In" vs. man coverages off the rub by #2. "Gun" automatically
lengthens routes by a step.

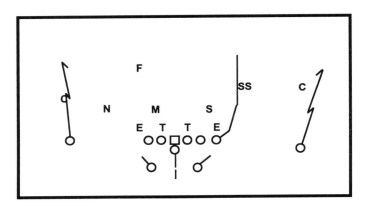

DIAGRAM 3-30
SPLIT RIP 91 DOUBLE STUTTER
A fully protected triple-move route that has an excellent chance
to move the chains on long-yardage downs if one of the
cornerbacks is isolated without any inside help from underneath.

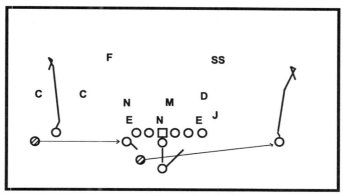

DIAGRAM 3-31
SHIFT TO RIP HIP F94 STOP
Same basic idea as Stutter combination above—a fully
protected route trying to isolate a particular break on the
outside. In this case, a special shift is used to try to
create the isolation for Z.

2-Minute Drill

Obviously, in two-minute and hurry-up situations, we want to have passes available to us that can use the sideline and get us out of bounds. If defenses in this situation do not use coverage techniques that defend this outside edge, we are perfectly willing to use a couple of basic plays on the sideline repeatedly to march us right down the field.

The two best representatives of this idea in the quick passing game are the 92 Quick Out and 94 Stop. Operating mostly from open sets, such as "Flex" or "Rex 6," the quarterback can choose sides (mostly working the boundary to conserve time), knowing that he'll have a Seam inside to help hold the safety on the side he chooses. He also has the freedom to bring in an extra man to protect from the backside if he senses blitz or wants an extra double team on a particular rusher.

Normally, these plays will have been game planned and called because we are reasonably certain that the particular opponent will allow us to throw cleanly to the singled outside route. However, the quarterback must also be aware that, at times, two-minute defenses will cause problems for his basic Out-Seam or Stop-Seam read. In other words, sometimes a short defender over the Seam may widen really quickly, which would normally tell the quarterback to go to the Seam immediately, but many times a two-minute type defense will also have a safety over the top left to intercept the Seam. In these cases, we have to be aware of the "Get Open" as a late outlet player if our original read does not hold up.

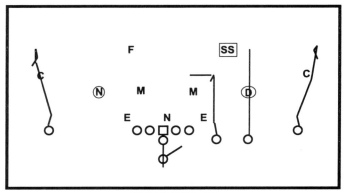

DIAGRAM 3-32
REX 6 94 VS. PREVENT DEFENSE

More and more, however, defenses are evolving in their two-minute packages to include some kind of hard corner on the outsides to prevent people from taking easy chunks on the outside as we have just described. In these cases, the "Quick Smash" is a very valuable tool to work the sidelines, because, especially into the boundary, the Hitch can hold that corner and open up a big hole behind for the Quick Smash.

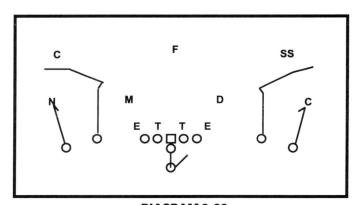

DIAGRAM 3-33
FLEX 96 QUICK SMASH VS. HARD CORNER PREVENT
Hitches hold down N and C; QB flattens Quick Smashes with
ball to lead them toward sideline and in front of deep C and SS.

The other general school of thought that complements the "work-the-sideline" idea is to get chunks of yardage large enough to justify staying in bounds, specifically working on the thought that you will get a first down, stop the clock temporarily (in high school and college), and be up to run another play before much clock has run off. One specific package to do this with is a concept borrowed from the 49ers, lining up a wide trips set away from a single receiver. Many teams assume, when this set is used in the last minute to 45 seconds of a half, that it is a "Hail Mary" formation, and many teams also over-rotate to the trips. This adjustment creates a very favorable situation for the Slant, who can often catch the ball on the move in an open lane and advance for big gains. We will then tag the trips side with an "In" combination to free up #1 in that same lane, should the underneath structure lean on the singled Slant instead. Either way, we have the chance to hit a good athlete in the softened underbelly of a prevent defense as he is running full speed.

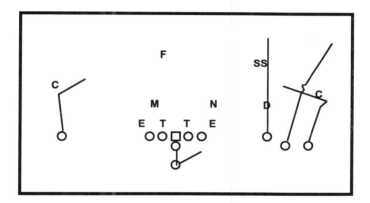

DIAGRAM 3-34
REX 6 (WIDE) 93 Z IN B SLANT
QB works singled Slant if under coverage gives him the lane; hits In on the move if they don't. Either has a chance to make large gains on R.A.C. vs. softened two-minute defense.

CHAPTER 4

Building and Teaching a Full Blitz-Beating Progression with the Quick Passing Game

Because of the popularity of pressure defenses in today's football, it goes without saying that any offense must have good ways to deal with all varieties of defensive blitzes. Generally, if you have any type of success throwing the ball against a base defense, one of the first alternatives a defensive coordinator will resort to is to use additional rushers to test your protection scheme to see if it holds up and to see if you have effective answers. These answers must not just exist on the blackboard or on paper, but must be provided through a careful, meticulous teaching progression that everyone, starting with the quarterback, can understand and execute.

This chapter shows how such a progression can be built from the ground up with the quick passing game as its centerpiece. In our case, we will use a few routes outside the quick game in our blitz-beating package (specifically the Vertical Switch and Post/Corner combinations), but a complete and thorough answer for blitzes can easily be found within the quick game without the need of these additional five-step type routes.

Step One: Creating a Positive Mentality toward the Blitz

Important to the teaching of a blitz-beating progression is the approach and mentality you impart to your players where the blitz is concerned. We have always taught our players from day one that the blitz is an opportunity that provides us a chance to attack and make a big play. In other words, we're going to take a positive, aggressive approach. A key component of this approach is the fact that our players understand very early that we have a PLAN, and that they have been given specific answers to back up this sort of confidence.

Too often, coaches convey a certain fear of the blitz to their players that results in a defensive, "escapist" approach. This approach plays right into the defense's hands, because part of the blitz's effect is created by the perceived threat that creates tentativeness on the offense's part. In other words, the defense has seized the initiative and become the aggressor, dictating to the offense and relegating them to a passive, reactive role. By virtue of our basic approach, we do not let this change happen.

We are not saying that "escaping" bad plays is not a part of dealing with the blitz at times. By taking a positive, proactive stance from the beginning, however, we feel that we can always get back to the escape because of the way we have planned, while keeping "attack" as a first priority gives us a big-play dimension we would not otherwise have.

The simple axiom that we give our players to summarize our blitz approach is: "Recognize it, Protect it, and Attack it." This axiom provides a simple teaching phrase that both portrays our mentality and provides a skeleton upon which we can build the rest of our teaching progression. When we have a breakdown, we can always point back to one of these simple areas and effectively teach: any failure to beat the blitz is likely to have occurred because we failed to RECOGNIZE the blitz, because, through a wrong scheme or a one-on-one breakdown we did not PROTECT effectively, or did not ATTACK as we should. The ability to bring all the elements of blitz-beating back down to these areas helps keep things clear in the minds of our players.

Practice Emphasis

For these ideas to effectively take hold, the proper practice emphasis must be given to the blitz. This emphasis will extend not only to the line and backs regarding protection, but also to the quarterback in recognizing, checking, and adjusting his footwork, and receivers in adjusting their routes as necessary.

For us, our practice emphasis will begin with a full offensive practice during the second week of pre-season practice that is devoted to working against the blitz and beginning our blitz teaching progression. This practice will include blitzes not only in pass rush situations, but "run blitzes" as well.

Once this foundation has been established, we next begin to designate ten- to fifteen-minute blocks within each practice as "blitz periods." This blitz period will always involve the line, protecting backs, and at least one quarterback; sometimes it will include receivers as well.

Questions to Answer/Forms of Blitz

To be able to best attack the blitz from week to week or play to play, it is important to answer some basic questions that help identify where the rush is coming from, how coverage is being played behind it, and where the holes are that can be exploited. A discussion of some of the questions we will ask follows.

How many are rushing?

Specifically, we want to know how many rush in relationship to the number of people we have protecting. Generally, we're most concerned with situations in which their number of rushers potentially exceeds our number of protectors.

If the two numbers are equal, related questions would include:

- Are they trying to overload a particular side to break down our protection?

- Are they trying to guarantee a one-on-one matchup for one of their players or against one of ours? Who and how?

Recent defensive developments, specifically the zone blitz, have forced us, at times, to answer these related questions as well:

- Are they trying to absorb a block or blocks with a player who will ultimately drop in order to free someone else to rush? Who and how?

- Are they trying to trigger a hot breakoff by a receiver while dropping someone into that specific throwing lane?

Is it a "Tight" Blitz or a "Soft" Blitz?

This question is important because the answer dictates to us exactly what types of shots we can take at the blitz downfield. In "soft" blitzing schemes, the number of rushers has been increased, but the secondary is playing "soft" to keep everything in front of them so they don't give up the big play. This tactic is becoming more and more prevalent on third and long: extra rushers will be brought to force a quick throw by the quarterback, while pass defenders are in a position to make the quick tackle in front of the first-down marker. Obviously we have to have a different plan for this type of approach than against a "tight" blitz, which in our terminology means that defenders are locked down in a closer relationship to receivers, often trying to smother them and prevent separation long enough for the rush to cause problems. In this case we would be much more apt to try to exploit the defense deep.

Are they playing Man or Zone behind the blitz?

Once we have established the general approach of the defense, we want to know more specifics about their coverage scheme. Generally, different types of blitzes will dictate that man coverage be played by the secondary. If they are playing man, there is one further bit of information we want to know:

- Do they "Banjo" within their man coverage or "lock"?

As noted, "zone blitzes" in various forms are becoming more and more common, in which secondary people are dropping within a zone scheme of some sort. In these cases, we will also ask:

- Which zones are being vacated by the blitzers?

- Is there an attempt to cover up these voids with a lineman dropping?

What is the Free Safety's role when he comes out of the middle? Is he in coverage to the weakside, coverage to the strongside, a blitzer, or a potential robber?

The free safety's function is very important to us in terms of matchups and where we want to go with the ball in our blitz checks. His alignment also tells us who is likely to be blitzing. For example, if he is aligned in a coverage position to the same side as the strong safety, he is probably there to assume the strong safety's coverage position while the strong safety rushes.

We also want to understand his coverage position related to people we may call in to block. If he is over a tight end, for example, and our check makes the tight end a blocker, the middle that the free safety had originally left open by his alignment may no longer be open because he can now become a "free" player. We need to be very careful about throwing into the middle in this case, and would prefer to throw away from the tight end.

Beginning the Teaching Progression

Before diving fully into our step-by-step teaching progression, it is important to understand that we deal with the blitz on two different levels: blitzes we can recognize pre-snap and deal with from a checkoff standpoint, and blitzes we have to adjust to "on the move." Specifically, the latter category refers to situations in which a player we had counted as a "coverage player" in our pre-snap checklist quickly became a "rush player" not accounted for in the protection. This scenario is one we would like to avoid as much as possible—we would much rather have the control of dealing with things pre-snap—but we must build in and practice ways to deal with these situations when they occur.

Certain types of formations can help us in this regard because they make blitzes more recognizable by making it more difficult for people who line up in coverage initially to effectively rush. Most formations of this type fall into the category of "wider" sets, generally involving four spread receivers. Certainly, the use of these kinds of looks is one of the preventive measures we will feature to minimize the number of times we have to resort to "on the move" blitz adjustments.

Basic Philosophies: Protection Checks vs. "Hot"

Two fundamental philosophies exist regarding how the blitz should be attacked. While it is important, especially at the higher levels of football, to have the ability to do both, our philosophy has always been to use protection checks any time we can, thus avoiding the need for "hot" throws as much as possible.

Our reasons for having this philosophy revolve around our quarterback. At the levels we have coached, we have had limited practice time and young, inexperienced quarterbacks. In many cases, "hot" breakoffs add an additional thought process to all the other things we ask him to do, making his job exponentially more difficult. By matching people up man for man in blocking people through a "protect first" concept, we eliminate the "hot" thought process and allow fewer clean shots on our passer.

Again, we are not saying that we never throw "hot," because we do have to sight adjust when we do not recognize blitzes prior to the snap, and at times in which we intentionally create "hot" situations through our protection call. In the case of the latter, however, we marry up the routes we use out of hot protection in such a way that the "hot" read and the quarterback's basic read are either off of the exact same person or in close proximity to each other so that we are not adding an extra worry for our trigger man.

At the professional level, higher percentages of "hot" principles are used for a number of reasons:

1) Because of the athleticism of their players, defenses can much more easily "bluff" the blitz and then play base coverage. To check extra protectors every time a blitz look was shown would leave NFL offenses at a severe disadvantage when it was a "bluff."

2) The multiplicity of sets that NFL teams use, at times, also make disguising and bluffing easier.

3) NFL teams have a much greater amount of time to get "hot" principles fully taught and practiced, and their quarterbacks are the "best of the best" by the time they reach that level, making it practical to use "hot" on a wider scale.

Of course, this more widespread use of "hot" concepts is one of the things that spawned the evolution of "zone blitzes," which is another reason we are leery about selling out too much to "hot" schemes. Two of the zone blitz's main principles are to:

1) Absorb blocks with people who are actually not rushing but dropping (defensive linemen), freeing up rush lanes for people who are rushing.

2) Trigger "hot" breakoffs by offenses with rushes by linebackers and secondary people, and, by studying the opposition's "hot" tendencies, drop unexpected people (linemen or LBs) directly in the path of those "hot" routes.

A basic example of these ideas is illustrated below.

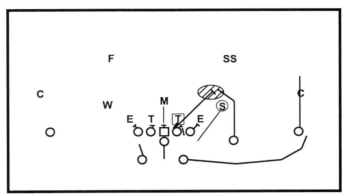

DIAGRAM 4-1
BASIC ZONE BLITZ CONCEPT
Rush by M & S triggers a "hot" breakoff to a Slant by #2. T steps to
the guard to "absorb" his block and make it hard for him to come off to
S in time. T then drops into the "hot" breakoff lane that the QB
anticipates being open due to the rush.

Being fully protected averts some of these snafus (For our basic menu on beating zone blitzes, see Appendix M).

Our approach to attacking the blitz is not the only approach; using predominantly "hot" routes certainly has its advantages. We have merely outlined our thought process and what we have had success with in our situation.

The Starting Point: Finding the Free Safety
Because our primary concern in attacking the blitz is getting a blocker "married up" to each potential rusher, and because the free safety's position provides us critical clues as to how many rushers we may face, we start our teaching progression with the identification of where the free safety is aligned.

To understand why the free safety is so vital, it is important to go back to the fact that our blitz/protection philosophy begins with the idea that defenses must commit one person to coverage for each spread receiver we have plus one. In other words, if we split four receivers into the formation, the defense must cover with at least five; if we have split three, they must cover with four, and so on. As long as the defense covers in this manner, we will have enough blockers to match up with potential rushers one for one.

Covering with at least one more than the offense has split means that, at the very least, there is one safety deep who is not locked into man coverage with someone or in a rush position. If the quarterback can identify the free safety in a deep position, he knows we have the numbers to match up in protection.

Examples of how this approach fits together from different types of formations are illustrated below, with potential rushers enclosed in squares and committed coverage people circled.

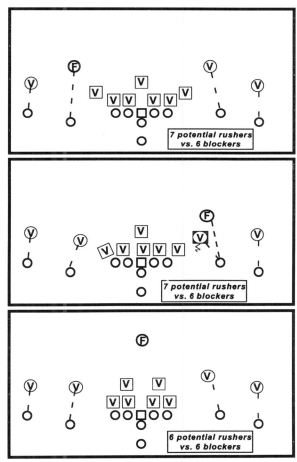

DIAGRAMS 4-2 THROUGH 4-4
"FLEX" FORMATION AGAINST DIFFERENT RUSH SCENARIOS:
POTENTIAL RUSHERS BOXED, COVERAGE PEOPLE CIRCLED
7 potential rushers with the Free Safety in a coverage position
on the same side as the Strong Safety (2), 7 potential rushers
with the Free Safety in a coverage position away from the
Strong Safety (3), and 6 potential rushers with the Free safety in
the deep middle (4)

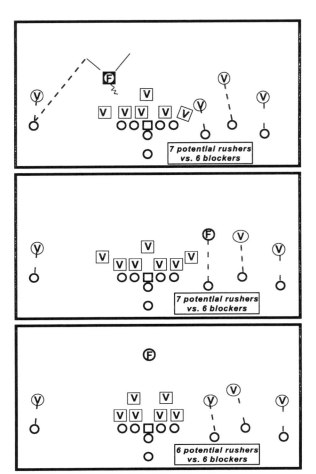

DIAGRAMS 4-5 THROUGH 4-7
"REX 6" FORMATION AGAINST DIFFERENT RUSH SCENARIOS:
POTENTIAL RUSHERS BOXED, COVERAGE PEOPLE CIRCLED
7 potential rushers with the Free Safety in a potential double
team, rush, or "free" position away from the Strong Safety (5)
7 potential rushers with the Free Safety in a coverage position
on the same side as the Strong Safety (6), and 6 potential
rushers with the Free safety in the deep middle (7)

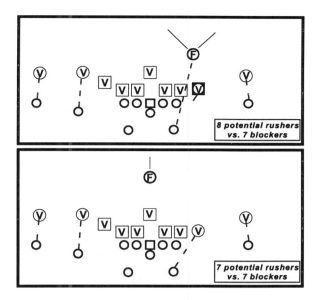

DIAGRAMS 4-8 AND 4-9
"SPLIT LEX" FORMATION AGAINST DIFFERENT RUSH SCENARIOS:
POTENTIAL RUSHERS BOXED, COVERAGE PEOPLE CIRCLED
8 potential rushers with the Free Safety in a potential coverage, or
"free" position away from the Strong Safety (8) and 7 potential
rushers with the Free safety in the deep middle (9)

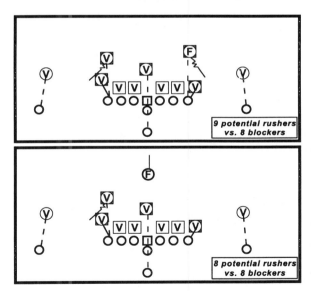

DIAGRAMS 4-10 AND 4-11
"RAM" FORMATION AGAINST DIFFERENT RUSH SCENARIOS:
POTENTIAL RUSHERS BOXED, COVERAGE PEOPLE CIRCLED
9 potential rushers with the Free Safety in a potential coverage or
rush position away from the Strong Safety (10) and 8 potential
rushers with the Free safety in the deep middle (11)

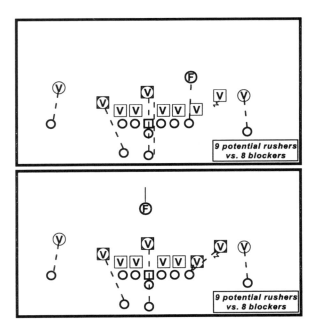

DIAGRAMS 4-12 AND 4-13
"BLACK RIP" FORMATION AGAINST DIFFERENT RUSH SCENARIOS:
POTENTIAL RUSHERS BOXED, COVERAGE PEOPLE CIRCLED
9 potential rushers with the Free Safety in a coverage on the same
side as the Strong Safety (12) and 8 potential rushers with the Free
safety in the deep middle (13)

If the quarterback sees that the free safety is out of the middle, he immediately knows that we probably have a protection problem. By virtue of taking the free safety out of the middle of the field and having him do some other job—specifically covering someone man-to-man or rushing himself—the defense has freed an extra man to rush and can now outnumber our blockers.

Seeing this problem, the quarterback has three basic options: check protection and throw quick, check protection and throw deep, or "gamble," not checking protection, and hope that the ball can be delivered before the unblocked man can get there.

We will primarily emphasize the first two options, building toward the third option only after the quarterback has some experience handling the blitz. This plan relates back to our "protect first" philosophy.

To check protection, the quarterback simply motions to the man he wants to come in to protect, calling his position, e.g., "*Y, Y, Y,*" or "*X, X, X.*" If the man he wants to protect is already in a closed position, he simply calls his position. The called-in protector blocks the end man on the line of scrimmage, with the tackle next to him having the ability (especially if the tackle is uncovered) to make a call that will put them in a tandem to "zone" protect the end man on the line of scrimmage and the linebacker over the tackle. This maneuver offers the man called to block a "check release" option if both the down lineman and linebacker do not rush. In a single back set, this action dictates that the running back initially works away from the called in protector, the line making whatever calls they would normally make to fit him in and match themselves up. Most times, we also tell the back that he can "cheat" to get closer to the man he is assigned to. In other words, he offsets himself to the side of his protection responsibility.

In making his protection check, the quarterback can also use more generalized checks to keep more than one man in. "Stay," "Max," and "Colt" would be examples of these kinds of calls.

These adjustments made, the quarterback may also need to change the route, depending on what was originally called and which of the two options he chooses. This change is done within our normal cadence.

We teach our quarterbacks to consider a number of factors in deciding whether to check to a deep throw or check to a quick throw. The major factors are down and distance, matchups, and the depth at which the man defenders are playing. Obviously, we don't want to take too many deep shots on third and three, and we do not want to be throwing quick too much of the time on third and 12. In the same way, the number of deep throws should be limited if we are getting loose, soft coverage.

As you will see, many of the routes we use as our "base" blitz checks give us the ability to throw deep or throw quickly.

Following are some examples of this checking process, showing the "throw deep" option as well as the "throw quick" option.

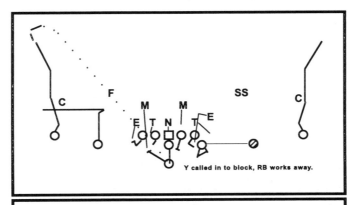

Y called in to block, RB works away.

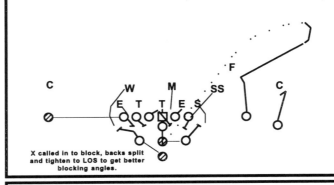

X called in to block, backs split
and tighten to LOS to get better
blocking angles.

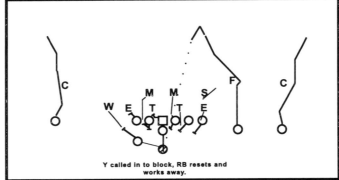

Y called in to block, RB resets and
works away.

DIAGRAMS 4-15 THROUGH 4-17
EXAMPLES OF PROTECTING AND CHECKING DEEP
Flex Check Y 198 Fade (15)
Rex Check X 96 Quick Smash (16)
Rip 8 Check Y 99 Fade (17)

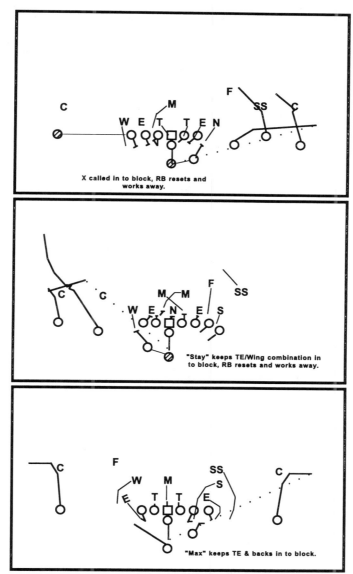

DIAGRAMS 4-18 THROUGH 4-20
EXAMPLES OF PROTECTING AND CHECKING QUICK
Rex 6 Check X 93 Slant
Larry Plus Check Stay 190 In
Strong Rip Check Max 92 Quick Out

"Gambling" without a protection check: When and Why?

"Gambling" without a protection check, either with the play called or a pass that
was checked to without adding a protector, should be done only when certain
criteria are met:

- First of all, the quarterback and the line must be able to clearly identify and communicate with each other to is being left unblocked. If confusion exists, it is highly possible that not one, but two unblocked players will come storming in on our passer. Clear communication between the quarterback and the line allows the line to create a situation where they can best match up and secure things from inside out. Usually, this quarterback/line communication amounts to the quarterback shouting the number of the unblocked player to the line and having the center or playside guard echo the number back to him.

- Second, the quarterback should have a route within the pass he is executing that quickly gets into the area that would be vacated by the unblocked rusher.

- Third, the quarterback has to be willing to stand in, deliver the ball, and take a hit shortly after the ball is thrown.

If the quarterback does not clearly understand these three things, he is much better off getting himself protected. As noted earlier, we progress a considerable amount in the teaching and working of the other two approaches before we get to this option. Illustrated below are two situations in which we would be willing to "gamble."

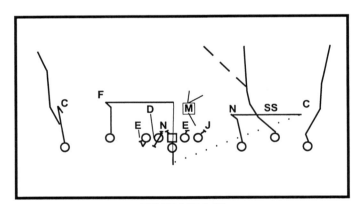

DIAGRAM 4-21
EMPTY HOT 90 F OUT
QB can "gamble" because:
a) He has a "Box" route coming into the area M would vacate if
he rushed b) He has a quick receiver available in the "Out"
working off a rub that can become available very early

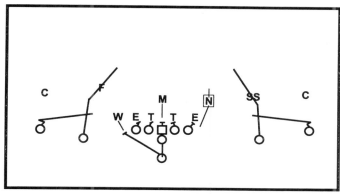

DIAGRAM 4-22
FLEX 97 SHORT
QB can gamble because he has two quick routes coming into his
vision that can replace the unaccounted for N if he comes. Is
especially workable since interior Slant can turn into a big play.

Dealing with "Blitzes on the Move"

All the elements that have been discussed up to this point have involved scenarios
in which the quarterback was able to recognize the presence of extra rushers *prior
to* the snap of the ball. There are times, however, when people who had been
counted as "coverage people" before the snap blitz off the edge of the formation.
Obviously, we must prepare for this possibility.

The way that we deal with this scenario is to sight adjust with our receivers. In
other words, they are made responsible for the coverage people over or nearest
them if they rush. If one of these players does rush, an automatic breakoff route
combination is activated on that side of the formation, with the players shouting an
alert call such as "Fire! Fire! Fire!" as they see the rush developing. This alert tells
the quarterback that he must abort his initial read and get the ball to one of his
sight-adjusting receivers in a hurry. Ideally, we like to use our receiver splits in such a
way that a secondary person blitzing will have to "prowl" before the snap to get
close enough to stunt. This "prowling" will alert the receivers, and subsequently
the quarterback, that something is up, enabling us to either make a full check or be
better prepared to sight adjust.

Of the three or four basic sight adjustments that we practice overall, we will carry
into a game one or two of them, based on the types of blitzes teams use. These
combinations enable us to get the ball off very quickly and attack defenses in spots
where they have left themselves vulnerable. Generally, we will start a game using
one that will be automatic on any "Fire" call, with the idea that if we find our
"alternate" combination would work better, or if we have had to sight adjust
enough times that we need a change-up, we will switch to a different combination
as the "automatic" on the sidelines or at halftime.

Below are three basic sight adjust combinations as they apply to one-, two-, and three-receiver sides. All of them are simply extensions of route combinations we use in our basic quick passing game, so actual new learning is limited.

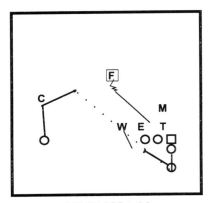

DIAGRAM 4-23
BASIC SIGHT ADJUSTMENT TO A
SINGLE RECEIVER SIDE: SLANT

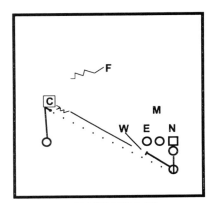

DIAGRAM 4-24
ALTERNATE SIGHT ADJUSTMENT
TO A SINGLE RECEIVER SIDE: HITCH

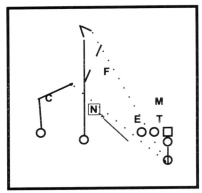

DIAGRAM 4-25
"SLANT/SEAM" SIGHT ADJUST-
MENT PACKAGE: TWO RECEIVERS

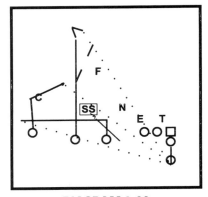

DIAGRAM 4-26
"SLANT/SEAM" SIGHT ADJUST-
MENT PACKAGE: THREE RECEIVERS

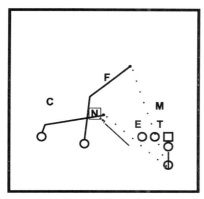

DIAGRAM 4-27
"SHORT" SIGHT ADJUSTMENT
PACKAGE: TWO RECEIVERS

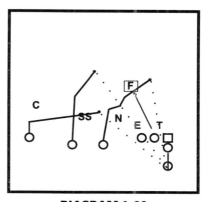

DIAGRAM 4-28
"SHORT" SIGHT ADJUSTMENT
PACKAGE: THREE RECEIVERS

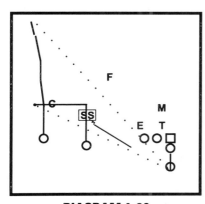

DIAGRAM 4-29
"FADE/OUT" SIGHT ADJUST-
MENT PACKAGE: TWO RECEIVERS

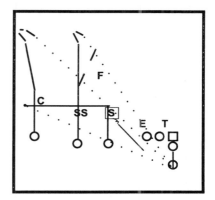

DIAGRAM 4-30
"FADE/OUT" SIGHT ADJUSTMENT
PACKAGE: THREE RECEIVERS

Base Blitz-Beating Route Combinations

How many different pass routes you place at your quarterback's disposal in terms of blitz checks depends on how much blitzing your opponents do. One or two blitz checks may be more than sufficient for a full year in many cases. Which routes you establish as your base blitz checks should revolve first and foremost around what things your quarterback throws well and what routes your receivers can execute and gain separation with. Ideally, within that framework you would like the ability to effectively attack all kinds of techniques and at both short and deep depths.

Five of the quick routes we have presented in the book could easily function as "base" blitz checks because of some distinct strengths they possess. A summary of those routes and their strengths follows.

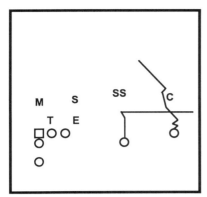

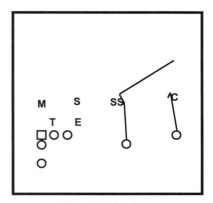

DIAGRAM 4-31
93-193 SLANT AS A BASE BLITZ CHECK:
-Simple check that can be delivered fast
-Has a big play chance in that the Slant can be hit on the move and run through open middle
-Shoot a safe "quick throw" on the outside

DIAGRAM 4-32
96-196 QK SMASH AS A BASE BLITZ CHECK:
-Qk Smash a good deep shot vs. inside leverage man defenders, can't banjo to it
-Hitch a solid, "quick" throw vs. soft blitzes
-Good vs. zone blitzes that drop linemen ... away from the danger
-#2's break sequences well with 97-197

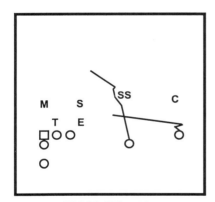

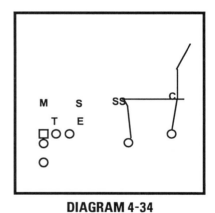

DIAGRAM 4-33
97-197 SHORT AS A BASE BLITZ CHECK:
-Inside Slant the quickest path to exploiting the deep middle
-Short coming into QB's vision a good, quick throw running away from C
-Good 1-2 combination vs. basic zone being played behind blitz
-#2's break sequences well with 96-196

DIAGRAM 4-34
98-198 FADE/OUT AS A BASE BLITZ CHECK:
-Fade as a deep throw and Break Out as a short throw both *very* good against all types of man coverage
-Safe, effective way to combat the zone blitz with dropping linemen

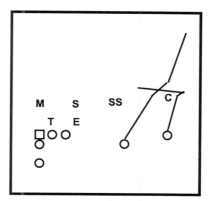

DIAGRAM 4-35
90-190 IN AS A BASE BLITZ CHECK:
Added leverage of a pick to get a
receiver running free with the ball
through the middle; Picker's route has a
chance to go big if a switch or banjo is
busted by man defenders

Blitz-Beating "Accessories" vs. Specific Blitz Types

In addition to basic blitz checks, certain routes within the quick package may be very useful on a game-plan basis to best take advantage of certain types of blitzes. A table illustrating those blitzes and routes that can attack them follows.

Attacking Specific Types of Blitzes

TYPE:	PLAYS	RATIONALE:

Tight	93 Dupe
	96 and
	96 Whip
	
	98
	99
	
	90 Out
		Two Slants that can gain separation and run free
		Good leverage to get Qk Smash deep; Whip
		  a good way to turn and separate from tight C
		Fade or Break Out both good ways to gain separation
		Inside and outside Vertical routes can take
		  advantage of speed mismatches
		Pick for the Out; Picker may have a chance to
		  get up over the top as well.

Soft	91 and 92
	93 Stick
	
	94
	
	97
		Quick, safe throws—can spin and make RAC yds
		Inside Stick a good, quick look; Slant may have
		  a hole and a good RAC lane behind him
		Good way to gain 8-11 on the edge against a
		  soft corner who doesn't want to give up Fade
		Short can catch the ball on the run, separating
		  from cornerback

Locked	93 93 Seam 98 90 In 90 Out	Slant has no inside help if he beats his man Slant has a chance to rub underneath Seam Trips version creates natural picks for Break Out Hard for people to fight through picks

Banjos	93 Dupe
	96 Whip
	
	97
	90 In
	90 Out
		No inside help for man over outside Slant
		If inside defender switches, he gets leveraged
		  by Whip running away from him; if he doesn't,
		  he's stuck on Quick Smash
		Two inside releases—nothing to "switch."
		In and Out with pickers cross at a point in the
		  route development that makes it hard to time
		  switch correctly; defenders' hips already
		  turned, hard to "re-recover."

Basic Zone Cov	91 Dupe
	
	93 Dupe
	93 Stick
	
	97
		Two quick, stationary throws with men working
		  into open areas
		Inside Slant good to adjust into open voids
		Stick safe and quick, Slant has chance to get into
		  open cavity, running free through vacated zone
		Two people working into voids left by zone—
		  should have solid 2 on 1 vs. any variety

FS Weak		Check protection in from strongside, go
		  weakside with singled Fades and Slant
		  combinations.

FS Strong		Pick best matchup side, gain protector from other side.

Formation Ideas for Combating the Blitz

Certain types of sets and movement are useful when dealing with steady diets of the blitz. Some of the concepts that we have found helpful are discussed below.

Wide Sets

As a general rule, the easiest way in our minds to attack the blitz has been to spread people out. Why? One of the most difficult things about dealing with heavy rush schemes and large numbers of players in the box is sorting out who is rushing and who is not, particularly for the linemen. In wider sets, the number of people who can be in the box is dramatically reduced if each receiver is going to have a player over him. This reduces the number of fronts, stacks, and variations that can be used to confuse protection schemes. Against base defenses, wide sets normally face either a 4-1, 4-2, or 3-2 front, all of which tend to be balanced and somewhat "vanilla." Blitz defenses usually entail 4-3 or 5-2 fronts.

Further, if a secondary player is going to "blitz on the move" after aligning in a coverage position, he will have to tip his hand somewhat to have a reasonable chance of getting to the quarterback in time.

The other advantage of wide sets is that they increase the operating space for the four quick receivers who have been deployed, increasing the chances of a big run after catch.

"Ram" Two Tight End Sets

Sets from our "Ram" package with two tight ends and two split receivers, either together or on opposite sides, also pose some problems for blitzing defenses. First of all, they widen the rush angles for outside blitzers, giving them a more circuitous course than normal. This split-second difference is key to getting the ball off cleanly.

Second, two tight end sets limit the number of blitz and stunt schemes that can be used without compromising "gap soundness." In other words, sound defensive football, especially against the run, revolves around having a player responsible for every gap. Double tight end sets give defenses two more gaps to account for than they might normally have in a set with no tight ends. Ram sets, therefore, are valuable on early downs or downs where the run is a viable threat; defenses will be less apt to stay in blitzes that leave gaps undefended if they think the run is a threat, especially from a strong run set like the Ram package.

Finally, two tight end sets are helpful because they provide nine big people immediately available for pass protection. Even in situations in which there are not seven or eight men rushing, this alignment can be valuable in terms of gaining double teams, especially if the route being run does not depend on having four receivers in the pattern.

Split Backs

Formations employing "Split" backs are one of the most time-tested ideas in dealing with heavy pass rushes. The pre-positioning of the backs gets them in an ideal spot to serve as pass protectors; they have a much shorter distance to go, and can therefore meet rushers at a point much farther away from the quarterback.

Having ready pass protectors on both sides is also a luxury that enables the line to use their full repertoire of calls that will help them gain the best matchups for themselves. They can make "big on big" calls to either side or "slide" the protection to either side to gain double teams.

Lastly, backs from a split position can function well as "erasers" when their assigned rusher doesn't come. Their backfield positioning enables them to move to a lot of different spots to provide help or cover up mistakes that have been made. This freedom is another tool that can help us counter the confusion that sometimes results from effectively executed zone blitzes.

Backfield Motion

Since so much of our blitz philosophy relates to *attacking* the blitz in a "proactive" way, backfield motion is a good fit for us. Backfield motion forces the defense to very quickly reveal who is covering whom. Often, it is the free safety who is forced to make the motion adjustment, or better yet, a linebacker running from an inside position to a wide coverage position.

Properly planned and utilized, backfield motion can change matchups very quickly in the offense's favor and/or disrupt the choreography of a pre-called blitz scheme. Some teams will check out of the blitz altogether and check back into a basic form of zone coverage. When we can force this adjustment, we have truly seized the initiative.

CHAPTER 5

Quick Passing Game Teaching
and Installation Philosophy

An effective installation and teaching progression, especially in working with a multiple offense, is paramount to players being able to understand and execute what's being asked of them. Even more, having an understanding as a coach of the nuts and bolts of actually *when* and *how* a new idea or ideas fit into the rest of the structure is important if the new idea is ever going to be used.

For these and other reasons, we give careful attention to planning when things go in, in what order, how much goes in at one time, and how things are going to get drilled and repeated. Through experience, we have developed several principles we try to use that we feel help provide the best foundation of learning for our players. A brief discussion of each principle follows, and they can be seen in action throughout the installation schedule example provided afterward.

Priority of the Quick Game

One of the first things you will notice in studying our installation schedule is that, within the passing game, our 90 series of quick passes gets top priority in every way. This principle accomplishes a number of things. First, it communicates to our players the central role and importance of the quick passing game within our offense. Since it is a complete "package" in and of itself, we are establishing through it the foundation for several other concepts in our offense (e.g., formations, motion, numbering of receivers, checks, reads, etc.) as we progress through our teaching.

Second, this scheduling gives our quarterbacks and receivers a chance to have success and build confidence early because of the high-percentage nature of the throws. The defense is often ahead in early camp, which can make deep passing patterns look bad because of the defense's proficiency and the offense's unpolished timing. Instead of eroding confidence by taking too many of these lumps, we emphasize a good dose of the quicks to make sure we are completing passes while the timing necessary for the deeper routes develops.

Third, and perhaps most important, this principle ensures that our quick passes will get a maximum amount of repetition and polish. In stressful situations, players and coaches always have confidence in and revert back to those things which have been emphasized the most. We want the quick game to be one of those things we can hang our hats on in the clutch.

Grouping vs. Memorization

One of the things we have found helps learning is pointing out similarities that exist between packages, placing them in certain "groups" of learning rather than making each one an entirely separate learning entity. For example, we classify our 91 Hitch, 92 Quick Out, 94 Stop, and 99 Fade/Seam as a group of passes having a "core" definition in which #2 will always have a Seam and #3 a Get Open. Now, instead of players having to commit to memory rules for three different receivers in four separate packages, they just learn the differences in the four, namely, the route of #1, knowing that once they've learned #2 and #3 for one of the routes, they know them all. The number of individual elements to learn in this case has gone from twelve (4 routes times 3 assignments) down to six, cutting the burden in half.

Another example of this principle is the fact that, even though it is diagrammed separately for clarity, we do not introduce our packages in such a way that "Doubles" and "Trips" rules have to be memorized separately. In general, #2 and #1 will stay the same regardless of a Trips or Doubles rule, so in those cases we reduce potential learning problems substantially by just teaching #1, #2, and #3 with the idea that #3 obviously doesn't exist in Doubles, but nothing else changes. From that point it is easy to note that 93, 95, and 98 are the *exceptions*, for which special learning must be done. Even in this case, we can (and will) teach 93 and 98 together, telling them that the inside most receiver always has an out-breaking route.

The "grouping" principle applies to installation scheduling as well as teaching, which helps not only in terms of the mental learning, but also the skill training. For example, because the 91, 92, 94, and 99 all have Seam and Get Open routes in their structure, they will go in together so that a heavy, effective emphasis of those routes can get done in drill work on that particular day. At other times, we have put in 91 and 96 on the same day so that we could get the overlapping work on Hitches, or 98 and 99 on the same day to really emphasize Fades.

A "Whole/Part" Approach

In our case, we have had consistent success using a "whole/part" approach to teaching. In other words, players are exposed to the entire offense on a surface level initially, tackling the "whole" thing and learning how its structures work. This approach equips us with a "toolbox" full of tools that can be employed in various ways from various combinations. It will also later enable us to go the entire season without adding things from week to week; we have enough tools that we can merely distribute them in different combinations.

Then, bit by bit, we go into more detail on each "part," focusing on what our players can do best using more specific combinations and detailed teaching. As this process occurs, things are *reviewed* for our players, and the initial learning is reinforced. The parts of the whole not geared to each group's talents are de-emphasized or discarded.

For pre-season work, this principle translates to a distinctly two-phased camp schedule. The first phase we refer to as a "learning and fundamentals" phase, in which fundamental skills are emphasized, and players are exposed to the "whole" of the offense. The second phase is known as the "refining and situational" phase, in which those "parts" get more specific, detailed work, and we begin to apply the first week's learning to situational football.

Levels of Learning

Consistent with the "whole/part" concept is a way of teaching that we call "levels of learning." Obviously, the ultimate goal of all of our teaching is for each player to understand exactly what to do on a given play and the exact technique required. Without technique, everything else breaks down.

This technique, however, must be taught and ingrained into players with patience, and in the proper sequence, one skill at a time, or the result will be confused and frustrated players. To this end, we always deal at all positions with a building process that we refer to as "levels of learning," which progresses as follows:

1. **The Big Picture.** Whenever introducing any kind of route or concept, we first want to create an overall understanding of what we are trying to accomplish. This foundation will be established well before we deal with any sort of assignment, rules, or techniques. We feel that once this "background" is created for players, learning is enhanced; all their assignments and techniques will make sense to the players because it is easy for them to see how they work toward this overall purpose they already understand, rather than simply memorizing. Understanding the big picture also helps players adjust and react properly for situations that come up that can not always be taught; it helps develop their instincts.

2. **Individual Jobs.** This level could also be titled "where to get." Once all the players have been shown the larger picture of how they are all supposed to work as a whole, we begin talking to them about what they as individuals must do to help make the entire thing function. This teaching will include a general understanding of the players' "mission" as well as the actual assignment itself. The first day we put in a route, about the only thing we hit hard in practice is seeing that they understand it and can execute it up to this point. In other words, we are only worried about them getting to the right place to begin with

(not necessarily teaching "how" at this point). The finer teaching points in the next stage of learning are not dealt with until a bit later, because they only confuse the issue the first several times a player is working to get a basic feel for what he is doing.

3. **Technique Details.** If the previous level of learning we talked about was "where to get," this stage would naturally follow as "how to get there." Again, it is our basic belief that learning happens quickly and most effectively when the knowledge that players acquire makes sense to them as they discover it, rather that trying to randomly cram and recall things. We find that once players understand the general mission they have and where they have to get, some of the technique work teaches itself because players naturally begin to acquire those skills through survival instinct; they adjust on their own, which can be, in effect, an improvement in technique. The specific technique work that does have to be taught makes sense because, again, players see its relevance to the overall task that they now know well.

4. **Specific Adjustments to Specific Defenses.** By the time this level of learning is reached, the players have a solid foundation of understanding and a box full of technique "tools" that can be applied to the specific defenses and techniques we face. Specific coverage work, obviously, is vital to success, but if it had been presented earlier in the learning process, and if particular adjustments to particular defensive looks were made a matter of memorization, the drills and teaching used would result in less total comprehension and less effective execution. To a wide receiver, for example, who has progressed through the previous levels properly, specific coverage adjustment is no more than, "On this route, I have to _____ this way, using _____ technique. Because Cover _____ is trying to _____, I must make sure that I really emphasize _____ within the technique and get a _____ relationship on the _____." Coverage adjustment is just a natural extension of a logical process he has grown to understand.

Sample pages from our playbook in Appendix A demonstrate how this process is carried out. The first page of any given route package is an introduction to the route's philosophy, uses, and "*big picture.*" It gives all players a feel for what we are trying to accomplish with the play. We call this the "cover page," and one exists for each of our route packages.

The next page, the "rules sheet," takes us to the next level of learning, detailing and illustrating individual assignments. It also begins the process of dealing with technique details.

The final two pages continue the teaching of technique details, and deal with specific adjustments (and reads) against specific coverages for our quarterbacks and receivers, respectively.

In this way, the "levels of learning" process is consistent throughout: the same steps we go through to install things on the field are used in building the playbook. This consistency is particularly valuable because different players will learn best in different ways; some learn best on the field, some in meetings, some by studying their playbook. Having these same teaching steps practiced throughout all of these modes gives any type of player/learner the same opportunity to grow into the same depth of understanding about a play.

Package-Building Progression
Related to this idea of progressive teaching is the concept of installation by "package-building." In other words, we no longer put in a basic 91, 92, 93, and 94 one day, and then come back a week later to try to add tags to each of those routes. Instead, we'll trim to a minimum the number of new routes being introduced, and, as the day goes on, add those additional tags and adjustments so that we have an entire package when we're through. For example, we might put in 91 and 92 on a given day, which will mean that by the end of the day that we will have added to our arsenal 91, 91 Stutter, 91 Dupe, 92, 92 Go, and 92 Stutter, all out of the variety of formations and motion concepts we wanted to see, all of it being practiced in increasing amounts. Again, this way of doing things goes back to the idea that players' skills and learning are helped when they see things naturally build off each other.

This manner of teaching works for us in a 2-day, 4-element rotation. Three of the elements are practices of varying intensity, the fourth element a meeting. The first part of this structure is a night meeting, in which the new ideas for the next day are introduced, included in which are film clips of what we want them to look like. Players will be given a script for the next morning's 7-on-7 so that they know exactly how we're going to apply the basic route for the first time (See Chapter 6 for an illustration of a typical "installation drill" that has maximized our initial learning process).

Part two, then, is the light morning practice, in which only the basic, untagged route is used, and from very generic and familiar formation combinations.

Part three is a heavy afternoon practice in which we will still use mostly untagged routes, with a few simple exceptions, but change the formations a bit, possibly adding a bit of motion to them. Then, either late in that second practice or early in the third, late afternoon/evening practice (part four), we teach the tags that we want to add to our day's packages. Those tags get practiced in the last session, along with the very best of the formation/motion applications we want to use.

At the meeting that night, then, we do two things: first, we review the whole of what was installed that day, and second, we put in the generic, basic form of the next day's concepts. The script of the next morning will be composed of two parts: first, the exact calls of the last practice from the night before, so that repetitions are gained for our tags and our highest class combinations, and second, the "vanilla" versions of the new passes installed.

Following are two forms of our typical installation sequence: the first shows, in overview form, our two-week installation plan as it relates to our passing game, specifically illustrating how our "four-step" process works to build learning. The second form is an expanded version for the first seven days of installation, showing more fully how we plan for the implementation of formations, motion, and specific skills training (see Appendix R).

DAY 1

A.M. WALK-THRU
Install: 91 Hitch   92 Quick Out
7 on 7:   Basic 91 & 92   Uncovered

P.M. #1
Install: 91 Go 91 Dupe 91 Stutter 92 Go   92 Stutter
Team: 91 & 92 from different sets
               91 & 92 tags—basic versions

P.M. #2
Install: 94 Stop   99 Fade/Seam
7 on 7:   94 & 99—basic

NIGHT MEETING
Review: 91 92 94 99 basic rules & tags
Install: 93 Slant   98 Fade/Out

EMPHASIS
Drops/Reads: 2 & 3 step—left & right   Seam Read
Cuts: Hitch Quick Out Stop Fade Seam

DAY 2

A.M. WALK-THRU
Install: 93 Slant   98 Fade/Out
7 on 7:   Review previous p.m. script 93 & 98—basic

P.M. #1
Install: 93 Dupe 93 Seam   93 Dog
Team: 93 & 98 from different sets
               93 tags—basic sets
               1 x 91   1 x 92   1 x 99

P.M. #2
Install: Add simple motion to 91, 92, 93, 98, 99
7 on 7:   Review previous p.m. script 93 & 98—basic

NIGHT MEETING
Review: 93 and 98 packages
Install: 96 Quick Smash 97 Short

EMPHASIS
Drops/Reads: 2 & 3 step Flat cov read   C read
Cuts: Slant Shoot Breakout Seam Fade

DAY 3

A.M. WALK-THRU
Install: 96 Quick Smash   97 Short
7 on 7:   Review p.m script   96 & 97—Basic

P.M. #1
Install: 96 Whip   97 Corner
Team: 96 & 97 from different sets

P.M. #2
Install: Squeezed 96 adjustment   Motion Hitch for 96
                         Snug motion for 96 Whip
7 on 7:   All varieties of 96 & 97 x 10Review calls x5

NIGHT MEETING
Review: 96 & 97 packages
Introduce: "Read" passing game   Hook route   Flood route

EMPHASIS
Drops/Reads: 2 & 3 step   C read   Short read
Cuts: Hitch Quick Smash   Short   Inside Slant

DAY 4

A.M. WALK-THRU
Install: Hook route   Flood route
7 on 7:   Review previous p.m. script Hook & Flood—basic

P.M. #1
Install: "Switch" tag for Hook and Flood routes
Team: Hook and Flood from different sets & basic motion
                         Hook and Flood "Switch" from basic sets

P.M. #2
Install: Total pass review
7 on 7:   Total pass review

NIGHT MEETING
Review: Flood & Hook   Q &A   Written test
Install: 95 Turn   90 Wheel

EMPHASIS
Drops/Reads: 5 step   Read flat cov
Cuts: Hook   Flat   Sail

DAY 5

A.M. WALK-THRU
Install: 95 Turn   90 Wheel
7 on 7: 95 Turn & 90 Wheel from basic sets

P.M. #1
Install: "Switch" tag for 95
Team: 95 from different sets   95 Switch—basic

P.M. #2
Install: 95 from motion
7 on 7: 3 x 90 Wheel   4 x 95 & variations
4 x Hook/Flood   3 x Overall 90 review

NIGHT MEETING
Review: 95 & 90 Wheel packages
Install: Mesh   Smash   "Bunch" concept

EMPHASIS
Drops/Reads: 2 & 3 step   Wheel read   Turn read
Cuts: Turn   Shoot   Wheel   Split

DAY 6

A.M. WALK-THRU
Install: Mesh Route   Smash route
7 on 7: Review previous p.m. script Mesh/Smash—basic

P.M. #1
Install: "Bunch" calls and traffic rules
Team: Mesh & Smash from regular and Bunched sets

P.M. #2
Install: 95 Trade and 98 from Bunched sets
7 on 7: 5 x 95/98 Bunched 6 x Mesh/Smash w/motion
3 x Read route review   2 x 90 series review

NIGHT MEETING
Review: Mesh   Smash   Bunch calls   95 Trade
Install: Verticals: Deep & Snake   Comeback   "B" Tags

EMPHASIS
Drops/Reads: 5 step   Read flat cov   C Read
Cuts: Whip Read   Smash   Flat   Read Seam

DAY 7

A.M. WALK-THRU
Install: Vertical routes: Deep & Snake
7 on 7:   10 x Verticals   5 x Bunch review

P.M. #1
Install: Comeback
Team: Verticals from different sets Comeback—basic

P.M. #2
Install: Basic motion for Comeback & Verticals
7 on 7:   6 x Verticals   6 x Comeback   3 x Review

NIGHT MEETING
Review: Vertical routes   Comeback   Written test
Install: Begin teaching situational football

EMPHASIS
Drops/Reads: 5 step
Cuts: Snake   Go   Comeback

CONCLUDE "LEARNING/FUNDAMENTAL" PHASE

"SITUATIONAL/REFINING" PHASE SUMMARY

DAY 8		DAY 9	
Situations:	1st & 10 Backed up Blitz day	**Situations:**	2nd & Long 3d & 4-7 3d & Long Blitz period
Review:	91 92 94 98 99	**Review:**	93 95 96 97 90Whl
DAY 10		DAY 11	
Situations:	4 minute 3 & Short 3 & 3-6 Blitz period	**Situations:**	Red Zone/Goalline +25 +15 +8 +5 +3
Review:	Hook/Flood/Smash	**Review:**	Mesh/Verts/Cmbk
DAY 12			
Total review/scrimmage, including Blitz walk-through			

EXPANDED INSTALLATION SCHEDULE: "LEARNING/FUNDAMENTALS" PHASE, DAYS 1-7

Day/Practice	Formations and Motions	Route Packages	Individual Cuts	Coverages	QB Skills	WR Skills
1/am	Basic Rip/Rex/Ron (static) HB numbered positions	91-191 Orange 92-192 Black	Hitch Seam Quick Out	Cov 3	Stance/exchange 2 step drop	Stance & start Uncovered courses/blocks
/pm1			91 Go 91 Dupe 91 Stutter 92 Go 92 Stutter	Hitch & Go Hitch Stutter Out & Up Out Stutter		Uncovered ID/throws Seam Read Basic Pop-Up drill
/pm2			94-194 99-199	Stop Fade	3 step drop (hold)	Sideline catches Vertical read
2/am	Basic motion system Split/Strong/Weak/Brown/Black	93-193 98-198	Slant Shoot Fade	Cov 1 Free BkOut	Pre-snap routine Id Read Player Coverage recogntn	6 second rule Coverage recogntn 3 step drop (quick) Flat defender read
/pm1	In/Out Plus/Minus	93 Dog	Dog 93 Dupe	Basic Read Drill	Basic weave mech.	1st short inside C read
/pm2	"Flex," Flip/Flop/Flash		93 Seam			
3/am	Ray/Larry Roy/Loy	96-196 97-197	Quick Smash Short	Cov 2	Id Danger Player	Pressure turn-RAC Hi-Lo Read off C
/pm1	Snug motion	96 Whip	Whip	97 Corner	Trajectory work	Jam releases intro
/pm2	"Squeeze" & "Bunch" calls	Twin	Squeezed Hitch			Bunch traffic rules

EXPANDED INSTALLATION SCHEDULE: "LEARNING/FUNDAMENTALS" PHASE, DAYS 1-7

Day/Practice	Formations and Motions	Route Packages	Individual Cuts	Coverages	QB Skills	WR Skills
4/am	Ram-Lion pkg X & Z Over Return motion	3 - Hook 5 - Flood	Hook Flat Sail	Pocket presence/hot air	5 step drop	Drag principle
/pm1		"Switch" tag for 3 & 5				Jam releases part II
/pm2						
5/am	Trace motion Pair/Slot/Wing	95-195 90-190 Wheel	Turn Split Read Go Wheel		Ball away from press 1st short inside C read	Catch/Tuck/Turn v. zones (split N/S)
/pm1	Shuffle motion	95 Switch				Underneath reversal Jam releases at variable depths
/pm2						
6/am	Green/Blue	6 - Smash 7 - Mesh	Smash Seam Read Whip Read	Cov 4	Army throw	Sideline turn-up Adv. weave tech Advanced Bunch traffic concepts Motion concept vs. jam
/pm1						
/pm2		7 Stem 7 Arrow 95 Trade Bunched 93 & 98				
7/am		8 - Snake 9 - Deep	Ins Snake Outs Snake	Quarters	306-307 Action 336-337 Action	Go
/pm1	Right & Left	2 - Comeback	Comeback		Scramble Rules Safe hook slide	Scramble Rules
/pm2						

CHAPTER 6

General Principles of Practice and Drilling

Vital to the success of any offensive concept or play is the manner in which it is first taught and then drilled and practiced on the field. These activities are the critical links that will determine how well all our offensive scheming and theory come to life during games and have consistent success.

It is for that reason that we felt Chapter 5 and the following three chapters were vital parts of any comprehensive book about the quick passing game; they represent the next logical building block. The philosophy, concepts, and detailed teaching progression must, without a doubt, be sound and thorough, but it is our conviction that they are wasted if not practiced and perfected the right way. This chapter builds on the ideas about installation and teaching from the previous chapter with a discussion of how to best take that teaching to the practice field. Clearly, every coach has his own way of conducting drills and practice; what follows is simply some successful methods we have used throughout the years in implementing the quick passing game.

In our case, we have a certain set of criteria and basic principles we take into account in laying out practice drills. These are the things we feel we must have incorporated throughout our classroom time and our practice if we are to make the most of our precious opportunities to improve.

Principles of Drilling
For drills to accomplish what they are designed to accomplish, they need to possess four basic qualities:

1. **Purpose.** Each drill we utilize in practice must have a very specific, well-defined purpose. Both the players and coaches must understand exactly what we are trying to accomplish, and what skills we want to improve each time the drill is conducted. This understanding of "purpose" is a key weapon against things like the boredom of daily routine and concentration-robbing exhaustion, both of which affect the quality of the work your players get done. Being given a specific direction and goal takes their attention away from how tired they are or how badly they want to get practice over with and refocuses it on improvement.

We emphasize and remind our players of these things during meetings, in the classroom, and as we coach on the run on the practice field. It is our goal, through constant reminders, to keep the sense of purpose and improvement heightened throughout every practice.

2. **Isolate specific skills.** As much as possible, we work to isolate the specific skills and concepts we have decided we want improved in each practice segment, much as a lab scientist seeks to control all the extraneous elements not being specifically tested in an experiment. By eliminating factors that could distract players from the specific point we are getting across, focus is once again enhanced, and players get good practice at doing things the right way.

    For us, then, this focus requires our input on the field to relate specifically to those purposes we have laid out, not to other unrelated flaws that we may see. For example, if we are working with a quarterback on a specific read drill, we are not going to complicate things for him by coaching him really hard at the same time on his drop mechanics. We have found that if we try to teach or account for too many things at once, players' focus gets clouded and much less gets accomplished.

3. **Create a realistic picture.** For any drill that we create to ever make it to the practice field, we must believe it has game relevance. We want to hone skills and create pictures that have direct application to what will happen on game day. When pressure and stress set in on game day, calm is maintained and execution successful most often when players have a sense that they have seen the things facing them before and have already developed ways to deal with them. The confidence and success rate of your players goes up when things appear familiar to them, and the skills that they must use to be successful have been ingrained so they are automatic. Practice time is too valuable a resource to spend on doing anything that does not accomplish this purpose.

4. **Fast tempo: Maximized repetitions, minimized idleness.** Finally, we look to construct drills that can involve as many people as possible, so that players are always learning by doing, not standing in line. We sell our players on the value of operating practice constantly at a brisk tempo so opportunities to improve are maximized. Keeping things moving and lively in this manner works with our other drill goals because it helps limit distractions and maintain focus.

    As a result, our coaching is "on the run," giving players a key focus/correction point as they sprint back to the end of the line. Again, that focus/correction point will be related to the specific thing we are trying to accomplish, but will not impede the continual, natural flow of the drill.

Another result of this philosophy is that we give very specific attention to how the drills can be aligned and function in such a manner that involves as many people as possible working at once. This strategy facilitates the fast tempo, "learn by doing" style and prevents the potential repetitions that are lost when players are standing in line. *In every drill we do, one of the coaches present is responsible for establishing and maintaining the tempo that we want.*

An example of how our installation and drilling principles come together is illustrated below in a typical, basic drill we use when first installing a route package.

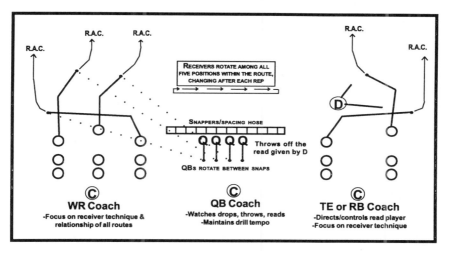

DIAGRAM 6-1
INSTALLATION DRILL SET-UP: 93-193 SLANT

This particular drill is designed to "rep" the basic assignments of the route we are installing as many times as possible on a basic level. It allows as many receivers as possible to be on the move at a time, and uses four quarterbacks for throwing. Each receiver is functioning in each of the different positions so the route is learned on the broadest possible level; this knowledge will help us take full advantage of our formation structures later.

The skills being isolated at this particular stage are the simple mechanics of throwing, catching, elementary route running, and run after catch, with the players understanding by our emphasis and the tempo we force them to maintain that the goal is to get as many quality repetitions at the different positions as possible within our time frame.

For the quarterbacks we begin building their sight picture by creating a rudimentary "read" situation at one of the locations. This read defender is controlled by a coach on each play to ensure that we get exactly what we want. As we get further along in the teaching progression, we will add additional read players on the other side so that different sight pictures are being presented and the quarterback's thought and reaction process is trained repeatedly.

Equally important is the fact that each of our coaches has specific areas on which he is focusing: They have been arranged so they can not only do their work with maximum effectiveness, but also give us the ability as an offensive staff to observe and coach every player in the drill.

The chapters that follow show more specific ways we use to train our players in the quick passing game based on these practice and drill fundamentals, first with the quarterbacks (Chapter 7), then with receivers (Chapter 8).

Quarterback Training Overview

The careful, step-by-step training of the quarterback is the single most important thing that takes place in any offense that emphasizes the pass to any degree at all. Unfortunately, the quarterback is many times the position on the field receiving the *least* individual attention. Quarterback training for us is a year-round proposition both mentally and physically.

We break down our total quarterback development program into five general areas: ball-handling, footwork and drops, actual throwing mechanics, pre-snap disciplines and checks, and reads/decision making.

Within these areas, we try to adhere to a number of basic teaching principles. First, we constantly make an effort to evaluate and see the things we are doing from the quarterback's standpoint. Without this approach, we would have a tendency, first of all, to overload the quarterback with more thought processes than he can handle at a given time, and second, to lose sight of the fact that the game looks much different to him from the heat of the pocket than it does to us on the blackboard or watching film. Our teaching is only effective to the degree that it can be understood and carried out from his perspective. One practical approach is to coach, many times, from a position behind the quarterback so we can see the play developing as he does.

Second, as we do with all positions, we coach every snap, every throw, and every repetition of everything they do. Particularly where it concerns his throwing motion, quarterbacks have to be sold on the fact that every time they throw a ball, a habit—bad or good—is reinforced. "Every throw is important," we tell them. The players must also understand exactly *why* what they did was either good or bad. "Good job" does not necessarily reinforce specifically what the quarterback did that made the play successful.

This coaching, however, is only part of the job; the quarterback must also be trained. In other words, quarterbacks will only be able to effectively integrate the information and feedback being given if they do it over and over and over again. This principle is the reason we work so hard on establishing and maintaining a practice tempo: our coaching is only going to be good to the extent that it is thoroughly trained.

Finally, we make a concerted effort to reinforce the leadership role the quarterback must occupy. This goal can be accomplished in a number of ways—giving him more responsibility, holding him to a higher standard, keeping him a step ahead in the learning process and practice schedule so he becomes a source of stability and understanding for his teammates, "forcing" him to grow up, or reaffirming our confidence in him in front of the rest of the team—but fundamental to them all is understanding that the quarterback position is *not* like all the other positions on the field. Not only are the demands placed on him different and more sophisticated than the demands placed on other players, he is the one in whom the other ten will have to believe during the most critical points of a game and of a season. The way we handle our quarterback as coaches should foster and build up this confidence his teammates have.

In this chapter we will touch on a number of areas that we feel are of particular importance to the quarterback's functioning within the quick passing game. First, we will discuss the different elements of his pre-snap procedure, which is a crucial but often overlooked aspect of quarterback play. Second, the details of the two- and three-step drops that are used in the quick passing game will be discussed. Third, we will address the matter of "read players" and "danger players" in the decision-making process. Fourth, two fundamental drills that are integral to our quarterback development and can be built to train a number of important quarterback skills will be introduced and illustrated.

Pre-Snap Routine

As we emphasize throughout this text, the success of any play is largely determined by what happens on our part *before* the snap. Nowhere is this concept more true than with the quarterback. Upon the snap, he will enter a two-four second "whirlwind" of activity in which he must execute a number of quick decisions while still being sound in whatever physical mechanics he uses. To function at his best in this fast-paced environment, the quarterback must, through his pre-snap work, provide himself with a clear picture of what he is looking for, an understanding of what things can happen based on how the defense aligns, and a plan for how he will react in each scenario.

To help him accomplish this goal, we provide the quarterback with a regimented routine he goes through every time he breaks the huddle. By laying out his routine in a specific, point-by-point manner, we leave nothing to chance and give the quarterback security and confidence because he knows all of his bases have been covered. Our checklist for him is as follows:

1) Get up to the line and get your hands under center immediately. This position provides the threat of the snap, forcing the defense to get to their final position. By doing all your surveying and cadence work from this position, you

avoid many of the problems that can be caused by defensive "stems" and other pre-snap jockeying on their part.

2) As you are arriving under center, find the free safety to determine if he is in some sort of deep coverage. If he is not deep, but in a removed coverage position, you know that you may be in a blitz/protection check situation.

3) Scan coverage from right to left:
   a) Is anyone uncovered?
   b) Are there any "gimmes" such as an easy Hitch you can check to or a busted defensive alignment that has left someone wide open?
   c) Confirm the coverage call you are hearing from your receivers and determine the number of defenders committed to coverage. (See Appendix O for basic coverage tips)

4) Come back and scan the front from left to right:
   a) Are there any overloads or unsound adjustments?
   b) Find any techniques relevant to a run check, or number in the box as it relates to a run/pass check.
   c) If pass, understand which of your linemen may have a tough 1 on 1 matchup and where heat might come from on the pass rush (advanced).

5) Clearly identify your "Read" and "Danger" players if it is a pass or an option play.

Drops

In both high school and college, a high percentage of bad throws result from poor drops. A pass drop has two basic goals:

1) Get the quarterback to his prescribed depth in the correct timing to deliver the ball.

2) Get the quarterback's feet and body balanced, positioned, and directed in such a way that he can make a fundamentally sound, "full body" throw.

Common to any drop we use is the emphasis that is placed on creating separation from the line of scrimmage on the first step. We call this first step a "reach step." A good reach step starts with a good stance. A quarterback should be balanced, standing slightly pigeon-toed under center, with his weight distributed so he can drive off his opposite foot immediately and without a false step. As he pushes off the line in this manner, the quarterback should strain to get as much depth as possible, to the point where he feels like he is leaning slightly backwards. We constantly challenge our quarterbacks to try to get more and more depth on their first step, stretching themselves to the point that they are no longer balanced.

Also common to both the two- and three-step drop is the idea that the quarterback must get his momentum directed forward, toward the throw as he delivers the ball. The posture we want as he sets to throw is a forward lean with his chin directly over his front knee, front shoulder down, and feet no wider than shoulder width apart, with the weight on the balls of his back foot ready to drive off it on the throw. His body lean should approximate the following figure.

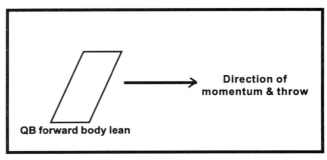

FIGURE 7-1
QB FORWARD BODY LEAN OFF LAST STEP OF HIS DROP

Another aspect of the drop that we train is ball positioning. In general, the ball should be carried in such a way that it is a comfortable, natural extension of the quarterback's movement, yet also enable him to get the ball into throwing position as quickly and efficiently as possible. We have gotten the best results when the ball is carried at chest level, pushed back with the front hand to a position on the quarterback's rear breast, allowing the ball to be taken from the drop position to the throwing motion with no wasted movement. *The quarterback should keep both hands on the ball at all times, until he starts his throwing motion.* Adherence to this point will prevent a variety of problems: fumbles on contact and the "patting" of the ball are two disasters that can be virtually eliminated if this habit of two-handed ball toting is forged early on.

The Two-Step Drop
The two-step drop is a sped-up drop we have developed that maximizes the quick timing of certain routes and helps the quarterback get his momentum going in the direction of the throw. In the right situations, it can help the productivity—specifically the run after catch—of certain, timed routes by getting the ball in the receiver's hands a count or two sooner than it would arrive from a three-step drop. Routes that can benefit greatly from this include the 91/191 Hitch, 92/192 Quick Out, 95/195 Turn, and 97/197 Short.

While it has definite benefits, the two-step drop is not for every route or every situation. The deeper quick route packages we use, such as 94/194 Stop, 96/196 Quick Smash, and 99/199 Fade/Seam, will never employ a two-step drop because of timing considerations. Further, in cases where the offensive line is not "holding its ground" in its execution of 90/190 protection but giving ground instead, the two-step drop can become a real problem because the quarterback will have too little space to operate since the two-step drop is shallower than the three-step drop.

The two-step drop always begins with a reach step by the foot opposite the quarterback's throwing hand. The second step will get his throwing side foot in a position to push off and swing his hips through for a fully powered throw. He then drives off that foot and begins his throwing motion between the second and third step. On his third step, all his momentum is directed downhill toward the target. This process is illustrated in detail both to the right and left in the diagrams that follow.

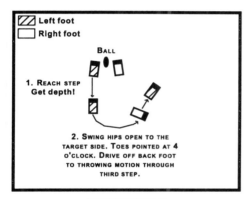

DIAGRAM 7-2
TWO-STEP DROP TO THE RIGHT
(RIGHT-HANDED PASSER)

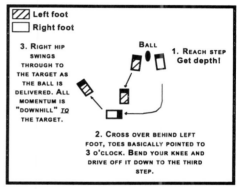

DIAGRAM 7-3
TWO-STEP DROP TO THE LEFT
(RIGHT HANDED PASSER)

The Three-Step Drop

The more common quarterback drop in the quick passing game is the three-step drop. Unlike the two-step drop, the quarterback's shoulders immediately turn perpendicular to the line of scrimmage as he takes his reach step. In taking the reach step, the foot opposite his throwing arm pivots and pushes, and the leg to the side of the throwing hand is propelled by this push to *strain* to its maximum depth. Again, this reach step should strain the quarterback almost to the point where he's leaning backwards.

The quarterback's second and third steps are "gather steps," which get his body into the forward leaning posture from which he will make the throw. He attains this position by "throwing his hips" behind him as he pushes off the first step. This action gets his hips under and then behind him, which naturally puts the body in a forward leaning position, chin over front knee. The throwing of the hips also means that the last two steps will not be distinct, individual steps as much as a sort of "hippity hop." His second and third steps hit the ground in quick succession, his third step not gaining much additional depth. As his second and third steps hit, the front knee bends and the feet land in a compact position, ready to drive off the back foot for a full-body throw. If the quarterback does not use this "hippity hop" but overextends on steps two and/or three, he will not be able to create the forward body lean and his feet will be too far apart, resulting in a limited power base from which to throw.

The fact that the "hippity hop" of steps two and three are for body positioning rather than gaining a lot of depth makes the depth of the reach step that much more important. We teach the "hippity hop" in this manner because we want the quarterback in a position to throw the ball immediately off the third step. On routes that develop a bit deeper and do not rely on such fast rhythm, we can lengthen the second step to gain more depth, using a "bounce up" by the quarterback off his third step to gain this body positioning. This technique is referred to as a "3 and hold" drop, and is used on routes like 94-194 Stop, 96-196 Whip, 97-197 Plant, and 98-198 Hang.

Another key element of the three-step drop is the quarterback's head and chin positioning. Especially on throws to the left (for a right-handed quarterback), it is important that the quarterback tuck his chin into his front shoulder and turn his head to the left third of the field so he can see what he needs to see. On throws to the left, right-handed quarterbacks often make reads and throws too late, because they have not seen the read developing during their whole drop, and, in effect, start their read too late.

"Read Players" and "Danger Players"

One of the quarterback's key concerns is understanding and accounting for both "read" and "danger" players in the route. By "danger player," we usually mean the defender immediately inside the defender we're reading. He is considered a "danger" because he has the potential, with an unusually active drop, to disrupt our basic read at times. Safeties playing unusually tight alignments, such as in some forms of Cover 4, can also become danger players because of their potential to "rob" from above when relieved of any deep coverage responsibility.

The read player is always the reference point for finding the "danger" player; danger players are generally defined by their relative position to the player we are reading, so it is impossible to know who the danger player is without identifying the read player. The following is summary of the "read player" and the potential danger player or players for each of our basic route packages.

Route	Read Player	Danger Player(s)
91-191	Flat coverage	Next LB in, Cov 4 Hash safe
92-192	Flat coverage	Next LB in, Cov 4 Hash safe
93-193	Flat coverage	Next LB in, Cov 4 Hash safe
94-194	Flat coverage	Next LB in, Cov 4 Hash safe
95-195	1st short inside C	Next LB in
96-196	Cornerback	Cover 3 flat coverage
97-197	1st short inside C	Next LB in, Cov 4 Hash saf
98-198	Cornerback	Cover 2/4 Hash safe, Cov 4 OLB
99-199	Hash or free safe	Sinking Cover 2/4 cornerback

It is the quarterback's job to ensure that the danger player does not become a factor in the play; most interceptions are a result of a danger player entering the throwing lane unexpectedly. This danger player can be accounted for in either or both of these two basic ways:

1) A pre-snap read that either prompts him to work to a side opposite the most "dangerous" of the danger players or tells him that none of the potential danger players realistically threaten the throwing lane.
2) Clear peripheral vision during his read that enables him to see not only the throwing lane provided by his read, but in front of the lane to see any potential invasion of it.

Some different examples of how the thought process might work in accounting for the danger player follow.

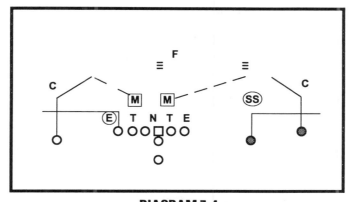

DIAGRAM 7-4
MIRRORED ROUTE ON A HASHMARK, example 1
The danger player on the right (M) has much further to go than
the danger player on the left (M) to get in a throwing lane
because of their position and field width. QB should go right.

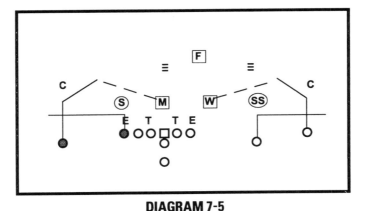

DIAGRAM 7-5
MIRRORED ROUTE ON A HASHMARK, example 2
Because of the linebacker structure, the danger player on the
left (M) has as far or farther to go to threaten a throwing lane
than the danger player on the right (W). With the FS in position
to be a potential <u>2nd</u> danger player on the right side, the
quarterback should work the left side.

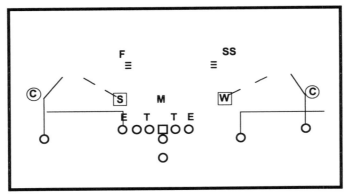

DIAGRAM 7-6
MIRRORED ROUTE IN THE MIDDLE OF THE FIELD
Danger players a definite consideration on both sides: QB
should pick a side based on drop tendencies of S & W, must
account for where they are before throwing Slant. If he thinks
they'll disrupt the read on either side, he should check to a tag
for #2 that can hold them (Seam, Stick, Dupe)

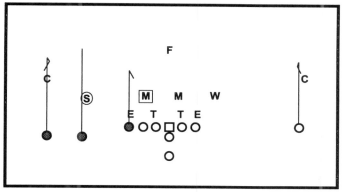

DIAGRAM 7-7
ASYMMETRICAL ROUTE (194 STOP CALLED), example 1
Quarterback can see through his pre-snap read that **M** as the
danger player on the left should not be a factor for two
reasons: 1) His positioning will not easily allow him to cover
the distance between him and the Seam's throwing lane, and
2) He would have to fight through #3's vertical release to get
there. QB should proceed with play to the left.

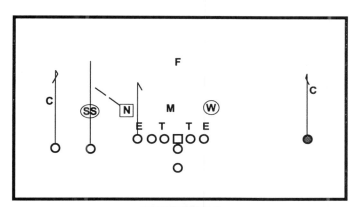

DIAGRAM 7-8
ASYMMETRICAL ROUTE (194 STOP CALLED), example 2
N, as the danger player on the left, now in a position to easily
get in the Seam lane and disrupt the read. QB should check out
of this strongside combination, or, if he feels good about the
lane being afforded the single receiver on the right, throw the
ball to the right.

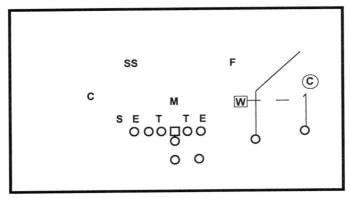

DIAGRAM 7-9
BASIC QUICK SMASH
W is a <u>potential</u>, but not a <u>definitive</u> threat to the Hitch from
where he is positioned. If QB's read of C takes him to the Hitch,
he must see slightly <u>in front of</u> his throwing lane to ensure that
W is not threatening the throw.

Drills
Throwing Routine

Very early in the training of our quarterbacks, we establish a precise, step-by-step throwing routine that isolates all the different aspects of the throwing motion. It is a "pre-practice" regiment through which they will go every day. The quarterbacks are taught exactly what each part of the routine is developing in the throwing motion, and are given goals related to different parts of their throw on a daily or weekly basis. The key to getting the most out of this routine is not the "going through the motion" of it, but the quarterback's understanding and awareness of what he is trying to improve through each throw. We tell them that every throw is important because it develops or reinforces a habit that will determine how consistently accurate they will be in a game. We also try to heighten this awareness by having them pick a very specific target for each of these stationary throws (e.g., bottom of the right number) to make each throw and throwing motion a focused one. Active dialogue will be maintained by the coach throughout the routine, literally coaching almost every throw, good or bad.

This routine for us consists of the following (with the emphasis in parentheses):

1. Throwing from the knee with the high elbow (emphasizing wrist cock and high elbow).

2. Throwing from the knee, rotating shoulders (emphasizing the "push—pull" of the non-throwing arm that forces hip rotation and helps power the ball).

3. Throw from standing, facing parallel (emphasizing hip rotation, as well as finishing the throw with good back bend and follow through).

4. Throw with the non-throwing shoulder facing your partner (Work on powering the throw by driving off the back foot and transferring your weight in sync with good hip rotation. Also work on full follow through. Quarterback should finish with his throwing hand in a position to "take a dollar from his opposite pocket").

5. Throw with your throwing shoulder facing your partner (forces hip rotation).

6. Throw from a miniature drop (emphasizing the drive off the back foot, sinking the back knee and transferring weight to the front foot so that the throw is powered by the lower body, not the arm; also emphasizing the "6-inch step", or prevention of overstriding).

7. Throwing from full drops, with partner offset right or left. (Work on specifics of each drop: depth on first step, proper forward "chin over knee" lean on the last step, as well as opening hips correctly to offset target)

Each quarterback executes five to eight of each of these throws in a typical day's routine. Throughout the season, we will emphasize more of one phase or another depending on areas that need refinement. Our quarterbacks must have the mentality that they never stop improving their throwing motion and are constantly seeking to become more consistently accurate.

"Pop-up" Drills

One of the first drills we use to train basic quarterback fundamentals is what we call the "Pop-up Drill." It is valuable not only in its basic form, but because it offers a number of different elements that can be added to train different aspects of quarterback play.

The starting point in the Pop-up Drill is simply to place two receivers 8-10 yards away from the quarterback, spaced horizontally 5-6 yards apart (the depths and relative positions of the receivers can be changed to simulate different throws for the quarterback). The quarterback takes a two- or three-step drop, and as he hits his last step, a coach points to one of the two receivers. The receiver to whom he points "pops up" by lifting his hands, essentially calling for the ball. The quarterback completes his drop, "resets" his hips toward the player he is throwing to, and delivers the ball to the "popped up" player. The receiver executes a catch and tuck using correct hand position, turns tightly, and accelerates upfield 5 to 6 yards.

This basic drill allows the quarterback to work on his drop and turning his hips toward the target so that he is not throwing against or across his body. It breaks the read and throw process down to its barest elements. For receivers, this is a time to get repetitions at using correct hand position for the type of throw they get, tucking the ball, and making a tight, upfield turn for the run after catch.

The next step is to put pop-up receivers in positions approximating where they would end up in different route packages. This "approximation" includes not only depth and lateral location on the field, but also the positioning of their body as it would be out of their final break. They assume the same relative angle to the line of scrimmage and head position they would have if they just finished their route. Adding this step gives the quarterbacks training in throwing to the actual spots they will be targeting in live action. It also trains receivers to make catches and turns in the actual position they will have to make them in game situations. This practice is a critical part of training receivers to catch the ball.

A third receiver can easily be added to this drill to create the feel of a route's "trips rule" as well. Nothing changes except that the coach may now designate any one of three receivers who have assumed the position they would have out of the break. This is most effectively used with route packages in which all three receivers are a viable part of the quarterback's initial read: 93/193 Slant, 95/195 Turn, 97/197 Short, and 98/198 Fade for example.

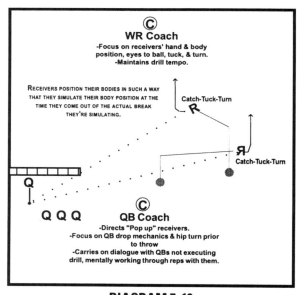

DIAGRAM 7-10
POP-UP DRILL WITH RECEIVERS IN POSITIONS THAT
SIMULATE THE FINAL BREAK POINTS OF A BASIC
ROUTE—e.g. 93 SLANT

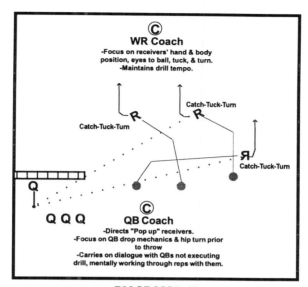

DIAGRAM 7-11
POP-UP DRILL WITH 3 RECEIVERS IN POSITIONS
SIMULATING FINAL BREAK POINTS OF A BASIC ROUTE—
e.g. 93 SLANT

Next, we can add "trajectory" training into the mix with the quarterbacks. This step is accomplished by placing a defender five yards in front of each receiver directly in his path to the quarterback. Now, when he makes his throw to the pop-up receiver, he will be throwing over a defender to get it there, a defender who raises his hands along with the receiver if pointed to. The quarterback wants to not only get it over the defender, but he wants to snap it down to the receiver on the other side rather than just sailing it or floating it high to get the ball over. He accomplishes this goal in two ways: first, he must focus on a good, high release point, and second, he must overemphasize his wrist snap as he releases the ball.

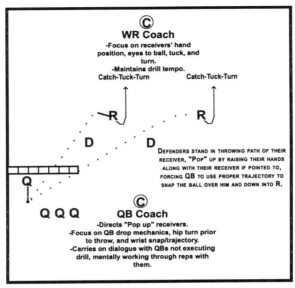

DIAGRAM 7-12
POP-UP DRILL WITH "TRAJECTORY" EMPHASIS ADDED

Finally, the Pop-up Drill can be done in a "hot air" situation. The quarterback executes the drill exactly as he normally would, except we have added a simulated pass rush. Three defenders who line up stacked initially begin to rush, one at a time, after the quarterback hits his second or third step. They run by him within a foot or two, being very careful never to touch any part of his arm, waving, yelling, and trying to distract the quarterback in any way possible. They may even brush his thigh pad on the way by. Now the quarterback must execute with lots of things going on around him. He must maintain his focus downfield, feeling the rush rather than looking at it, stepping up out of the "hot air" into "clean air" when necessary to make his throw. Since his eyes are the giveaway to whether focus is being maintained or not, many times this phase of the drill is done with the quarterback coach positioned in front of the quarterback rather than behind. This position enables the coach to see where the quarterback's eyes go, while still being able to see his drop, hip turn, etc.

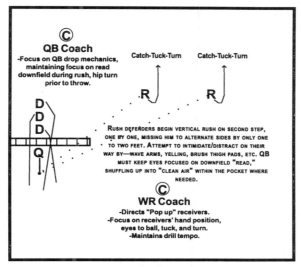

DIAGRAM 7-13
POP-UP DRILL WITH "HOT AIR"/RUSH ELEMENT ADDED

One of the real strengths of this pop-up format is that any or all of the "interchangeable parts" may be used in combinations at the same time, gradually building to a fuller and fuller picture of what actual games feel and look like to the quarterback. The different aspects can be employed individually, all together, or in some combination in between, depending on which particular skills need the most training and focus. It also provides a very specific teaching progression that may be followed, helping the quarterback to understand exactly what is being taught and what the coach is looking for.

Read Drill

The next type of drill that is very basic to our quarterback training is the "Read Drill." Like the Pop-up Drill, our Read Drill starts with a very simple core, and can then have different elements added to hone different skills.

The initial premise of the Read Drill is simply to have two receivers positioned a certain distance apart from each other, much like the Pop-up Drill, station a defender between them, and as the quarterback drops, direct the defender to cover one receiver or the other.

For the quarterback to execute his read and delivery in the correct timing, the reading process must be honed to the point that he responds to what he sees rather than thinking about it. Effective reading is a process of "trained feel." The quarterback, through countless repetitions, becomes conditioned to react in an immediate, correct way to certain "sight pictures." The basis of the Read Drill is to present the quarterback with sight pictures, and train him to react to those sight pictures with greater and greater proficiency.

The Read Drill can be run on two basic levels: as a "still" drill in which receivers assume positions and body postures as though they had already completed the route and stand stationary, or as a full-speed drill in which they run full routes triggered by the quarterback's call. The "still" drill allows quarterbacks to get a lot of repetitions at the reads and throws they will have to make at a very rapid rate; the full-speed drill does not get the same number of repetitions, but enables receivers to get much more meaningful work on route technique. Our general approach has been to use still drills initially in the training process to keep things as simple and focused as possible for the quarterbacks, later working up to full-speed drills.

The Read Drill in its basic form as it would apply to the 91-191 Hitch package is shown below.

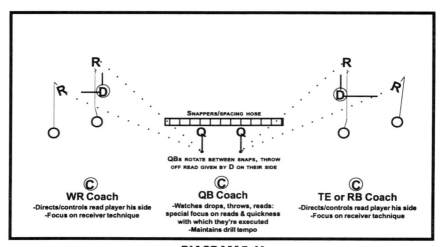

DIAGRAM 7-14
BASIC READ DRILL: 91-191 HITCH

Certain routes within certain route packages warrant the kind of "trajectory" training we use in the Pop-up Drill. That element can also be added to a basic Read Drill. This step is shown with the "Seam" route in the illustration that follows.

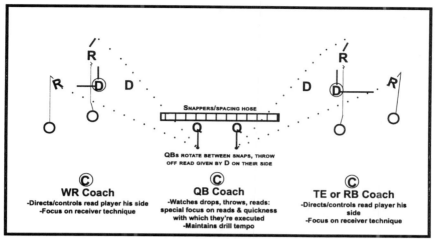

DIAGRAM 7-15
BASIC READ DRILL WITH TRAJECTORY ELEMENT
ADDED FOR SEAM

As we discussed earlier in the chapter, it is vital that quarterbacks be trained to identify and account for "danger" players who have the potential to disrupt the basic read. One way we can begin to create this feel and understanding is by adding such danger players to the basic Read Drill. The danger player is controlled by the same coach controlling the read player. If the quarterback is told by his basic read to throw the Seam, in this example, and sees the danger player entering his throwing lane as he turns to throw the Seam, the ball should be thrown away, at least for the purposes of this drill.

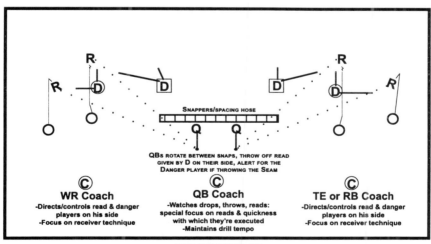

DIAGRAM 7-16
BASIC READ DRILL WITH "DANGER PLAYER" ADDED

As with the Pop-up Drill, the "hot air" element may be added to the Read Drill to develop pocket presence on the quarterback's part. Again, we use three successive rushers brushing closely by the passer in an attempt to create "heat" and distraction. Generally, this phase is done in a "still drill" format except later in the season when we are polishing route combinations we know well. We use this approach because rushers *plus* the read *plus* the prospect of having to hit inexperienced receivers on time presents too many problems to effectively develop the skills we want to develop.

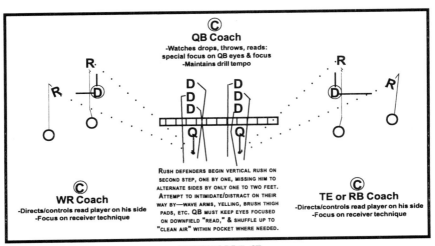

DIAGRAM 7-17
BASIC READ DRILL WITH "HOT AIR" ADDED

CHAPTER 8

Receiver Training Overview

As people who have both spent extensive time in our careers as receivers coaches, we have always thought that really specific attention to the details of receiver technique is one of the most overlooked parts of the passing game, and an area that, with the proper work, could quickly improve the passing proficiency of any given offense. "Technique," we have always preached, "turns average receivers into very good ones, and good receivers into great ones."

This technique, however, has to be taught and ingrained into players with patience and in the proper sequence, one skill at a time, or the result will be confused and frustrated players. To this end, we always deal at all positions with the "levels of learning" building process discussed in Chapter 5.

This chapter is not meant to be a comprehensive "Receivers Manual"; rather, we will accomplish two things. First, we will discuss principles of basic receiver techniques that are crucial to any individual pattern. These principles, to us, are many of the "fundamentals" of a receiver's job that will be drilled and emphasized and talked about all year long. In our case, we break down those fundamentals into five areas: mental approach, blocking, route technique, catching, and run after catch.

Second, very specific attention will be given to beating the "jam." This area is one that, if not addressed consistently and properly, can very quickly destroy the entire route and all its careful design.

These elements, along with the illustrations of specific route technique for the different cuts found in Volume 1 and 2 (a reference guide for these is included at the end of this chapter), will provide a well-rounded picture of what it takes to be a successful receiver within the quick passing game.

Receiver Fundamentals

As noted, there are a number of fundamental "ingredients" that must be drilled and taught to receivers for them to be consistently successful. While many of these ideas resemble common sense, they will, when taught and emphasized over and over again, result in sound receiver play. Nine times out of ten, when there is a receiver breakdown during a game, that problem can be traced directly to one of these fundamental areas. As a result, these are the things our players will hear us talk about and demonstrate in the classroom, in film sessions, and in all areas of practice literally from day one, with the idea that "you get what you emphasize," or more specifically, "you get what you *demand*."

Fundamental Area #1: Receivers' Mental Approach

1. **A Physical Mentality.** The first part of the "mentality" we try to build in our receivers is one of being very physical and very aggressive. Many times the athletes you get at this position are not as geared toward aggression and contact as players at other positions, occasionally to the extreme of being "prima donnas." We have found that if we do not make a concerted effort to instill a hard-nosed toughness into them, too many times we end up, by default, with receivers who are soft, get pushed around, will not make the tough catch over the middle, and will not block for their teammates. Therefore, within the other drills we do, numerous ways are found to force receivers to become physical players, to teach them to not only withstand but thrive on contact, conditioning them to expect contact and training them to be the giver rather than the recipient of contact.

2. **"Six-Second Rule."** We believe much of the success or failure of plays is determined before the snap ever occurs. For that reason, our receivers are told that the most important part of any play occurs in the six seconds between the huddle and the snap. The "Six-Second Rule," then, is a mental checklist that our receivers are taught to go through every time they break the huddle. This discipline enables them to "play with a plan," another major tenet of our receiver play.

   Players who have such a plan and know exactly what they are doing, as well as how to adjust to contingencies, perform aggressively and confidently rather than in a tentative, uncertain fashion. The checklist that receivers are given in the Six-Second Rule is as follows:

   1. Formation, including "Am I on or off the ball?"
   2. Split
   3. Uncovered situation?
   4. If run—identify whom to block and plan your release
   5. If pass—what route? what release? potential adjustments/conversions?
   6. Identify coverage and *call it.* (See Appendix O for specific clues on how to do so)

   While the items on this checklist are elementary, the consistent, regimented practice of going through it makes all the difference. Notice that the snap count does not appear on the list; receivers are expected to watch the ball and come off the line of scrimmage only after they *see* the ball snapped. In this way, receivers should never have an illegal procedure penalty whistled against them. With a good, balanced stance, and a powerful start free of false steps, receivers can still get into the pattern without any loss of timing, and their six-second checklist will have prepared them for what they will see when their eyes turn to engage those of the man over them as they release after the snap.

3. **"Levels of Learning" and Understanding the "Big Picture."** As described in Chapter 5, we try to teach all aspects of our offense through "levels of learning" that build an understanding of not only "what," but also "why" and "how" in everything players do. The "level" that we particularly emphasize and reemphasize with receivers is the understanding of each play's "big picture." Receivers have a tendency to narrow their focus to their assignment only. As they gain more repetitions, we try to broaden this focus and reemphasize how their assignment fits in with everyone else and what they are trying to do. Once receivers begin to take this approach, correct adjustments on the run begin to happen naturally because they understand the whole play as a complete mechanism and know what must happen for it to be successful. This "big picture" will ultimately grow to encompass not only the routes of other receivers, but also protection, the quarterback's drop, and the particular formation and motion that are being used.

4. **"Go to School" Every Play.** Because football is a game of "punch and counterpunch" that has numerous twists and turns over the course of a game, and because the winner is often the team that makes the best adjustments, we want our players to constantly be gathering and cataloguing information throughout the entire sixty minutes. By "going to school" each play and learning something about the people defending them or about the defense in general, receivers can learn things that help them as individuals or us as a team make key, in-game adjustments. This information can relate to releases, blocking angles, specific patterns, defender techniques, coverage, or any number of other things. A "go to school" emphasis creates an alertness that leads to better execution and higher quality adjustments.

5. **"Educated Freedom."** As players gain a solid grasp of our offense, they begin to understand and use the freedom naturally provided by our system. The bottom line behind this freedom they are given is that their single most important job is to get open, and specifically to get open on a timing and in a place that allows the quarterback to get the ball to them. *We do not want any assignment to be so rigid that it makes it impossible for this basic priority to be fulfilled.*

This freedom is also typified by this example: a receiver whose assignment is to run a Hitch has the cornerback over him slip and fall, with no one behind him to cover deep. The receiver's logical reaction should be to take full advantage of this, go deep, and score.

Any freedom that is exercised, however, must be done for a definite reason, which is why we say "educated freedom." Again, we go back to the basic criteria of getting open, but also being open in such a way that the quarterback can get to you. Understanding this particular parameter makes the freedom functional and prevents all kinds of erroneous adjustments and miscommunication.

This "educated freedom" is a gradual growth process. We talk about it in general terms initially with our players, but don't really begin to instill it until players have a solid grip on what their assignments are. Once this freedom really takes hold, however, it maximizes the productivity of our passing game and gives us numerous positive plays throughout a season that we would not have otherwise had, nor could we have planned for.

Fundamental Area #2: Blocking

Since our focus is the quick passing game, we will not deal in much detail here about the specifics of how we train our receivers to block; suffice it to say that blocking gets the same emphasis and regard within a receiver's game in our program as anything else they do. Getting receivers to take great pride in their blocking ties in very closely with establishing the physical mentality that was discussed in the last section. A phrase we use a lot in talking about blocking is that it is "90 percent want to, 10 percent technique." We will give a great deal of time in practice to developing that 10 percent, working on releases, body positioning and lean, rolling through the hips, working the feet to maintain contact, and so forth, but we are always driving home the importance of the "want to." This "want to" is vital not only on running plays, but in blocking for other receivers on passes when they catch the ball.

In drill situations, the best way to work on receivers' blocking after another has caught a pass is simply to insist that players do it every time during seven-on-seven and team drills. We do not blow the whistle on a play until each receiver is formed up and engaged on a defender after the catch.

Fundamental Area #3: Route Running Technique

A well-run route does two basic jobs: first, it gets the receiver to the spot the quarterback expects him to be in the correct timing, and second, it does so in such a way as to create an effect on a certain defender or defenders that gets him open. Within all the technique details we teach, we work to keep ourselves and our players focused on these two simple goals.

This focus helps keep players from "losing the forest for the trees," and it also keeps us as a staff open to those occasional "new" techniques that are developed almost by accident. Sometimes resourceful athletes may, guided by a survival instinct, do something differently than the "book" would suggest. To us, if such an approach does those two basic jobs in a more effective way than we had been teaching it, that is what we want done, at least by that particular player. This flexibility helps us to keep growing, and also ties in quite naturally with our concept of "educated freedom."

We could discuss and identify a nearly limitless number of things related to precise, optimum route running; many of these points are detailed in the route technique diagrams in Volumes One and Two. In general, however, we have pinpointed several broader ideas that all good routes have in common:

A balanced stance and an effective start free of false steps. Because the receiver's fundamental job has to do with getting to a certain spot at a certain time, absolutely no movement can be wasted in getting there. An overlooked but crucial aspect of any pass route is the stance and start. Without a balanced stance that enables the receiver to push off and attack quickly without wasting a step or two, the timing of the route will never be what it should. Early in practice, receivers must give intent focus to developing a comfortable, yet functional stance that gets them off the ball as quickly as possible; they must also develop the habit of driving off their back foot and rolling over their front foot so that false steps are eliminated. We really bear down on this concept early in camp so the right stance and start become so natural that our players do not have to think about it.

An initial "stem" or "weave" that looks the same every time and establishes the desired relationship on the defender. We want everything receivers do to be smooth and fluid, providing no tip-off to the defender about what the final intentions of the route are. Achieving this consistency takes constant attention to detail by both the player and the coach during practice, but three key ingredients must be present for us to get the desired effect:

- Smooth, exaggerated arm drive by the receiver
- Intent eye contact—"staring" at the defender
- Weight over the toes at all times; "fight the height." The surest way a receiver can advertise his final break to a defender is to raise up. This tendency must be battled constantly.

As for the "weave," our receivers generally attack the defender's technique. If the defender is playing inside technique, our receivers release inside at him, either to drive him further inside to help an outside break, or to gain inside leverage if breaking inside. The reverse is true for a defender playing outside technique. Receivers are always to release directly at the shoulder of the defender on the side to which they want to get. Attacking this landmark gets the receiver the kind of relationship that is needed to break either inside or out; it keeps receivers from having to make their final break across the body of the defender, which causes real problems in getting open.

At least one distinct misdirection move against man coverage. Depending on the route being run, the athleticism of the defender, and the type of coverage, this move can range from a simple "nod" (a change of direction without losing speed) to a hard, double-move fake. One of our main principles in the passing game is the need for separation against man coverage. A misdirection move or moves executed convincingly are a key part of gaining this separation.

An effective BURST just before the final break. This burst is accomplished more with body language than actual acceleration: in many cases, we tell receivers to drop their head and pump their arms in rapid succession in the two to three steps immediately preceding the break. This action communicates to the defender that the receiver is going to try to run by, prompting him to turn and run out of his backpedal. Once the defender is out of his backpedal, breaking on the route is much more difficult and separation is increased.

Great body control and distinct breaks. Body control is enhanced by three key fundamentals: low hips and a low center of gravity; the weight being distributed *forward,* over the toes; and control of acceleration, which is the ability to appear to be at full speed while in reality being fully under control.

Distinct breaks are a product of the elbows, head, and shoulders as well as this body control. They must lead the rest of the body by *snapping* around rather than gradually turning around. This motion, in turn, will prepare receivers to receive the ball much more quickly.

Fundamental Area #4: Catching the Football

In training the catching skills of our receivers, we try to teach in simple phrases and focus points just as we do in other areas. The basic phrases we use to teach include "focus and follow," "hand position," "soften and squeeze," and "habits." When we say "focus and follow," we are referring to the habit of focusing the eyes on the ball from the time the receiver picks it up until the time it is safely tucked under his arm. Undisciplined eyes that disengage from the ball earlier than they should probably account for more drops than any other factor.

"Hand position" is something we work very hard on in our off-season and pre-practice routines. Players should instinctively, through endless training, get their hands in the correct position for the type of throw they are receiving. In general, that means having their pinkies together and elbows squeezed for a ball coming in over the shoulder, having their index fingers and thumbs overlapping to form a triangle on balls above their waist, and their pinkies together, elbows squeezed with their palms turned up, prepared to act as a "spatula" on balls below their waist. These habits can only be ingrained by catching ball after ball in the proper fashion.

"Soften and squeeze" refers to the receiver's hands "giving" with the ball, then squeezing it with his fingertips upon the catch. This technique is especially important on balls that are thrown directly into the receiver's body, helping to eliminate those passes that smack directly off of rigid hands and back to the ground.

The "habits" that we emphasize relate to balanced body position when at all possible, consistent practice of the three ideas noted above, and most of all, the act of tucking the football away every single time they catch it. To us, tucking the ball means setting it in a secure position under the armpit in which it is covered by the forearm, and at the point by the palm of the hand. At no time during any practice do we allow our receivers to catch a ball without tucking it away.

In addition to the endless repetition of catching balls the correct way over and over and the use of these focus phrases, the manner in which receivers are handled in this phase of their game has a great deal to do with their productivity. Too often, receiver coaches simply shout, "Catch the ball!" when a player drops a pass. This approach not only tells the receiver something he already knew and thus does nothing to improve his catching, it is often counterproductive in terms of the unnecessary pressure it puts on that player. While we are more than willing to climb all over receivers for mental mistakes, lack of effort, and so forth, dropped passes is not an area in which we are apt to scream. Rather than yelling "Catch the ball!" after a drop, we prefer to coach players very specifically on why they did not catch the ball and what specifically they can do to catch it the next time. Often, the player will be able to tell you himself. By addressing it this way, even asking them, "What could you have done to have caught it?", that counterproductive pressure has been replaced by constructive coaching that will make that player better.

Fundamental Area #5: The Run After Catch
Again, this area is one where we are of the strong conviction that you get what you emphasize. In addition to the specific teaching and drill work we will do for run after the catch, we treat it just like blocking by expecting our players to practice running after the catch every time they make a grab in any sort of practice situation. We also communicate very clearly to them that 50 to 60 percent of all yards gained in the passing game are gained after the catch. Running after the catch must become, just like blocking, almost a competitive matter among the players in which they take great personal pride.

Following is an illustration of a typical drill we use to train the run after catch. In this example, we are working on the tight turn the receiver must make off a defender's leverage after catching the Hitch. Defenders, controlled by the coach, attack through one shoulder or another as the man catches his Hitch route. The receiver must feel the defender, execute a tight turn away from his pressure, then accelerate straight up the field. The defenders are carrying dummies which they use to initiate contact on the way by. This method is another way we train receivers to become physical and to expect and thrive on contact.

Full discussion of the coaching points given our receivers for the run after catch on all routes is contained in Appendix D.

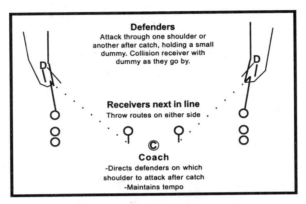

DIAGRAM 8-1
RUN AFTER CATCH DRILL FOR THE
HITCH ROUTE

Defeating the Jam

Defeating the jam consistently is a product of sound technique that is emphasized and practiced constantly. In other words, techniques are very important, but as or more important is the emphasis they get on a day-to-day basis, and the amount of quality, full-speed repetitions they can be given in practice. Even on days we do not have specific practice periods blocked off for jam release work, our receivers are forced to confront and defeat jams in their ten to twelve minutes of pre-practice route running.

Basic Principles

When we first introduce our jam-defeating progression, we give our receivers four basic "focus" points that are central to all of our other work:

1) **Attack the jam with a plan.** As part of their normal six-second rule, receivers facing a jam defender must formulate a clear plan in terms of their footwork and specific method of release *before* the ball is snapped. This plan allows them to play with initiative and aggression they would not have if they simply began to run their pattern without a clear vision of what they were going to do, reacting instead of acting.

Much of the jamming defender's "game" lies in being the aggressor and the attacker; by matching his initiative and aggression, receivers neutralize this effect, keep themselves from being pushed around, and are able to make more positive adjustments on the fly.

2) **Quick feet and short steps.** Until the jam is completely defeated, it is vital that all steps be extremely quick and choppy. This action gives receivers the ability to "wiggle" and change directions quickly, which is vital to a clean escape. Longer strides make the receiver an easy target for the jam, since they provide no immediate flexibility for direction change.

   To the extent individual receivers are comfortable, we will often "shorten up" their stance to facilitate this. In other words, we will shorten the stagger between their front and back foot in their stance, giving them added ability to work in either direction quickly.

3) **Get their hands before they get yours.** Obviously, the jamming defender's primary tools are his hands, and his whole purpose is to use them to impede the receiver's progress and destroy the timing of the route. The "battle of the hands," then, becomes the focal point of the whole process; receivers win this battle by taking aggressive action to knock defenders' hands and arms away, thus preventing them from being engaged.

   To emphasize this and break the jam-beating process down to its barest elements, we will, many times, begin by lining pairs of receivers up across from each other, with one holding out his hands. The other receiver is instructed simply to "slap his hands out of the way," first with their left hand, then their right. Later, we begin to add to this process their initial footwork before the slap, and later still incorporate the slap and the footwork into a full-fledged release technique.

4) **Violence.** Too often, receivers take too "nice" of an approach to releases and are not forceful and decisive enough in their actions. This approach results in their being engaged and hounded by their defender longer than they should be. To gain separation, which is what a receiver needs to get away cleanly, all the movements of his shoulders, hands, and arms, must be decisive, forceful, and most of all, violent. This violence is what gets and keeps the defender's hands away, turns his shoulders, and creates space, all of which add up to a successful release.

Alignment Principles
In addition to these focus points, we use the flexibility we have in our alignment as an aid to our receivers. In most cases, we leave the decision regarding which split receivers line up "on" the ball up to our players. A key guideline we give them in

making these decisions is that, most of the time, the receiver(s) with the most immediate jam threat over him (them) should be off the ball. This positioning is helpful because it provides an extra yard or so of separation, allowing the receiver more maneuverability and a better chance to gain the desired relationship on his defender.

The Starting Point: Misdirection Steps

The very first thing a receiver must do in releasing against the jam is to attack the defender with a series of short, choppy steps. Some coaches refer to this process as "patting the feet," because it gives the illusion of a great deal of movement while the receiver is, in reality, not advancing very far upfield at all. He does not want to advance up the field because of the separation factor. Initially, he wants to maintain that distance between himself and the defender so he remains out of reach.

What the receiver does want to do through these short, misdirection steps is create lateral movement on the part of the defender, ideally to the point where his shoulders and/or hips turn in the direction opposite the direction of the receiver's desired final release. This turn gives the receiver a "soft shoulder" so he can more easily attack with his release move to get by.

The misdirection step sequences are generally either two or three very quick steps. Regardless of the number, the final step will be in the direction opposite the direction the receiver wants to ultimately go. He is trying to sell the defender on the fact that he is going in a certain way to create a lean or a turn in that direction. On his final misdirection step, he gives extra emphasis to a head and shoulder fake in the direction of the last step to help this sales process. As he hits on the final misdirection step, he plants on the foot opposite his final direction and drives to the soft shoulder he has created. Examples of two- and three-step misdirection sequences are shown below. In our case we primarily use three-step sequences, with two-step versions as change-ups.

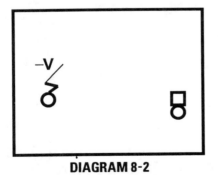

DIAGRAM 8-2
2 STEP MOVE TO RELEASE
INSIDE: "In-Out"

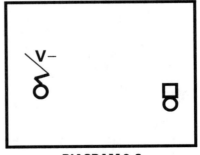

DIAGRAM 8-3
2 STEP MOVE TO RELEASE
OUTSIDE: "Out-In"

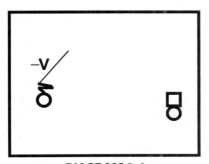

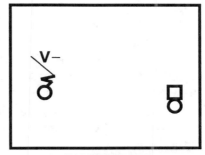

DIAGRAM 8-4
3 STEP MOVE TO RELEASE
INSIDE: "Out-In-Out"

DIAGRAM 8-5
3 STEP MOVE TO RELEASE
OUTSIDE: "In-Out-In"

Important to the execution of the misdirection steps are eye contact and arm drive. These two elements help create a certain body language that sells the defender on the receiver's intentions. It is also critical that he keeps his weight centered and balanced in everything he does rather than leaning or lunging; any lack of balance on his part is apt to be exploited by the jamming defender.

Release Moves

We employ four basic release moves to get by a jam defender as he tries to collision. They go by different names, but in our case we refer to them as the "Swim," "Low Swim," "Rip," and "Slam and Spin." Again, the moves are only as good as the violence with which they are executed and the effectiveness of the misdirection steps. It is also very important for the receiver to make himself "skinny" as he gets by, leaning and twisting in such a way that he minimizes the amount of his body that the defender can cling to as he clears him. After getting clearance, receivers must, on most routes, reestablish their position behind the defender and work vertically up the field. We refer to this process as "stacking" or "restacking" the defender.

1) **The Swim.** This technique is probably the most basic and familiar move from our inventory. As the receiver drives off his final misdirection step, he targets the defender's wrist or forearm on the side he wants to get to, slapping it violently with his near arm. The key is not only initiating contact with the defender's wrist/forearm, but also the violence with which the receiver thrusts it out of his way. Done properly, he will not only push the defender's hands out of the way, but he will also turn that whole side of the defender's body and give himself a freer lane through which to escape. Done improperly, he may (or may not) get the hand moved, but will still have a shoulder to work through as he tries to go by. Worse, the defender may be able to use his opposite hand to jam

the receiver in his rib area as he tries to go by. Gaining this "body turn" of the defender with a good, strong slap prevents a host of potential problems.

As the receiver is slapping the arm away, his opposite arm must come quickly up and over the defender's shoulder on the side to which he is escaping. This maneuver should be done in such a way that he gets his arm up as straight and quickly as possible so it can get above the defender and over to the clean air on the other side. It is this step that can, at times, make this move difficult to execute for a receiver who is at a height disadvantage compared to his defender; lack of wingspan against a taller defender makes it difficult to get "up and over."

2) **The Low Swim.** The Low Swim is similar to the basic Swim in terms of the actual action of the move, but differs in a lot of other respects. It, like the Swim, targets the wrist to the forearm of the defender to the side the receiver is going, except he targets that wrist with his opposite arm. In a sense, he "hooks" the defender's wrist/forearm up and over the top, creating the same body turn with the violence of his slap. As this body turn is created, he twists to make himself "skinny" as his body follows the path carved out by his opposite arm's low swim.

The advantage of this technique over the more traditional swim is that, because it does not require an off arm getting up and over a defender to be successful, it can work regardless of height. Because the receiver has to reach across the body of the defender to execute the move, however, it is more dependent on his creating some kind of movement on the defender's part with his misdirection steps.

3) **The Rip.** The Rip, like the Low Swim, is an opposite arm technique, except that instead of swimming over the top of the target arm of the defender, the receiver creates separation by dropping his opposite shoulder and ripping up underneath and through the defender's target arm to the side he is going. Again, violence is the key, as is the ability to gain some kind of movement through the misdirection steps. Receivers must also get their shoulder dropped sufficiently to get underneath the armpit of their defender.

4) **"Slam and Spin."** The most unorthodox move of these four, "Slam and Spin" is a good change-up on certain routes. It is a "rule breaker" in the sense that it does not apply many of the basic escape rules that have held for the other three.

In executing a Slam and Spin, the receiver sprints straight at the defender and initiates contact, leaning forward so he "bounces" off the defender as a result of the contact. As he bounces, he spins 180 degrees to the side to which he is trying to release, getting cleanly past the defender before he can recover.

Ironically, this release uses contact to create the necessary separation, banking on the fact that the receiver can recover before the defender does due to the fact that the receiver initiated the contact.

Because of the time it takes to execute, Slam and Spin is only good on certain routes, and basically serves as a change of pace to the other releases. Among the individual cuts in the quick passing game that can conceivably make use of it are the Fade, the Break Out, the Short, the Seam, and the Stop.

Our practice with these release techniques has been to introduce all of them to the players, and encourage them to fully develop at least two, and possibly three of them so they provide themselves with different options during the course of a game. Having different "tools" not only helps keep them from being predictable to their opponent, it also gives them the ability to cope with different types of defenders, different game conditions, and so forth.

Using Escape Techniques at Different Levels

One important aspect of training receivers against the jam is to make them understand that the release moves are not for the line of scrimmage only. They can and will be collisioned at all different times within a pattern and must practice all the different times jams can occur. For example, Cover 2 cornerbacks, depending on the specific teaching they have received and their own individual preference, may jam in the first yard or two of the receiver's release, or they might not engage until the receiver has released 5-6 yards.

Other examples of situations for which receivers have to be prepared include jamming and walling techniques of flat defenders against vertical releases (which can happen anywhere between four and seven yards deep), and attempted collisions by cornerbacks as receivers make their final break on "double move" routes such as the Hitch and Go or Slant "Dog."

One way to help train receivers in this area is a simple drill we call the "variable depth escape move drill." In this drill, pairs of defenders and receivers face each other, with the coach standing behind the receivers. The coach calls out to the receivers the side to which they are to release, while signalling to the defenders the depth at which they are to jam. Receivers are to go through a full jam defeating sequence, including misdirection steps, the actual escape move when the defender works to engage them, and clean acceleration past the defender to a depth of 15 yards.

As the drill progresses, the initial alignment depth of the defenders can be changed, and the coach can make it more difficult for his receivers by signalling the defenders as to which side their man is going to attempt to release. The most important thing, however, is that receivers are training themselves to automatically put their basic release moves into action at any point on the field where a man attempts to collision them.

An illustration of this drill is shown below.

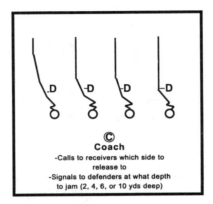

DIAGRAM 8-6
VARIABLE DEPTH ESCAPE MOVE DRILL

The Use of Motion Against the Jam
A simple tool that can be effective against the jam is pre-snap motion. Regardless of what category of motion is being used—short motion, motion across, "Return" motion, etc.—it can help the receiver gain a half-step or so laterally in the direction he wants to go. This little bit of difference means a lot in terms of beating the defender to a spot and being in a good relationship to effectively use an escape move once he has reached that spot. It provides that "soft shoulder" we have mentioned previously.

Route Illustration Reference Guide
The specific techniques involved in executing the different routes involved in the quick passing game against specific coverage have been illustrated within the route package chapters in the Volume One and Two. Following is a reference list of where those specific diagrams are located.

Volume	Diagram	Description
2	3-2	Short vs. zone
	3-3	Short vs. man
	3-4	Inside Slant vs. man
	3-5	Inside Slant vs. Cover 2/4
2	4-7	Box vs. zone
	4-8	Box vs. man
	4-9	In combination vs. tight man
	4-10	In combination vs. soft corner/zone
	4-11	In combination vs. Cover 2/4
	4-12	Out combination vs. man
	4-13	Out combination vs. zone
2	5-4	Split vs. loose man
	5-5	Split vs. tight man
	5-6	Split vs. zone

CHAPTER 9

Final Thoughts on the Quick Passing Game

We began this book by discussing the idea of our jobs as coaches in relation to enhancing our players' *percentages* of likely success, and how the quick passing game could improve our effectiveness in that regard. This book has attempted to equip you with a comprehensive series of tools, working from the ground up, that will enable you to realize the full benefits of those enhanced percentages that eventually translate into wins.

It has been our experience that the amount of success we have enjoyed in implementing new things into our offense is proportional to the amount of commitment we give it. When we say commitment, we mean both in the short-term sense of studying, understanding, and teaching it to the most minuscule detail, and in the long-term sense of gearing ourselves to live with it and let it grow and evolve over the course of two or three seasons (as opposed to ditching it mid-season if it wasn't performing as spectacularly as the guy at the clinic promised).

To be as prosperous as it can and should be, the quick passing game fully demands this type of commitment. This commitment is made not in terms of changing your philosophy to throwing every down, but in terms of first studying and teaching it with great attention to the fine points, and then to using it in those situations you have preordained (even if it falls outside your usual comfort zone), and also giving it a chance to improve and grow as your players gain proficiency, even if it looks bad at first.

As we discussed at some length in our previous book regarding the "Bunch" concept, we only commit our time and resources as an offense to those things that are first of all sound; second, able to provide us with specific benefits; third, fit within the philosophy and structure of our system; and fourth, have the ability to adapt and grow and survive when defenses make initial adjustments to it. Subjecting ideas to these criteria keep us from wasting our time and our players' time by chasing "fads" which pop up so often in football.

The quick passing game in general, as well as the specific route packages we have laid out here, all meet those requirements and go well beyond them. Not only does the quick passing game have a strong, firm philosophical base that provides numerous benefits and has stood the test of time and numerous defensive trends, it has the ability to naturally fit into most any offensive coach's basic structure of attack. For this reason we feel that the quick game is not an optional, accessory item in our offense, but rather a vital, core component that more than rewards any amount of commitment we give it. We sincerely hope that your commitment to the quick passing game proves just as beneficial and rewarding for you.

Playbook Sample:
Illustrating "Levels of Learning"

Following is a sampling of how one of the quick routes discussed in this book would progress through our playbook. As discussed in Chapter 5, we try to build any type of learning we do through a progression that we call "levels of learning." This approach carries over into the design and writing of our playbook.

The first page we refer to as a "cover page," and it introduces players to the route's "big picture." After reading this introduction, they have a framework in their mind about what we are trying to accomplish, and they see the reasons for having it in our offense and why it would be called in given situations.

The next page, known as the "rules page," begins to get down to the "nuts and bolts" of the route package. Each player is introduced to and has illustrated his assignments for the play. This page also progresses from the "individual assignments" level of learning into a bit of the "technique" and "specific adjustments to specific defenses" levels, though those things are secondary at that point.

The final page deals with the specifics of those last two levels in greater detail, completing the learning process. These specifics are the finer points that really give the learning its depth, and are some of the things that really make the difference between success and mediocrity. At the same time, they could not possibly be digested properly had the other levels of learning not been solidly in place before. In this case, the "QB Thought Process" sheet has been included to show these detail points as they relate to the quarterback. We also have similar sheets that break down those specific adjustments for receivers, linemen, and backs.

Certainly, we are not trying to espouse this process nor these playbook pages as revolutionary; many of you likely use a similar teaching progression and have pages that serve similar functions. However, we felt it important to include these pages because of our firm conviction that nothing in the entire body of this book is worth anything to you unless it can be effectively taught, and providing tools to help that teaching makes this text much more complete and useful. For us, we feel that talking about how we teach in specific, explicit terms is vital to maximizing our potential as teachers.

"Fade/Out"—mirrored definition

The "Fade/Out," or 98/198 route is the first of our two Fade packages. This particular Fade package was designed to attack the cornerback; with a Fade running deep over the top of him and an Out coming to him, in 2-deep coverage, he must make a choice, because the safety's influence, short of playing extremely wide, will be negated by our splits, timing, and technique. Against soft corners, we have a chance to create mismatches for the Out against slower strong safeties and linebackers while the corner is run off by the Fade.

When, in a Trips rule, a Seam is inserted between the Out and Fade, we gain some extra benefits as well, among them possible rubs, a possible high-low off a strong safety, and a way to hold 2-deep safeties on the hash. This combination also lends itself to numerous formation and motion concepts that give it different personalities.

Because of this versatility, we can create 98/198 combinations for a variety of occasions. It is one of the four or five major patterns we will begin looking to once we are inside an opponent's 15; it can be good on 3rd and 4 to 6 as well to account for a number of different basic coverage possibilities. Certain types of prevent coverage make it a strong possibility in 2-minute scenarios, and the right matchups can make it very useful when it is 3rd and long or if we are "Coming Out."

VARIATIONS		
Action/Protection	Tags/Adjustments	Formation Concepts
300	Hang/Hang-Twist	Motion Fade
		Motion Out
		Squeeze/Bunch
		Ram
		Rex In/Out; Pair

98-198 Fade/Out—Mirrored Definition

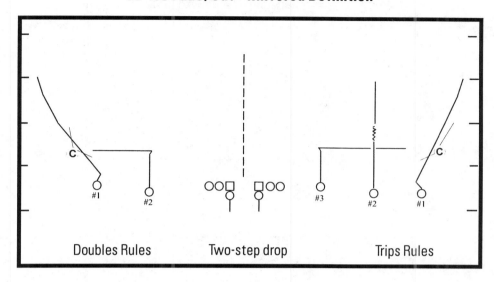

Doubles Rules   Two-step drop   Trips Rules

POS ASSIGNMENT

TRIPS

#1   Fade. Distinct technique based on coverage; basically, outside release and get to hole between S and C vs. Press, or use weave to pin C on hip and fade to ball outside if coverage is soft.

#2   Seam. Know who you are trying to beat; either short flat defender in Cover 3, or hash safety in 2/4. This dictates when and if you throttle/look for the ball. Get a clean release, attack quickly.

#3   Break out at 6. Push to 6 and break out, coming right off Seam's hip. Use misdirection move/collision vs. man cov. If a zone defender waits outside of you, settle and turn back inside to void.

DBLS

#1   Fade. (see above)

#2   Break out at 6. Same as above, with no seam to release underneath.

QB   2 Step drop. In general, work Fade to Out off corner's movement, favoring the Out if he's soft. Vs. 2 you may work Fade-Seam off safely in some cases.
Cov 1: Best Fade or Out matchup by down list
Cov 2: Fade to Out off C
Cov 3: Favor Out; poss. Out to Seam off SS in Trips
Cov 4: Favor Out off LB

COACHING POINTS

Box out defender on underthrows and catch at highest pt. in front of you. Over the shoulder—pinkies together, elbows squeezed.

Be nimble and avoid collisions, prepared to swim on the move.

Be ready for the ball out of the break, snapping head and shoulders around with hands ready. Get to sideline for R.A.C.

Blitz: 7 man pro-keep trips
'Q': Out or Fade
Outlet: Out
CP: Understand the throw required by different coverages—bullet in hole vs. hard C, lofted outside vs. soft C.

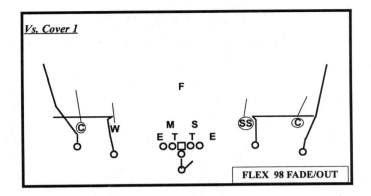

Vs. Cover 2

FLEX 98 FADE/OUT

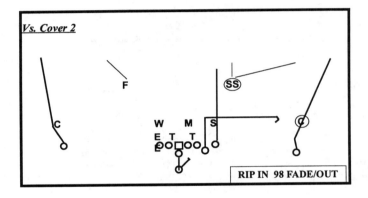

Vs. Cover 1

RIP IN 98 FADE/OUT

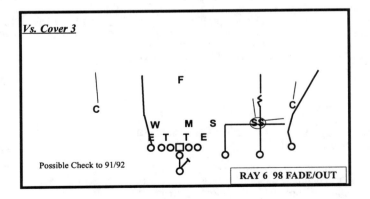

Vs. Cover 3

Possible Check to 91/92

RAY 6 98 FADE/OUT

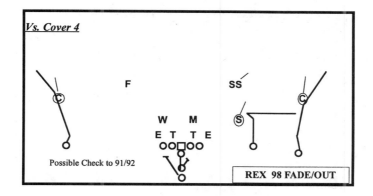

Vs. Cover 4

Possible Check to 91/92

REX 98 FADE/OUT

98-198 Fade/Out—QB Thought Process

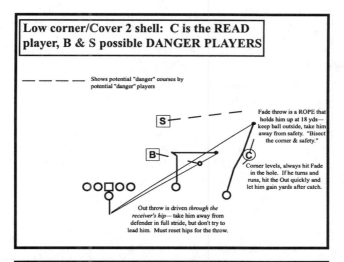

Low corner/Cover 2 shell: C is the READ player, B & S possible DANGER PLAYERS

— — — — Shows potential "danger" courses by potential "danger" players

Fade throw is a ROPE that holds him up at 18 yds— keep ball outside, take him away from safety. "Bisect the corner & safety."

Corner levels, always hit Fade in the hole. If he turns and runs, hit the Out quickly and let him gain yards after catch.

Out throw is driven *through the receiver's hip*— take him away from defender in full stride, but don't try to lead him. Must reset hips for the throw.

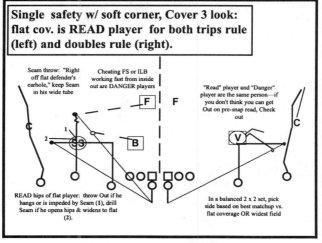

Single safety w/ soft corner, Cover 3 look: flat cov. is READ player for both trips rule (left) and doubles rule (right).

Seam throw: "Right off flat defender's earhole," keep Seam in his wide tube

Cheating FS or ILB working fast from inside out are DANGER players

"Read" player and "Danger" player are the same person—if you don't think you can get Out on pre-snap read, Check out

READ hips of flat player: throw Out if he hangs or is impeded by Seam (1), drill Seam if he opens hips & widens to flat (2).

In a balanced 2 x 2 set, pick side based on best matchup vs. flat coverage OR widest field

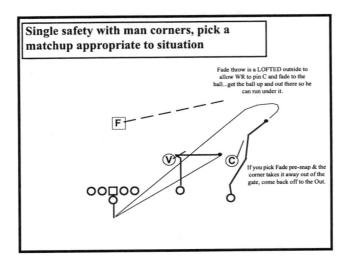

Single safety with man corners, pick a matchup appropriate to situation

Fade throw is a LOFTED outside to allow WR to pin C and fade to the ball...get the ball up and out there so he can run under it.

If you pick Fade pre-snap & the corner takes it away out of the gate, come back off to the Out.

1. Vs. any type of hard corner or 2-deep shell, the cornerback is always the read player. You're reading his hip turn and his relationship to the Fade. If his hips don't turn to run and he stays level, you'll always throw the Fade. If he turns his hips and runs, hit the Out NOW so he can run and make yards.

   The danger in these coverages depends on who's being thrown the ball. For the Fade, it's the safety coming recklessly off the hash to get over top of the Fade. You should be able to tell if he's going to be a danger by seeing his alignment pre-snap. For the Out, it's the first short defender inside the corner cutting underneath the Out.

2. Vs. single middle safety looks with SOFT, OUTSIDE corners (likely Cover 3), your read player is the flat defender. From a 2 x 2 set, you either throw the Out or you don't, based on whether or not he takes it away (check to a different play if you're sure he will pre-snap). From a 3 x 1 set, throw the Out quickly unless you see the flat coverage widen quickly, in which case you drive the Seam in where he left.

   The danger player also varies by our set: from a 2 x 2, you don't really have one—he's the same man as the read player. In a 3 x 1, it's usually an inside LB working inside out to get in the Seam's throwing lane, or possibly a FS cheating to jump the Seam.

3. Against middle safety defenses where you have a MAN look because of low, inside corners, you read based on the situation. If we need 5-6 yards, throw the Out, and pick the best side based on matchup and widest field. If the situation warrants that we can take a deeper shot, pick the Fade to the side of the

lowest corner, best matchup, and/or widest field. If he can't get open initially, come off to the Out. In either case, your read player is the one over the man you choose in your pre-snap read.

If you're throwing the Fade, you have a potential danger player in the free safety.

4. Types of throws.
    FADE: Against a hard corner, you must throw a rope into a spot halfway between the C & safety, holding the receiver up at 18 yards, stretching him toward the sideline. Against man or deep 1/3 corners, the throw is lofted to a spot deep and outside the receiver's original position, allowing him to pin his man, "fade" to the ball, and run under it. Vs. man where the defender has run over the top, you can use a deliberate underthrow back outside, allowing the receiver to come back and get it.
    OUT: Vital to this throw is the resetting of your feet and hips. Don't try to lead him, but do throw it right "through his hip," allowing him to catch the ball in full stride and run. FINISH the throw, follow through, take a dollar out of your pocket.
    SEAM: Drive off your back foot and drill the ball right off of the "earhole" of the flat coverage that widens. Ball is on a line, placed so that receiver can stay in his wide "tube" and not have to bend inside to get the ball at all.

Route Package Assignment Reference Table

This appendix is designed to provide for you a quick glance at the very basics of each of the route packages introduced in the book. Certainly it is not by any means a hard and fast "prescription" for how to set up a pass offense; rather, it is merely a summary of the different pattern concepts that were dealt with in previous chapters.

The other purpose served by this Appendix is that it closely approximates an actual teaching tool we have used during installation. Accounting for the fact that all kinds of different players learn and absorb things in different ways, we found it effective to provide this sort of reference chart for them that could summarize the information that, spread out over numerous practices and hundreds of playbook pages, might otherwise seem overwhelming. In other words, it was helpful for a lot of our guys to see that all this "stuff" that seemed to come at them in waves at times could actually be capsulized on one or two sheets of paper, and that the learning had a rhyme, reason, and organization to it. As they review the "skeleton" summary, details and drill work associated with those basics are recalled, and learning at all levels is reinforced.

In keeping with this idea, we have organized the table in "learning groups" by which players can see and translate similarities from one route to another. The same logic that drives the groupings for this table could drive an installation schedule in terms of the *order* in which things go in. Those "groups" are as follows:

- The first group is what we sometimes refer to as our "core" routes, meaning they all have the same "core" assignments of a *Seam* for #2 and a *Get Open* for #3.

- Next is the Quick Smash package, since it maintains the *Get Open* by #3, while changing the other routes outside. It serves as sort of a "transitional" route in this particular progression.

- Following the Quick Smash are the "Fade/Out" and "Slant" packages, which are grouped together because they both have Trips and Doubles rules that are substantially different, and share the common denominator that "the inside most receiver will always be breaking out."

- The "Short" is like the Quick Smash in that it doesn't neatly fit into any kind of group with other routes, but we put it here, following the Slant, since it has some elements of the Slant included in it.

- "Wheel" and "Turn" go together because of two significant things they have in common: first, they're the only "full field" quick routes we have that employ a distinct rule for backside receivers instead of being mirrored; and second, their backside assignments are the exact same.

- "In" and "Out" go together since their rules are special, being related to the player called.

This particular order and organization is by no means a "final word" of any kind. In fact, any number of approaches could be used with the same set of routes and be just as legitimate a means of organization, as long as it was built on a logical sequence. Routes with "Fades" on the outside could be grouped together, for example (i.e., the Fade/Out and Fade/Seam), while grouping the "Hitch" and "Quick Smash" together since they are alike except for the assignment of #2. The important thing is that we try to enhance learning through our organization and the way we progress through learning.

Route Assignment Table

ROUTE		#1	#2	#3
91-191 Hitch		Hitch/Fade	Seam	Get Open
92-192 Quick Out		Qk Out/Fade	Seam	Get Open
94-194 Stop		Stop	Seam	Get Open
99-199 Fade/Seam		Fade	Seam	Get Open
96-196 Quick Smash		Hitch	Qk Smash	Get Open
98-198 Fade/Out	2 REC	Fade	Break Out	
	3 REC	Fade	Seam	Break Out
93-193 Slant	2 REC	Slant	Shoot	
	3 REC	Slant	Slant	Shoot
97-197 Short		Short	Slant	Slant
95-195 Turn	2 REC	Shoot	Turn	
	3 REC	Go	Shoot	Turn
	BKSD	Slant	Split	
90-190 Wheel		Wheel	Slant	Split
	BKSD	Slant	Split	
In and Out Basic	FS	Hitch/Fade	Seam	Get Open
	BS	Hitch/Fade	Box	
90-190 In	CALLED RECEIVER: In		NEXT INSIDE: Fade Pick	
90-190 Out	CALLED RECEIVER: Out		NEXT OUTSIDE: Inside Pick	

Receiver Split Rules Summary

A key element in making our quick pass routes work are the splits taken by receivers. Each route has a specific spacing that creates the desired effect on defenses, times things up properly, and best enables the quarterback to make the read and throw.

Consistent with the rest of our teaching, we do not ask players to "memorize" split rules. Rather, as they understand the "big picture" of a given pattern and the job they are to accomplish within that big picture, the split rules make sense to them within that context. In this way, they learn rather than memorize.

Nevertheless, we still try to provide our players with every learning tool possible, understanding that different players learn in different ways. The table that follows is another example of such a tool, summarizing this critical part of our pass packages.

For both the #1 and #2 receivers, we have a "basic" split rule, which tells them how far to align outside the tackle or tight end on their side any time the ball is not on or near a hashmark. From that "basic" rule, their split may "adjust" plus or minus a few yards if they're aligned to the "short side" of the field or the "wide side." For example, if a receiver's basic split for a route is 14 yards, and his wide field adjustment is "+2," that would tell him to align 16 yards outside the tackle/tight end if he is set to the wide side.

"Boundary," or "short side" adjustments are expressed in terms of how far #1 should line up inside the sideline. An adjustment of "Sdl-6" would tell him to align 6 yards inside the sideline.

The fundamental rule for a #2 receiver is always to "split the difference" (abbreviated "SD") between the alignment of the #1 receiver and the tackle/tight end on his side. From this starting point, he is told to adjust in or out slightly depending on the route. "SD +2" would tell him to align two yards wider than his normal "halfway" point; "SD -2" would tell him to align two yards closer than halfway.

On some occasions when the #2 is set into the field's short side, we may give him a "break off 1st short" rule. This rule tells him that he simply must align wide enough so that he forces the first short defender to "declare," either breaking off the front or leaving him distinctly "uncovered."

Split Rules Summary Table

ROUTE		BASIC	BOUNDARY	WIDE SIDE
91-191 HITCH	#1	14 yds	Sdl - 6	
	#2	SD	Brk off 1st short	
92-192 QK OUT	#1	8yds		+2
	#2	SD	Brk off 1st short	
93-193 SLANT	#1	12yds	Sdl -6	+3
	#2	SD-1		
94-194 STOP	#1	10yds	Sdl -7	
	#2	SD		
95-195 TURN	#1	16yds +	Sdl -4	+3
	#2	Paired with #3----------------------------		
96-196 QK SMASH	#1	12-14yds	Sdl -6	
	#2	SD+2		
97-197 SHORT	#1	14-16yds	Sdl -4	On numbers
	#2	SD+2	Brk off 1st short	Opp Hash
98-198 FADE/OUT	#1	8-10yds vs. soft C 14yds vs. hard C		+3 v. hard C
	#2	SD-1		
99-199 FADE/SM	#1	8-10yds vs. soft C 14yds vs. hard C		+3 v. hard C
	#2	SD		
90-190 WHEEL	#1	Motion: +1 to +2 outside #2		
	#2	12yds	Sdl-6	+3

Run After the Catch Coaching Points Summary

Throughout the book, we have stressed the importance of maximizing the run after catch, or "R.A.C." It is one thing to be acquainted with the fact that R.A.C. accounts for 50 percent of all the yardage in the passing game, but quite another to consistently teach and emphasize the things that will make run after the catch as productive as it can be. None of the R.A.C. coaching points are particularly revolutionary; it is their consistent emphasis and practice that develop habits that create great R.A.C. results.

For us, this teaching and emphasis applies not only to the player doing the actual running after catch, the receiver, but the player doing the throwing as well. Where the ball is placed on the receiver's body and where it is thrown relative to defensive pressure have as much to do with what can be gained after the catch as the actual course the receiver takes.

On the following chart are the keys that are emphasized related to the run after catch for each individual pattern contained within our quick route packages, as they apply to both receiver and quarterback. Before discussing those specifics, however, there are some general rules that hold up for most any route:

Receivers
1. Must recognize man or zone on the move.
2. Against zones, "cut the throttle", and work to stay centered between two defenders in a dead spot. Catch and turn tightly to the side the quarterback gives you the ball and run north and south, splitting defenders. Maintain a forward body lean and fall forward upon being tackled.
3. Versus man, continue to separate and accelerate. Look for a place to turn up north and south and split people.
4. On outside routes, get to the sideline, going north and south. Defeat one defender at a time.
5. When another receiver catches the ball, find someone to block and maintain contact until the whistle blows.
6. Practice the run after catch, full speed, using the right technique, *every* time you catch a ball in practice; practice blocking for your buddy to the whistle each time you do not catch the ball.

Quarterbacks

1. In general, keep balls between the bottom of the receiver's number and his facemask unless making a safe throw or getting a completion requires otherwise. Balls below a receiver's waist "lock up" his hips and cripple the run after catch.
2. Timing is the key. The better the timing of your throw, the less time defenders have to settle and break up on receivers. When possible, get it in the receiver's hands while people are still dropping.
3. Must recognize zone or man coverage during the drop.
4. The right throw is always the one that leads the receiver away from pressure, or the defender nearest to making the tackle.
5. Against zones, stop the receiver in the hole. Never lead him through a zone into trouble. Put the ball on the number away from the nearest closing defender so that he can spin into the greatest amount of space for his run.
6. Versus man, lead the receiver further away from the player he is separating from. Extend him and do not hold him up.

A chart of the specific coaching points we use for each route package follows, in which you will see many of these basic principles reapplied.

ROUTE		RECEIVERS	QUARTERBACK
91- 191 Hitch	HITCH	Spin tightly away from DB pressure, usually outside; Get sideline, accelerate N/S	Deliver on time as you hit 2d/ 3d step—ball gone before he breaks. Throw to armpit away from CB attack angle.
	SEAM	Stay in your tube, stay vertical after catch and accelerate after catch, splitting defenders North and South.	Throw off flat defender's ear-hole immediately when he leaves; drive ball in slightly out front, keep WR in his tube
92- 192 Quick Out	QK OUT	Know where sideline is—snap head and shoulders around quickly after catch, get sideline, accelerate N/S	Open your hips and drive ball through his hip on time—finish throw so it stays helmet height or below.
	SEAM	Stay in your tube, stay vertical after catch and accelerate after catch, splitting defenders North and South.	Throw off flat defender's ear-hole immediately when he leaves; drive ball in slightly out front, keep WR in his tube
93- 193 Slant	SLANT	Continue accelerating away f/ C until you feel a threat f/ inside. When you do, turn N and split people. Pressure from inside may come early.	Lead WR further along a line that takes him away from pressure. Vs. an immediate inside threat, stop in the hole
	SHOOT	Snap head and shoulders around quickly, get the sideline. Vs. hard pursuing under cov, can stop and let him overrun	Open hips and drive ball through his hip on time—keep throw at shoulder height or below

94-194 Stop	**STOP**	Know where sideline is—snap head and shoulders around quickly after catch, get sideline, accelerate N/S	Offset your throw 1-2 yards to bring receiver away from CB pressure—optimum throw is at armpit height
	SEAM	Stay in your tube, stay vertical after catch and accelerate after catch, splitting defenders North and South.	Throw off flat defender's ear-hole immediately when he leaves; drive ball in slightly out front, keep WR in his tube
95-195 Turn	**TURN**	Tight, sudden 180 degree turn, accelerate North/South, SPLIT people and fall forward on contact	Put ball on number away from pressure, usually to outside. Firm but catchable ball at armpit height, on time
	SHOOT	Snap head and shoulders around quickly, get the sideline. Vs. hard pursuing under cov, can stop and let him overrun	Open hips and drive ball through his hip on time—keep throw at shoulder height or below
96-196 Quick Smash	**HITCH**	Spin tightly away from DB pressure, usually outside; Get sideline, accelerate N/S	Deliver ON TIME as you hit 2d/3d step—ball gone before he breaks. Throw to armpit away from CB attack angle.
	QK SMASH	Know where the sideline is, accelerate to get it, then beat one defender at a time running North and South	Loft and lead WR vs. man, don't slow him down; vs. zone, lead him on the angle that splits C and Saf w/ a firmer throw
97-197 Short	**SHORT**	Turn North *quickly*, finding the first vertical lane to run through. Split defenders, fall forward on contact.	Firm but catchable ball at chest level, out in front so he doesn't have to reach back.
	SLANT	Get North and South as quickly as you can and begin splitting defenders...do not continue inside.	Hit WR halfway between short defenders—ball may need driven in. Do not lead him into the next short defender.
98-198 Fade/Out	**FADE**	Continue accelerating up sideline vs. man or soft C. Vs. Cov 2 look, beat safety either side and get North	Vs. man/soft C, take him away f/ pressure to the sideline. Stop him in the hole with a rope vs. Cover 2
	BREAK-OUT	Accelerate until you get the sideline, snap head and shoulders around quickly, turn North and South	Open hips and drive ball through his hip on time—keep throw at shoulder height or below

99-199 Fade/ Seam	FADE	Continue accelerating up sideline vs. man or soft C. Vs. Cov 2 look, beat safety either side and get North	Vs. man/soft C, take him away f/ pressure to the sideline. Stop him in the hole with a rope vs. Cover 2
	SEAM	Stay in your tube, stay vertical after catch and accelerate after catch, splitting defenders North and South.	Throw off flat defender's ear-hole immediately when he leaves; drive ball in slightly out front, keep WR in his tube
90-190 In and Out	IN	Continue accelerating away f/ C until you feel a threat f/ inside. When you do, turn N and split people. Pressure from inside may come early.	Lead WR further along a line that takes him away from pressure. Vs. an immediate inside threat, stop in the hole
	OUT	Accelerate until you get the sideline, snap head and shoulders around quickly, turn North and South	Open hips and drive ball through his hip on time—keep throw at shoulder height or below

Scramble Rules Related to the Quick Passing Game

"Scramble rules" accomplish two specific things for us in our offense: first, they enable us to stay out of bad plays, creating a longer, legitimate opportunity for our quarterback to find a viable place to throw the ball and make yardage. Second, understanding where to go on a scramble opens up big plays for us, because coverage responsibilities and angles often break down late in the play.

Scramble rules are dependent on where a receiver is at the time the scramble begins: fundamentally, whether he is on the side to which the quarterback is scrambling or away from it, and also the depth and proximity to the scramble side sideline he is on. We divide the field into a "grid," with each square on the grid representing one of these relative positions, and each square having a rule as to where to go next as the scramble unfolds. If the scramble happens long enough that you move into a different area with a different rule that reroutes you, you may execute more than one different turn or scramble route.

Some general principles should be kept in mind on any scramble, summarized by the following:

1. Outside of a few select spots on the field, work toward the quarterback. Constantly work to get in his vision and make yourself available to him.

2. If you're coming from the "Away" side toward the quarterback, stay on your level; do not drift to different depths.

3. The addendum to rule #2: if someone ahead of you is on your level, move up to the next level on the grid.

4. When crossing, use Drag Principle rules, but only once you are in the quarterback's vision. Cut the throttle to stay open once you are in an open void, but only if you're in a place where the quarterback can see you.

5. Quarterbacks must keep some basic rules in mind from other parts of the passing game which include:

    a. Throw between people in clearly open lanes, not over them.
    b. Never try to drop a ball over a retreating defender.
    c. Never lose the ball late in the middle
    d. Always be aware of where the original line of scrimmage is.

A summary grid of our basic scramble rules is shown below, followed by illustrations of how those rules would apply to many of the basic routes introduced in the text.

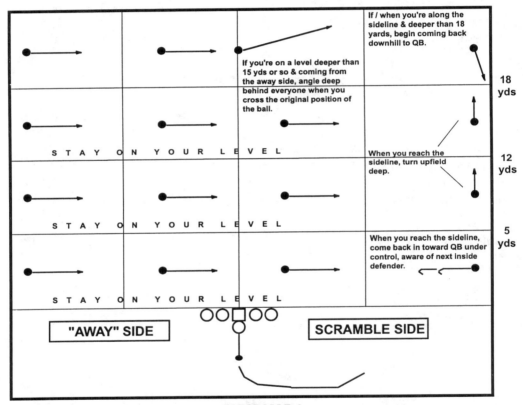

DIAGRAM E-1
BASIC SCRAMBLE RULES GRID

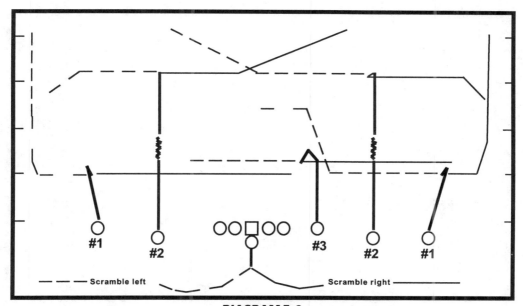

DIAGRAM E-2
91-191 "HITCH" PACKAGE SCRAMBLE COURSES

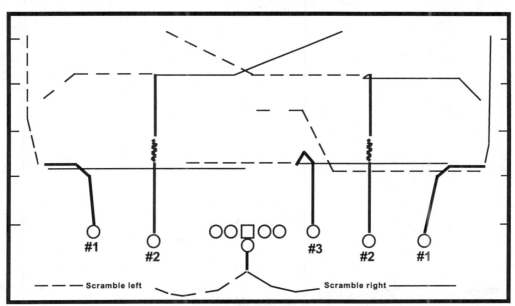

DIAGRAM E-3
92-192 "QUICK OUT" PACKAGE SCRAMBLE COURSES

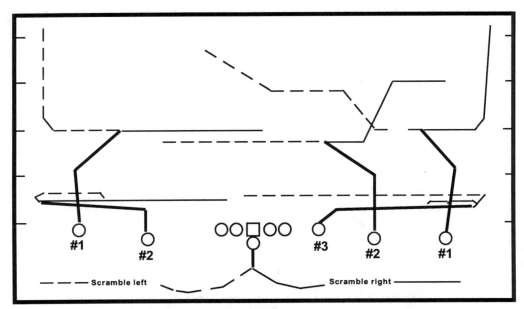

DIAGRAM E-4
93-193 " SLANT" PACKAGE SCRAMBLE COURSES

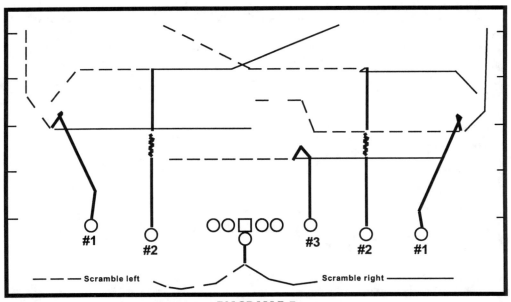

DIAGRAM E-5
94-194 "STOP" PACKAGE SCRAMBLE COURSES

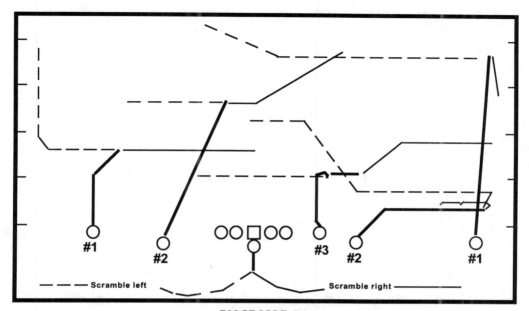

DIAGRAM E-6
95-195 "TURN" PACKAGE SCRAMBLE COURSES

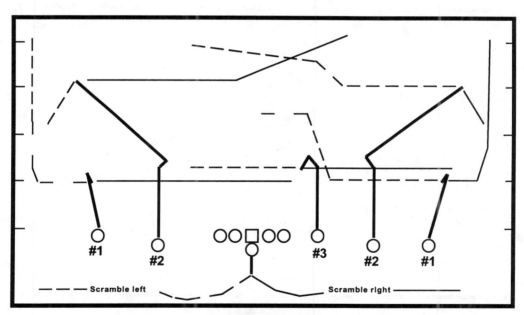

DIAGRAM E-7
96-196 "QUICK SMASH" PACKAGE SCRAMBLE COURSES

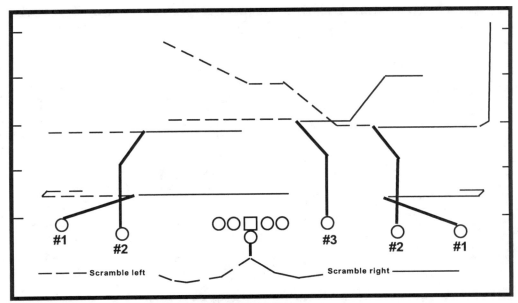

DIAGRAM E-8
97-197 "SHORT" PACKAGE SCRAMBLE COURSES

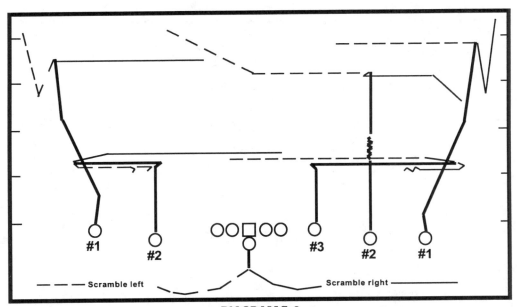

DIAGRAM E-9
98-198 "FADE/OUT" PACKAGE SCRAMBLE COURSES

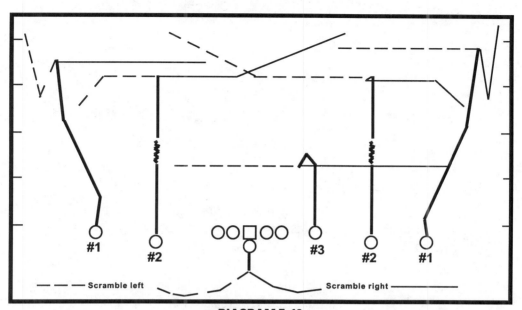

DIAGRAM E-10
99-199 "FADE-SEAM" PACKAGE SCRAMBLE COURSES

Fundamental Principles and Disciplines
of the Passing Game

This appendix could also be entitled: "How we do things and keys to our success." It contains principles and basic philosophy that underlie everything else we do in the passing game.

If you read *The Bunch Attack*, you are no doubt familiar with this section already. We have included it again because its ideas are universal to the passing game, quick or not, and continue to be critical to its success.

Some of the material within it relates to how we in our system have set our passing game up, our "recipe," if you will, while most of the rest reflects a specific list of the things we use to train our players' "instincts." This list, along with the "skills lists" in Appendix R, provides us with a concrete list of things we know we must practice if our people are going to make good decisions and react the right way in the heat of battle.

These things help good concepts on paper become the well-executed plays, play after play, that make the passing game successful. We refer to them as our "Dirty Dozen."

The "Dirty Dozen"
Cardinal Principles of Taylor Pass Offense

"How we do things and our basic keys to success"

1. **Multiplicity.** All plays can be run out of different formations.
   How: Small building blocks that speak to specific players.

2. **Route Adjustment.** Routes are run differently vs. different types of coverage.
   How: Pre-snap coverage calls, receivers and quarterback read on the move.

3. **Route Conversion.** Some routes are totally changed vs. some coverages.
   Why: Some routes simply will not work against some coverages.
   How: Pre-snap coverage calls, receivers and quarterback read on the move.

4. **Route Exchange.** Routes are run by the players relative to their position within each formation, generally numbered from the outside in (#1, #2, #3) on either side of the ball.
   Why: Different formations and motions put players in different positions, and this flexibility is key to creating positive matchups and being able to present a multiple look while keeping learning simple.
   How: Players learn the entire route package for each position when it is initially installed.

5. **Educated Freedom.** Players must always have a common sense approach to operating and running their routes, understanding that their job, first and foremost, is to get open in a way that the quarterback can find them.
   Example: Your assignment is a 10 yd Out, but your cornerback falls down and no one can cover you deep. Common sense and educated freedom say go deep, take the easy touchdown.

   Second, players should understand what their overall job is within a given route, and do whatever it takes to get that job accomplished. This concept is the beginning of having an "educated" freedom that enables players to use their freedom responsibly and productively. It is also the basis upon which finer technique details are built, because technique is only a means to most effectively get this job done.

6. **"Sandbox" Rules.** Each player within a route, by the design of the route, has a specific area assigned to him in which to get open, or a "sandbox." Receivers should ensure that their route stays out of the "sandbox" of any other player, lest that area get congested and our play ruined, by making whatever adjustments are necessary.

7. **Built-in Constants.** There are certain things built into the pass offense that do not change:

   a. If the Free Safety leaves the middle of the field, someone will be assigned to replace him and go deep down the middle.

   b. Vs. Cover 2, we will generally work to get three people deep.

   c. We will never throw the ball in the deep middle if a FS is there. (Covers 1 and 3)

d. Against hard-corner, Cover 2-type defenses, we will never attempt to throw a ball over the head of a cornerback who's retreating; take the short throw.

e. Crossing receivers never look back to make eye contact with the quarterback until they have recognized the coverage and are ready for the football; quarterbacks never deliver the ball to any kind of crossing receiver until they make eye contact.

f. Versus Zone coverages, receivers are to find and settle in holes between pass defenders; quarterbacks are to throw the ball to those holes and not lead them.

g. Versus Man coverages, receivers always work for separation, accelerating away from pressure, often after misdirection moves. Quarterbacks are to lead receivers and allow them to keep running away, maintaining that separation.

h. The quarterback will have a stationary outlet on most plays who is responsible for getting open and making the decision on whether or not he is open. The quarterback looks for eye contact and throws it if he gets it, meaning that the receiver has gotten to a hole and is open. Getting no eye contact, the ball is thrown away.

    Keys: The outlet must be made visible/available for quarterback. The quarterback must be aware of where outlet is and who can take the outlet away.

i. 'Q' receiver: within all of our patterns, we will have built in a player whose route enables him to break/be available quickly, so that the quarterback will always have a place to go with the ball if he gets early pressure. The quarterback must always understand where the Q or Qs are in relation to him, and the Q players must always be alert to get open quickly.

    Special note: Because of the timing and protection involved, (h) and (i) often don't apply to the quick passing game.

j. If there is a Flat route in the quarterback's initial read and down and distance do not warrant otherwise, we will always look to hit that Flat fast to maximize the R.A.C. yardage.

8. **Quarterbacks never pass up an open receiver to wait for another to get open.**

9. **Scramble Rules.** In the event of a scramble, receivers have definite breakoff courses based on the type of route they are running. Quarterbacks have definite escape lanes that are and are not available to them related to our different protections. They will never throw a ball late back into the middle on a scramble.

10. **Run After Catch.** All people involved in the passing game must be aware that over 50 percent of the yards gained in the passing game come after the catch. Receivers will be trained where to go after the catch based on coverage, and quarterback's will be trained to provide the specific types of throws that enable them to maximize their R.A.C. gains.

11. **Throwing the Ball Away.** Quarterback's are never to take a sack on 1st or 2d down.

12. **2d Down and Long.** When passing on 2d down and Long, the quarterback's primary responsibility is to get us to 3d and medium. The probability of success goes up greatly if 3d down yardage is less than 7.

Adapting the Quick Passing Game
to the "Shotgun"

Although it has not been dealt with specifically through most of the illustrations in the text, placing the quarterback in the "Shotgun" can be an effective way to help the quick passing game, particularly where the quarterback is concerned. Specifically, it helps the quarterback's *vision*, in relation to both his read and seeing potential blitzes. It helps with his *rhythm* and *drop*, because his footwork can be more relaxed and less strained since he already has good depth by virtue of lining up in the shotgun initially. It also helps against the *blitz*, because the depth the quarterback can reach after executing his drop from the shotgun makes him harder to reach.

Of course, if and how much of the shotgun you use will depend on a number of factors, including your center's ability to execute the shotgun snap, the quarterback's preference, the types of defenses you play, how much of your running game can be incorporated from it to provide balance, and your own general philosophy on the use of the shotgun.

When incorporating the shotgun with our quick, 90's routes, we generally make a few basic adjustments. First of all, we align the quarterback's heels at 4 to 4 1/2 yards, with any single back offset to the side of his protection call. If we are in two-back sets, they will generally be split. The depth of the backs places them just slightly behind, or deeper than the quarterback, so that the execution of run actions will be natural.

The quarterback takes a normal three-step drop, but the emphasis is now on a good, relaxed drop that gets his body into a strong, stable throwing position rather than on getting depth.

Receivers, in most cases, will maintain the route's timing by pushing their route an extra one to two steps (depending on the receiver and the route). This step or two essentially compensates for the time that the ball is in the air on its way to the quarterback, all the other timing being the same once the ball is in the quarterback's hands. Notable exceptions to this include the 94-194 Stop, because the original depth of the outside receivers is conducive to effective shotgun use as is, so no adjustment is made. Another such exception is the 96-196 Quick Smash, where the depth of #1 does not change because we do not want to change the spatial relationship between him and the Quick Smash over top; he compensates for the timing by hesitating a count before beginning his route.

On the chart below, the routes discussed in the text are divided into three basic categories: routes whose timing is distinctly helped by the use of the shotgun, routes whose timing is unaffected by the shotgun with the minor adjustments noted above, and routes that may need special attention to function properly from shotgun. The latter distinction doesn't mean they can not be used or effective from the gun, merely that more specific work with the timing is needed.

ENHANCED BY GUN	TIMING UNAFFECTED	NEED SPECIAL WORK
91-191 Stutter	91-191 Hitch	92-192 Qk Out
92-192 Stutter	91-191 Dupe	93-193 Slant
93-193 Dog	91-191 Go	95-195 Turn
94-194 Stop	92-192 Go	95-195 Switch
96-196 Whip	93-193 Stick	96-196 Qk. Smash
97-197 Plant	93-193 Dupe	97-197 Short
99-199 Swing	93-193 Seam	
90-190 In	95-195 Trade	
90-190 Out	97-197 Corner	
90-190 Wheel	98-198 Fade	
	99-199 Fade	

SHOTGUN ROUTE ADAPTATION CHART

Quick Passing Game Field Width Menu

A handful of the quick passing route concepts we have discussed in the text are definitely geared to be thrown to either the short side of the field or the wide side of the field. The illustration that follows summarizes the discussions of those routes and their optimum field width uses.

A tool that comes in particularly handy in making full use of the field width advantages of each route is the "B" tag that allows us to assign receivers on one side to execute a different route package than those on the other side; this tool and its relation to field width are specifically discussed in Chapter 2 and expanded a step further in Appendix I. This appendix is the type of visual aid that we ourselves would use to try to create effective route "pairings" with this tool.

WIDE FIELD MENU	SHORT SIDE MENU
90/190 In	92/192 Quick Out
91/191 Hitch	94/194 Stop
93/193 Slant	95/195 Turn (2 rec rule)
95/195 Turn (3 rec rule)	96/196 Qk Smash vs. Cov 2
96/196 Qk Smash vs. Man	98/198 Fade/Out vs. Cov 2
97/197 Short	
98/198 Fade/Out vs. Man	

QUICK PASSING GAME WIDE FIELD / SHORT FIELD MENU

Maximizing and Understanding the "B" Tag

As described in Chapter 17, we can create "packaged" sides that each operate separate route concepts through the use of the "B" tag. The benefits of this tool include the ability to deal with coverage variety and different techniques without checking at the line of scrimmage and the nearly limitless number of combinations it can provide.

However, it is vital with a mechanism as open-ended as the "B" tag that specific focus is maintained on exactly how and why it is to be used, and the exact reasons a certain "B" tag would be employed on the back end of a given route. Otherwise, the mind-boggling array of combinations becomes vague and muddies things within the total offensive package rather than helping it.

This focus and understanding is particularly important where it relates to the quarterback. If the B tag is going to be used and executed properly, he must be educated as to how the two packaged sides fit together, and under what circumstances he works one side or another.

For all these reasons, when we first began implementing the "B" tag in our offense, we created a reference chart like the one that follows. This reference chart contains the three to four *best* B tag pairings with each of our basic 90 series routes, along with the explanation of its use. This chart was a help not only to us in our practice scripting and long-range planning, but to our quarterbacks as well.

"B" Tag Combinations
- Reference Chart -

ROUTE	"B" TAGGED WITH:	HOW THEY WORK TOGETHER
91-191 HITCH	Slant Qk Smash Fade/Out In	Hitch vs. zone, Slant vs. man Hitch vs. soft corners, Qk Smash vs. hard Cs Hitch vs. soft corners, Out/Fade is a high % combination vs. a hard C Hitch vs. zone, In vs. man
92-192 QK OUT	Slant Short Fade/Out	Use Slant vs. tight man or wide flat coverage Short to wide field vs. hard C, Qk Out into the boundary vs. a soft C Qk Out vs. soft C, Fade/Out high % vs. hard C
93-193 SLANT	Stop Qk Smash Fade/Out	Stop into boundary if under cov overloads Slant side Go Qk Smash vs. hard, inside man under cov. Throw Break Out vs. hard, inside man cover
94-194 STOP	Hitch Qk Smash Fade/Out	3 x 1 sets--Hitch if wk flat defender can get to Stop Stop vs. soft C, Qk Smash vs. hard C Stop vs. soft C, Fade/Out vs. hard C
95-195 TURN	Hitch Stop Qk Smash	Higher % BS throw if under cov rotates to Turn Stretches BS under cov--Turn unless taken away 2 x 2 set--go Qk Smash vs. hard C
96-196 QK SMASH	Hitch Qk Out Fade/Seam	Throw Qk Smash unless Cover 3 Go Qk Out vs. Cover 3 Cloud or really soft zone 2 x 2--Go Fade/Seam if safeties are wide over #2
97-197 SHORT	Stop Turn In	Short vs. hard C, Stop vs. soft C 2 x 2 set--Turn to boundary if soft C, Short if hard C Go In vs. man or Cover 3 with wide flat cov.
98-198 FADE/OUT	Turn Fade/Seam Out	2 x 2 set--Fade/Out if hard C, Turn if soft C Stay with Fade/Out unless Cov 2 hash saf is wide Basic 98 vs. zone, go to Out if you recognize man
99-199 FADE/SEAM	Short In	Short if Cov 2 safeties high, Fade/Seam if they're tight In vs. medium to loose corners, Fade/Seam if tight

Using Sequence in the Quick Passing Game

No matter what system or philosophy is involved, a major key to an effective offensive package is having plays that "fit" together and work off one another in a logical sequence. When defenses begin anticipating and taking away certain aspects of the offense, the system naturally provides built-in answers that "sequence" with other parts of the system.

Even though the quick passing game is not in itself a system, but only one aspect of a system, it is no different in this regard. Sooner or later, no matter how well-executed and taught the plays are, defensive teams and players are going to find ways to limit their effectiveness. Therefore, built in to our quick passing game are routes and packages that work hand in hand so that when one route is taken away, another is instantly opened up.

This idea of sequence makes a big difference in many areas of offensive football. The first and most obvious is that it allows a coach to "set up" certain things during the course of calling a game. An example of this might be to establish the Hitch early and often, with the idea that you will run the Hitch and Go to strike deep at a key point later in the game.

During games, it also provides you as a play-caller with a certain amount of direction and focus when parts of your original plan are taken away for some reason. Because certain plays fit together in a sequenced fashion, the fact that a route is being taken away instantly tells you that something else is likely open.

Even beyond game settings, however, a solid sequence is important in actual teaching and practice. By showing players not only the "what" of your quick passing package but also the reasons "why," you create not only more educated players, but also confidence in your system that lets players know there is always an answer to any dilemma they might face in a game.

Since this "sequence" has such important implications for teaching, and practice as well as the actual calling of plays on game day, we have included this appendix to summarize how some of the routes discussed in the book can be paired together to answer defensive responses. In all the cases listed on the following chart, a "picture" is given to the defense—sometimes a single player, sometimes groups of people—that causes them to react in a certain way; the "complementary," or "sequenced" play, then, takes direct advantage of that reaction. A summary of how some of our packages fit together follows.

Sequenced Calls

Denotes a route combination not specifically discussed in this text

Running:	Can help set up:	Because:
91	91 Go	Corners in man or even deep 1/3 will begin to jump Hitch & become vulnerable over the top
91 Go	91 Stutter	Corner will turn hips and sprint to try & get over top of the H & G, opening break under him
92	92 Go	Corner will begin to break down & outside hard to tackle quick out--can't recover deep
93	93 Dog	Corner will turn hips and sprint to try & get over top of the Slant, opening break under him
Trips 93	95 Switch	Short defender inside #3 will begin to fly to Shoot or outside Slant; Turn gets right into hole he leaves
95	91	From wing sets, SS will anticipate Turn or close in run support, leaving wide flat area open for Hitch
95	95 Slant	Safeties may try to aggressively come up on Turn and jump it, leaving deep crease for Slant
96	93 Dupe	Safety on hash sees vertical release by #2, widens and is sold easily by nod because he
96	97	wants to work over the top deep outside to cover Qk Smash--hole in middle left for inside Slant
96 Whip	91 w/ #1 Whip*	Vs. Cover 3, active flat defender gets eager to jump Whip, opens the door for #2 Seam
97	96	Hash safety begins to close on Slant by #2, opens hole for Qk Smash to hole outside him
97	98	Short defender over #2 begins to play hard inside leverage to wall Slant--hips turn inside, opening Out
97	96 Whip	Corner in man or aggressive Cov 2 turns hips to try and close on Short; Whip can get back outside him.
98/99	In	Man or Cover 3 corner opens hips to the outside to run with Fade; easier to pick & run under
99	91 & 94	Picture looks the same to C, who's conscious of deep ball b/c of 99; gives ground, opens Hitch & Stop
99	93	Vs. low, hard C, he must turn his hips outside b/c of Fade threat. Slant can now break open under him.
Crossing Routes	96 Whip	Man coverage MUST close hard down inside to cover cross; Whip can come back out under him

Organizing a Multiple Offense: "Concept Sheets"

As we have mentioned periodically throughout the text, it is important in an offensive system such as ours that essentially provides limitless room for creativity and tinkering to organize ourselves in such a way that we keep focus on those combinations that are most effective and make the best use of our personnel. If this focus is not maintained, the vast multiplicity ceases to become functional to us and our players, and we have more "stuff" than we can effectively use or execute. In this text alone, for example, over 150 different formation/motion combinations have been illustrated as applied to this one phase of our offense. If not incorporated into a workable framework, that type of number can become unmanageable and counterproductive. If successfully "harnessed," on the other hand, it becomes a tremendous weapon against defenses.

One of the ways we bring our plays and formations into focus for optimum use is an off-season organizational tool that we call "concept sheets." To us, a "concept" in this setting simply refers to a certain way we might manipulate our formations and motion to create certain types of situations for our different routes. Any number of individual formation and motion combinations may fit into a different attack "concept," and so this particular tool helps group an unmanageable amount of formations into a manageable set of "groups" or "concepts."

This type of organization helps us in a number of ways. First of all, it helps us to script our practices, especially pre-season practices, with optimum efficiency. We understand the different types of things we want to be able to do with each route, and can make sure that the specific concepts we want repetitions on get adequate practice work. In other words, each formation we use has a specific purpose because of the way it fits in with a particular attack idea, rather than just being scripted at random.

Second, it helps us in our week-to-week game planning as we map out the different sets we want to use. Concept sheets provide us with specific "menus" of formations we can go to when we want to attack certain defenses in certain ways. The menus help us go one step further by allowing us to change formations from one week to the next, while essentially attacking in the same way.

Finally, this organization maximizes the creativity of our staff by giving all the different ideas that can be generated by the system a concrete outlet where those ideas can be documented and used rather than lost. Many coaches have lost good ideas either because they never worked their way in a practical sense into the game plan, or because they were originally hashed out on restaurant napkins and placemats, never to be heard from again.

The following sheets illustrate our two basic "concept sheet" forms and how they look for our basic 91-191 Hitch route. The first sheet is a "worksheet" upon which ideas can initially be worked out, the second a "summary" sheet that we eventually put in front of all the worksheets for a given route to serve as a quick reference guide.

FORMATION/CONCEPT WORKSHEET

PLAY: *91-191 Hitch*   **PAGE:** *1*

CONCEPT: General trips sets	NOTES	OTHER FORMATIONS
	> Can be used to dictate Cover 3 vs. teams that check out of 2/4 v. trips: guaranteed soft corner > Vs. teams that always set SS to formation, trips into boundary gives single receiver lots of running room.	Rip 8 (R 8) Rex In/Out Rip +/-/In/Out Rip Wing + Roy 6 - faster trips side combo Rex 10 - faster Seam to trips Rex 6 Flop - Z isolated weak *No split receiver weak:* Ram X/Z Ray 6 Ray Pair *Also:* Backfield motion concepts Y motion concepts

CONCEPT: Balanced, wide sets	NOTES	OTHER FORMATIONS
	> Get a true Seam read to both sides-- allows QB to pick best matchup, easier to control active flat coverage > With regular personnel, gives us a chance to force a LB into wide coverage-- chance for mismatch on the Seam	Flex Flip Flex Flop Flex Flash Flip Flop Roy 9 Roy 11 *Also:* "Expand" shift from Ram

CONCEPT: Ram Package	NOTES	OTHER FORMATIONS
	> Vs. Cover 3 teams, puts flat defenders in a bind: tighten for run support on the edge, or stay in a good inside-out coverage position > "Z Over" & "X Over" looks may *guarantee* Cover 3 *and* give us a good Seam matchup	Lion Ram X/Z Lion X/Z Tight Rip 11 *Also:* "Shrink" shift from Flex/Rex 6 Backfield motion concepts

CONCEPT: Backfield motion (2 x 2)	NOTES	OTHER FORMATIONS
	> Great way to attack "Cowboy" adjustments or locked LB coverage > Soft motion adjustments by outsidemost defender likely, helping the Hitch > Can open backside Seam if FS adjusts with motion	Black/Brown/Split backfields Rex/Roy H11 Tight Rip H11 Ram X H11 Rip H11 *Hot protection:* Ray 6 F11 Rip Plus H11 Rip 8 F11 Rex 6 F11

FORMATION/CONCEPT SUMMARY

91-191 HITCH (page 1)

DESCRIPTION	BASE SETS		OTHER SETS	
1 TRIPS SETS: Force Cover 3 / ensure a soft corner	Rex 6 Rex In/Out	Rip 8 Rip +/-/In	Rip 10 Roy 6/8/10 Ray 6 Ray Pair Rip H8/10	Rex 10 Ram X/Z Rex H6/8
2 TE TRIPS: Put OLB/Nickel in a Cover 2/4 shell in a bind	Rip 8 Rip 10	R 8	Ram X/Z Rip H8/10	Tt Ray 8
3 WIDE 2 x 2 SETS: 2 pure Seam reads, can also force an OLB into wide coverage	Flex Flop	Flip Flash	Flip Flop Roy 11	Roy 9
4 RAM PACKAGE Good way to balance up, since Cov 3 flat defenders must support the run	Ram Ram X/Z	Rip Hip Ray Hip	Tight Rip 11 Tight Rip H11	
5 BKFLD MO - 2 x 2 Attack Cowboy cov., possible soft C or LB coverage wide	Ray H11 Rex H11 Brown/Black/Split	Rip H11 Roy H11	Ram X H11 Ray 6 F11 Rip + H11	Tt Rip H11 Rip 8 F11 Rex 6 F11
6 BKFLD MO - 3 x 1 Possible soft C or LB coverage wide, may also force Cover 3 check	Rip H8/10 Ray H6/8 Brown/Black/Split	Rex H6/8	Rip Wing H10 Squeeze Rex H10	
7 "BROKEN BUNCH" Vs. Cov 3 & 4, puts pressure on 1st short defender--widen to help on #1, or lock down on #2 & #3?	Rex In/Out Ron Pair	Ray Pair Roy Pair	Squeeze Rex H10 Squeeze Rex 6 Z10	

Quick Passing Game Situational Menu

Because football is essentially a game of specific, important *situations* strung together one right after another, planning and educating your players as to what they mean has become more and more paramount to offensive success. Chapter 3 went into depth in describing some ways we try to equip our players to best succeed at situational football. This appendix is designed to pick up where that chapter left off, providing a broad-based reference guide that shows where the combinations illustrated in this book can be plugged in to the crucial situations we all face. Included are fourteen different game situations for which we will account, a brief summary of the points we emphasize with our players related to those situations, and a "menu" of plays from the quick passing game that are well-suited to succeeding in that particular scenario.

Please note that these are meant only to illustrate concepts as they would look within our particular system, not to prescribe some sort of "final word" on specific plays, formations, and combinations. Most of these same concepts can be fitted within your system and terminology, tailored to your players' specific talents, and adapted to attack the problems your opponents present.

Note also that most all of our basic quick route packages have some sort of application in almost every situation in one form or another. This knowledge points up one of the quick passing game's real strengths: its flexibility and capacity to provide excellent answers for all kinds of game situations.

First and Ten

- Priority one is to get us into second and six or less; we must have a completion and will not take a sack.
- Formations that look like base run formations can be effective to pull in outside defenders tighter and open outside throwing lanes. Play action throws are effective from these sets also.
- Wide sets are also a priority to clearly define blitzes, coverage, and quarterback reads.
- Packaged sides and "Run/Quick" checks an effective way to deal with front/coverage variety.

Refer to Diagram:	Formation	Play	Comments/Brief Summary
1: 6-15	Split Larry	192 Quick Out	Hi %, simple throw from base set
1: 6-16	Ram	191 Hitch	Quick edge throw from strong run set
1: 6-22	Blue Flex	192 Quick Out	Spread look for hi % throw outside
1: 7-19	Black Larry	Y193 H Shoot	Quick throw to backfield player in flat
1: 8-8	Roy	98 Fade/Out	Possible mismatch for Z on Out
2:1-13	Flex	96 Qk Smash	Spread set with easy throws outside
2:1-20	Ram X	96 Y Sit	Run set to pull in flat cov for Hitch
2: 1-28	Ram Z Snug	96 Whip	Whip an easy throw, good RAC v. man
2: 2-8	Weak Rip F Shuffle	94 Stop	Singled up Stop from run look
2: 3-18	Brown Larry	95 Switch	Run set, isolate 2 quick throws on LB
2: 3-35	Split Rip H Left	Hot 95 Switch	Safe 2-on-1 combo away from motn
2: 4-17	Shift to Larry	197 Short	Shift to iso Z on a LB vs. 8 man front
2: 4-21	Flex	197 Short	Basic wide set Short combo--hi %
2: 5-14	Brown Rip Y9	190 X In	Safe rub v. man teams on 1st down
2: 5-22	Rip 10 Z Trace	90 Z Out	Motn Out w/good matchup v. base D
2: 5-23	Flex	90 X & Z In	Field stretch, good vs. man or zone
2: 6-16	Brown R H11	190 Wheel	Qk stretch on weak flat coverage
2: 6-35	Squ Ram H Mo Chk	Wheel Turn	Motn check for best matchup
3: 1-8	Split Rip	Y321 Slant	Play action opens Slant/Shoot lane
3: 1-10	Ram	Max 324 Slant	Fully-protected Slant from a run set
3: 1-17	Rip 9	Y307 Fade	Play action fake to isolated BreakOut
3: 2-10	Squeeze Lex 7	198 B Slant	Pkgd sides stretch under coverage
3: 2-16	Flex	Chk 91 or Counter	Run/Qk check to guarantee good play
3: 2-18	Rex	Chk 92 or Iso	Run/Qk check to guarantee good play
3: 2-21	Liz 8	Check 98 or Zone	Run/Qk check to guarantee good play

Second and Long

- Biggest key is to gain yardage that will get us to third and 6 or less.
- Heavy blitz down for some teams; alert zone blitz also.
- Generally prefer high-percentage routes with built-in R.A.C. potential. This category will include formations that flip our faster players inside to get mismatches.
- May also build in a longer route that we'll take if they hand it to us on a platter.

Refer to Diagram:	Formation	Play	Comments/Brief Summary
1: 6-25	Lex 7	191 Hitch	Basic Hitch from wide set
1: 6-27	Blue R 8	92 Y Sit	Quick Out to gain yds, "Sit" outlet
1: 6-35	Empty	91 Hitch	Spread field for Seam/Hitch--R.A.C.
1: 6-37	L 8 F Left	Y91 Dupe	Bkfld motion to widen R.A.C. lanes
1: 7-18	Rip 8	93 Slant	Trips Slant to stretch under coverage
1: 8-19	Ray In H Return	98 Fade/Out	Potential rubs for Outs on both sides
1: 8-22	Blue Lou 7 Y7	Y199 Swing	Good yds for Swing if Fade not there
2: 1-18	Ray Out	96/196 Qk Smash	Yds for Hitch if Qk Smash not open
2: 3-12	Squ R 11 Y11	195 Turn	X Matched on LB running Turn
2: 4-25	Ram Z	Y197 Short	Broken off Short/Slant-good RAC lanes
2: 4-29	Grn Larry 10 F Left	Hot 197 Swg Y Sit	Mot stretches zones, opens RAC lanes
2: 5-24	Rip 8 F11	Hot 90 F In	Motion In stretches def, RAC lanes
2: 5-27	Split Rex	190 X In Swing	Swing helps vs. zones, good dump
2: 6-19	Rex Out F11	Hot 190 Wheel	Attack wkside of trips-- chance for deep shot or RAC for short throws
3: 1-23	Ray Plus F4	Y336 Short Z Plant	Plant a good stationary target in hole
3: 2-12	Empty	93 B Hitch	R.A.C. for Slant or safe Hitch avail.
3: 3-19	Strong Lou Y9	193 Stick B Stop	Hi % yds with Stick or Slant
3: 3-20	Grn Larry 10 F11	Y190 Wheel	Hi % Whl or Slant with deep poss.

Third and One to Two

- One of two approaches is warranted: either a sure, extremely high-percentage throw that can be guaranteed, or, in games where we need to roll the dice, a deep shot to take advantage of tightened defensive backs.
- Solid protection answers are essential, because we will often face "gapped" defenses with extra potential rushers.

Refer to Diagram:	Formation	Play	Comments/Brief Summary
2: 4-28	Ray Plus	Stay 97 Swing	Good protection with "Stay," Short & Swing are good, hi % throws
2: 6-17	Weak Rip F10	90 Wheel	Motn f/ a run set provides a deep shot w/ Wheel as a built-in dump
2: 6-33	Weak Rip Wing F10	90 Wheel Turn	2 hi % routes with a built-in deep shot
3: 1-18	Ray	Y336 Fade	Deep shot off play action w/ safe Out
3: 3-21	Brown Liz Z6	Y93	Easy throw to quick Shoot off motion
3: 3-22	Weak Rip Wing Z7	Y192 Go Z Sit	Deep dbl move shot w/ "Sit" guarantee

Third and Three

- Find highest percentage ways to throw the ball since most routes can get the first down by virtue of the catch.
- Coverage variety likely: use different types of packaged calls to account for different possibilities.
- Stationary routes facing the quarterback ideal.
- Tighter techniques likely; receivers must use distinct breaks and separation techniques.
- Can use tighter sets to pull in flat defenders to isolate outside receivers for easy throws.

Refer to Diagram:	Formation	Play	Comments/Brief Summary
1: 6-17	Rip Plus Wing	191 Hitch	Trips run edge creates soft C for Hitch
1: 6-18	Strong Rip Tight	92 Qk Out	Run set to pull in flat cov for Qk Out
1: 6-33	Brown Ray H9	192 Qk Out	Motion Quick Out to gain a soft C
1: 7-15	Brown Rip Y7	193 Slant H Shoot	Good chances for Shoots on both sides
1: 8-20	Larry Out H7	198 Fade/Out	Rubs for Break Out off motion
2: 1-29	Ray In X Snug	96 Whip	QB can pick bet. Whip & Wing Hitch
2: 3-11	Weak Rip Wing F10	95 Turn	Z running Shoot has a great chance
2: 3 -19	Strong Liz Z8	95 Switch	Creates natural pick for bkfld Shoot
2: 4 -20	Ron 11 H9	197 Short	Creates good lev & run for Short
2: 5-26	Empty	Hot 90 F & H Out	Horiz stretch w/picks, good matchups
2: 6-25	Ram H Mo Chk	Wheel	Motn chk creates best matchups/hi %
2: 6-30	Rip Plus	Sty 190 Wheel Turn	Solid pro w/ 4 to a side horiz stretch
3: 1-12	Roy	310 Dupe Hitch	Hi % Hitches in front of QB off P.A.
3: 1-22	L 8	Y324 Short	Hi % Short off Play Action
3: 2-1	Ray Out	97 B Turn	QB picks best of 2 hi % combos
3: 2-20	Rex Out	Chk 95 or Veer	Run/90s check guarantees hi % play
3: 3-23	Flex	Ck 91 Dupe/Trap	Run/90s check guarantees hi % play
3: 3-24	Split Rex	97 B Quick Out	Packaged Short & Quick Out
3: 3-25	Squ Rip Out Z7	190 Out B Turn	Pkged Outs acct for diff coverages

Third and Four to Six

- Coverage variety likely; expect opponent's *best* coverage.
- Often a blitz down, including zone blitzes. "Hot" throws are workable, but must see the throwing lane *clearly.*
- Some cuts won't get first down on their own—favor those that *do* unless we can create definite R.A.C. situations.
- If the Hitch is available on the outside, TAKE IT every time. By building them into call, we avoid the need to check.

Refer to Diagram:	Formation	Play	Comments/Brief Summary
1: 6-22	Blue Flex	192 Quick Out	Basic Quick Out vs. soft corner
1: 6-26	Black Ray H10	91 Hitch	Hitch off motion to get a soft C
1: 7-25	L 8 Y6	193 Slant	Creating a lane for singled Slant
1: 8-9	Larry 7	Y198 Fade/Out	Solid Break Out good v. man or zone
2:1-10	Ram H10	F96 Quick Smash	Motn creates matchup for Hitch or Smash
2: 1-26	Rex H9	196 Whip	Basic Whip/Qk Smash combinatn
2: 3-9	Lex In	195 Turn	"Broken Bunch" isolates LB 2 on 1
2: 3-23	Squ Lex 7	195 Trade	Two clear-outs for Turn from Bunch
2: 4-19	Lex 7	197 Short	3 Slants possible or Short w/ RAC
2: 4-22	Empty	97 or 197 Short	Wide set opens lanes for Short/Slants
2: 5-18	Roy 10 Z Trace	90 Z Out	Motion & a good matchup for Z off rub
2: 5-25	Empty	Hot 90 Z In	Field stretch makes Z viable v. man or zone
2: 6-24	Flex F11	Hot 190 Wheel	Wheel combo on 1 side with solid Slant/Stick combination backside
2: 6-34	Squeeze R 8 F10	Y 90 Wheel Turn	Motn disrupts def Bunch adjustments
3: 2-25	Flex H6	Chk 91 or 93	Hitch or Slant chk off man or zone cov
3: 3-26	Grn Liz Out H8	Y96 Whip	Whip/Smash combo or wksd Hitch
3: 3-27	Rip 9 Wing H10	95 B Hitch	Turn or Shoot w/ Z; bksd Hitch built in
3: 3-28	Blue Ray In Z Return	98 Fade/Out	2 good poss. for hi % Break Outs

Third and Seven to Eleven

- Often a blitz down, including zone blitzes. Would rather protect than "hot," because defenses often invite "hot" throws to tackle the man in front of the 1st down marker.
- Cover 2 Man from Nickel/Dime people common also.
- Gear plays to one of two categories: make distance with the catch, or throw short with distinct R.A.C. opportunity. Quarterbacks and receivers must understand which we are trying to do. Max protection and isolated edge throws are best for making distance with the catch.

Refer to Diagram:	Formation	Play	Comments/Brief Summary
1: 6-38	Flex	91 Y Slant	Interior Slant & outside Hitch account for different types of coverage
1: 6-41	Ram X	91 Go Y Sit	Dbl move vs. aggressive C w/outlet
1: 7-35	Rip 9	93 Seam	Big hole if 2d short def stuck inside Y
1: 7-37	Gun Flex	93 Double Dupe	Good man-beater for R.A.C.
2: 1-33	Twin	96 Dbl Whip	Squeezed Smashes or RAC Whips
2: 2-12	Rip 8	194 Stop	Good chance to isolate edge throw
2: 4-31	Lou 10	197 Dbl Corner	Good v. 2 Man: Corner or Short (RAC)
2: 4-33	Green Larry Pair X10	197 Plant	Plant a hi % throw to make the yards
2: 5-17	Flex H8	90 H In	Good chance for separation & RAC vs. Cover 2 Man
3: 3-29	Gun Flex	193 Stick B In	Two combinations with good RAC chances
3: 3-31	Shift to Rip Hip	F 94 Stop	Shift to single up a Stop

Third and Twelve or More

- Gear thinking the same way as 3rd and 7 to 11, knowing that soft corner techniques and Cover 4 varieties become more of a possibility.
- Do not force something into the teeth of a zone defense; the times we try to throw for it all, which are more rare in these situations, we will do so on the edge of the field.
- Try to create/find seams in the defense that will allow a sure throw and catch with R.A.C. potential.

Refer to Diagram:	Formation	Play	Comments/Brief Summary
1: 6-45	Split Larry	192 Stutter	Edge throw that can make the 1st
1: 7-26	Empty	Hot 93 Slant	Spread the field and hope someone can hit a seam on the run
1: 8-15	Flex	99 Fade/Seam	Vertical pressure on edges or Seam 2 on 1 vs. Cover 3 FS
2: 1-14	Rex Out	96 Quick Smash	Puts deep pressure on hash safety
2: 6-21	Rex 6 F10	Hot 90 Wheel	4 rec to a side--can isolate BSSlant for RAC or hope for an open seam FS
3: 3-30	Split Rip	91 Dbl Stutter	Mirrored triple move "Stutter" routes provide a chance for yardage vs. soft corners.

Coming Out Offense: Minus 15

- Often a time in which extra rushers will be brought from outside, with slants and scrapes likely as well; at least one TE to widen their rush and protect is ideal.
- Some teams play base coverage, while others' philosophy is to use this opportunity to attack, tightening things down.
- Basic throwing ideas: throw deep up the field to the outside, where no one can get it but us, or isolate someone on the edge of the field for safe throws so we are only dealing with one defender at a time.

Refer to Diagram:	Formation	Play	Comments/Brief Summary
1: 6-42	Rip 9	192 Go	Safe dbl move route on deep edges
1: 7-24	Rip Plus	Y 193 Slant	Singled slant wk from strong run set
1: 8-12	Ray H10	99 Fade/Seam	Deep shot from motn vs. crowded def
2: 1-24	Black Larry H10	96 Quick Smash	Hi-lo stretch on the edges from motn
2: 3-34	Str Rip Tight F Ret	95 Turn	Solid, hi % route from a tight run look
3: 1-16	Bear 9	Y 306 Stop	Play action pass to the outside from unbalanced set; Z should be isolated
3: 3-1	Rip Hip F Return	91 Go	Deep shot using motion to reveal cov
3: 3-2	Weak Ray Tight	Y 94 H Swing	Fully protected Stop w/ Swing dump
3: 3-3	Ram X	Max 324 Fade	High-low on the edge off play action

Red Zone: Plus 25

- Amount of man coverage and number of rushers likely to increase from here on in.
- "Speed of the game" begins to increase, holes in defenses close up quicker because of restricted field.
- Emphasize man-breaking routes, especially those with a TD shot built-in, while ideally having sound outlets vs. zones.
- Backfield motion can help gain TD leverage, because FS will more often be the "adjust player" and leave the middle.

Refer to Diagram:	Formation	Play	Comments/Brief Summary
1:6-43	Twin	92 Double Go	Double move routes f/ Bunched set
1: 7-29	Squ Brown Liz H5	193	Qk Shoot to wide field off two rubs
1: 7-33	L 8	93 Stick	Creating a crease for a deep Slant
1: 8-20	Larry Out H7	198	Fade, Seam, and Pressure Out all potentially good vs. Red Zone cover
1: 8-21	Ray 6	Y 99 Swing	Chance for deep Fade or Swing as a dump
2: 1-6	Rip 8 H11	Y 196	Creates matchup probs on Hitch & Smash
2: 2-15	Ram H11	Max 194	Special form/mo to create mismatch for the Stop route outside
2: 3-14	Larry Out F10	Hot 95 Turn	Motion to force coverage adjustment, deep Split possible
2: 5-15	Ram H Mo Chk	In	Good separation combo off motion check to help matchup
2: 6-18	Split Rex H10	90 Wheel	Shot at a Split or Slant/Wheel combo
3: 1-15	Strong Rex	336 Quick Smash	P.A. to freeze hash safeties for Corner-type route
3: 2-5	L 10	97 B Fade/Seam	Fade/Seam if a good deep matchup exists; Short as a zone layoff
3: 3-7	Rip 11	99 B Fade/Out	Packaged Fades acct for cov variety
3: 3-8	Squeeze Larry H11	196 Quick Smash	Mot Hitch w/ 2 deep shots inside it
3: 3-9	Strong Liz F10	90 Wheel	Split if FS leaves plus mirrored, man-beating Slants

Red Zone: Plus 15

- Corner-type routes and Fades now within TD reach.
- Blitz percentage now higher than it was before, as is the likelihood of the FS leaving the middle with motion.
- Receivers must work extra hard at making distinct breaks and gaining separation, since coverage techniques are tighter.
- Must build in answers for "lanes"/"Banjoed" man concepts.

Refer to Diagram:	Formation	Play	Comments/Brief Summary
1: 7-22	Larry H7	Y 193 Slant	Shoot rubbing off two Slants
1: 7-38	Brown Larry Z8	Max 193 Dog	Great dbl move route v. overplays of the Slant
1: 8-26	Squeeze Ray 6	98 Fade/Out	Break Out off 2 rubs f/ Bunched set
2: 1-5	Ray	96 Quick Smash	Qk Smash to corner of end zone
2: 3-26	Nasty Rip Plus	95 Slant	Deep Slant v. single coverage or Turn
2: 5-15	Larry Pair X Trace	Y 190 X In	In off two rubs f/motion & a Bunch look
2: 6-24	Flex F11	Hot 190 Wheel	Wheel combo FS, Slant/Stick BS
2: 6-31	Brown Liz H11	190 Wheel Turn	Bkfld motn provides mismatch opportunity
3: 1-20	Squ Ray 9 H6	Y 324 Fade	Squeezed Fade off motn & P.A.
3: 2-3	Roy H11	97 B In	Short and In both solid in this area
3: 3-10	Rip 8	90 Z In Stop	Singled Stop packaged with In
3: 3-11	Str Rip F Shuffle	329 Double Dog	Two man beating, double-move routes to the corner off P.A.
3: 3-12	Larry Out X Snug	96 Double Whip	Two routes to the corner with Whip lay-offs that are excellent vs. man

Red Zone: Plus 8

- Some sort of substitution package now likely, as is heavy blitzing on at least every other down.
- Biggest keys for quarterback: proper, quick rhythm and full vision of the lane through which he is throwing.
- Biggest keys for receivers: distinct separation moves and great head snap, hands ready to catch balls in tight spots.
- Intentional "hot" throwing can be done, but it must be very safe and calculated.
- Slants and Stops are now in scoring reach; create isolations.
- Play action is a viable option to throw behind or outside people.

Refer to Diagram:	Formation	Play	Comments/Brief Summary
1: 7-21	Blue Ray In H6	Badger 93	Trips rule Slant w/ good matchup for H on Shoot
1: 8-14	Ram	198 Fade/Out	Good chance to iso TE vs. LB on Out
2: 1-30	Rex Out Z Snug	96 Whip	Motion Whip running thru 2 rubs
2: 2-7	Ram	94 Stop	Basic goalline Fade/Stop
2: 4-20	Ron 11 H9	197 Short	Short motn concept w/ 197 to create problems for lanes & bumped man cov
2: 5-21	Green Rip 11 X10	90 X In	Rub for basic In off motion
3: 1-9	Ram X	F 324 Slant	Play action Trips Slant combination
3: 3-13	Ray 10	97 Short	Two rubs for Short with two possible Slant isolations
3: 3-14	Larry Pair X Return	Y198 Fade	Break Out off motion off two rubs
3: 3-15	Rex	93 Seam	Slant breaking in behind a Seam

Red Zone: Plus 4

- Must protect the football and not take a sack.
- Use motion to reveal coverage: lanes, bumped man, locked man, or pure zone.
- Separation and release techniques are now vital, as is head snap on final break since ball must be delivered in tight spots.
- On in-breaking routes, quarterback must be especially aware of the next defender in front of the man he is throwing to.
- Flat and Shoot-type routes are now within scoring reach; receivers must fall forward after catch, use proper body lean. Throws must not be late.
- Route combinations with rubs that can be delivered on fast rhythm are at a premium.

Refer to Diagram:	Formation	Play	Comments/Brief Summary
1: 7-36	Green Larry 10	Badger 93 Dupe	3 Slants--pick the best matchup
1: 8-25	Green Larry 10 X Ret	Badger 198 Fade	Squeezed Fade to corner or Break Out off motion & a rub
2: 1-31	Squeeze Ray	Max 96 Whip	Squeezed Whip concept
2: 3-12	Split Larry H6	95 Turn	Fast motion to open Turn & create good matchups
2: 4-19	Lex 7	197 Short	Short complete in a hurry if C gives too much ground; 2 Slants also
2: 5-20	Strong Rip Z9	190 X In	Motion picker to create quick rub for In
3: 3-16	Rip 9 Z7	193 Slant	Motion Shoot off two rubs by Slants; "America's two-point play"
3: 3-17	Black Rip	194 Stop	Great when C overplays the GL Fade
3: 3-18	Rip 9 F6	Hot 95 Turn	Quick hole opens vs. GL zones & bumped man adjustments

Four Minute / "Victory" Offense

- Priority #1: Get a completion, keep the clock running; use highest percentage throws.
- Play action can take advantage of aggressive perimeter run support playing from a tightened position.
- "Run/Quick" checks are an excellent tool to stay in high percentage plays, as are packaged route sides on downs where we must throw.

Refer to Diagram:	Formation	Play	Comments/Brief Summary
1: 6-28	Ram Z	F 192 Qk Out	Solidly protected Qk Out w/ Seam Read
1: 6-29	Larry Pair	191 Hitch	"Broken Bunch" to isolate Hitch
1: 7-36	Green Larry 10	193 Dupe	Double Slant concept—short throws
2: 1-15	Squeeze Rip 9	196 Qk Smash	Hitch can maneuver into open area like an option route from this pos.
2: 2-17	Shift to Rip Plus	194 Stop	Shift to stir the pot & get flat cov out of pos for sound possession throw on the edge
2: 3-8	Rip Plus	95 Turn	Very high percentage throw f/ run set
3: 2-15	Strong Liz	198 B Quick Out	Packaged side allows QB to pick best of two hi % throws
3: 3-4	Larry Plus	Chk Zone/191 Dupe	Solid "Run/Quick" chk on 1st or 2d down
3: 3-5	Brown L	Y324 Slant/Shoot	Play action to attack flat coverage
3: 3-6	Shift to Ray 11	Y93 Dupe B Hitch	Shift to create matchup problems; safe throws on either side for QB

Two Minute Offense

- Philosophies on two-minute coverage and when to go to prevent vary; offense must be able to account for both soft corner and hard corner varieties.
- Find the best way to gain yardage outside and get out of bounds; always understand who and where the defender is that is assigned to keep us in bounds.
- Wider sets are generally used to maximize the number of options.
- Interior throws can be made, but they must give us a great chance at making first-down yardage and stopping the clock.

Refer to Diagram:	Formation	Play	Comments/Brief Summary
1: 6-31	Split Roy	92 Qk Out	Safe way to gain yards and get the ball out of bounds
1: 8-8	Roy	98 Fade/Out	Basic Break Out can be good RAC while allowing rec to get out of bounds
1: 8-15	Flex	99 Fade/Seam	Deep Seam look 2 on 1 vs. 3 deep-type Prevent coverage
3: 3-32	Rex 6	94 Stop	Boundary throw to take adv of soft corners and get out of bounds
3: 3-33	Flex	96 Qk Smash	Method of getting out of bounds vs. hard corner Prevent coverage
3: 3-34	Cluster Rex 6	90 Z In	Stretches underneath coverage of soft prevent defenses...singled Slant or In off two rubs. Good RAC on both.

Basic Coverage Sheets

In introducing and discussing various defenses, Volume Chapter 5 mentioned a very effective visual, summarizing tool we borrowed from Sid Gillman, Jim Colletto, and others called a "coverage sheet." Through these coverage sheets, a good deal of useful information can be communicated to players very quickly regarding the different types of things they see from opponents on the field.

This appendix is a compilation of those coverage sheets as they would look to us for a number of basic coverages. Each of the sheets uses the same basic format, all of them asking the basic questions: "What is it?"; "How is it recognized?"; "What is the philosophy behind it?"; "Who on our schedule plays it?"; "What are the things we must do to beat it?"; and "What questions will we ask in trying to best attack it?" These questions help to break the body of information available on each coverage down into digestible chunks, and they are also designed to provide a deeper level of understanding as they progress, again following the "levels of learning" formula.

COVER 1 BLITZ

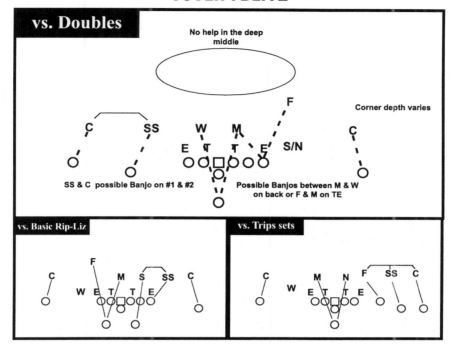

WHAT IS IT? A pure man-to-man coverage with no free safety in the middle that enables a maximum number of players to rush the passer.

HOW IS IT RECOGNIZED? There is no coverage deep in the middle, cornerbacks play inside man leverage, extra people lined up to rush off edge from various places.

WHAT IS THE PHILOSOPHY BEHIND IT? A roll of the dice that reflects extreme confidence in cornerbacks' and safeties' coverage ability. People playing this feel they will break down your protection before you can get people open into the deep middle.

WHO PLAYS IT? Anderson, Tri-State, ONU, Trinity, St. Ambrose, Iowa Wesleyan

WHAT ARE THE THINGS WE MUST DO TO BEAT IT?
- Make certain we are fully protected through checks and "Smoke" calls
- Use effective releases and violent misdirection moves: attack
- Lead receivers away from pressure so that they can run after catch
- Create and take advantage of good matchups
- Make use of rubs and picks
- Whenever possible, quickly get to the deep middle to make them pay.

WHAT KINDS OF QUESTIONS WILL WE ASK TO BEST ATTACK IT?
- Do the corners play loose or tight technique? Do they jam? When?
- Do they bump with motion or lock?
- Do they banjo? Play triangle techniques vs. Trips? Who? If they do not, how do they deal with rubs? Will they stay in it if we line up "Bunched"?
- Can we get a LB to move wide with a TE lined up as #1? Can we force a LB to cover a WR by lining him up inside or in the backfield?
- Do they try to roll to this out of Cover 2 shells? How late? What tips it?
- How do they handle backfield motion? With a LB? By bumping?
- Is the FS a blitzer? An adjustment cover player weak? Strong?
- How do they try to compensate for the hole in the deep middle?

COVER 1 FREE

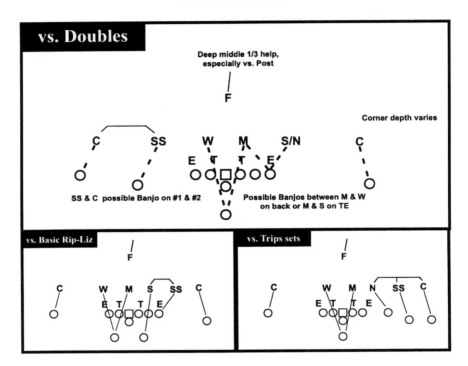

WHAT IS IT? A pure man-to-man coverage with a free safety left in the deep middle one-third to help, serving as a "center fielder."

HOW IS IT RECOGNIZED? Corners tightened down with inside leverage, staring straight at their receiver, a tighter strong safety, and/or defenders chasing motion men across the field instead of bumping or sliding.

WHAT IS THE PHILOSOPHY BEHIND IT? To play a pressuring-style of defense, gambling that their people can cover receivers one-on-one long enough for the front to pressure the quarterback, knowing that deep help in the middle can prevent them from giving up the big play.

WHO PLAYS IT? Tri-State, Olivet Nazarene, Iowa Wesleyan, Malone, Geneva

WHAT ARE THE THINGS WE MUST DO TO BEAT IT?
- Use effective releases and violent misdirection moves: attack
- Lead receivers away from pressure so that they can run after catch
- Create and take advantage of good matchups
- Make use of rubs and picks
- Avoid losing the ball deep down the middle where the FS is

WHAT KINDS OF QUESTIONS WILL WE ASK TO BEST ATTACK IT?
- Do the corners play loose or tight technique? Do they jam? When?
- Do they bump with motion or lock?
- Do they banjo? Who? If they do not, how do they deal with rubs?
- Can we get a LB to move wide with a TE lined up as #1? Can we force a LB to cover a WR by lining him up inside or in the backfield?
- What route(s) is the FS trying hardest to take away? Can he be moved?
- How do they handle backfield motion? With a LB? FS? By bumping?
- Will they stay in it if we line up in "Bunched" alignments?
- How do they handle flaring actions and backs out of the backfield?

BASIC COVER 2

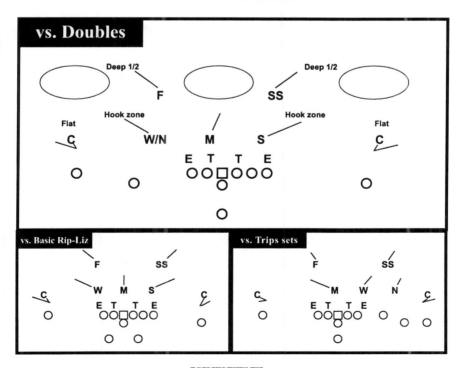

203

WHAT IS IT? Zone coverage that plays with two deep safeties each responsible for 1/2 of the field, and five short defenders in underneath zones, including two "hard" corners.

HOW IS IT RECOGNIZED? Corners are tightened down, normally to six yards or tighter, usually with outside leverage (i.e., you can see the stripe down the middle of their helmet). One deep safety is aligned in the vicinity of each hash at 12 yards or so.

WHAT IS THE PHILOSOPHY BEHIND IT? To cut down underneath throwing lanes with extra droppers, and to funnel routes to the inside with hard, low corners. Many times will entail physical cornerback play to try to destroy the timing of pass routes with the jam. Is generally a balanced coverage that also has ability to "bracket" single receivers. Also used as a run support defense vs. outside runs.

WHO PLAYS IT? Anderson, Walsh, Iowa Wesleyan, St. Xavier, Findlay

WHAT ARE THE THINGS WE MUST DO TO BEAT IT?
- Use purposeful, violent releases on the outside to maintain route timing
- Get people to the deep dead spots quickly and deliver the ball on time
- Get into open windows, with the quarterback stopping receivers in those windows
- Use formations to either isolate one underneath player on two receivers or cause an imbalance that favors us

WHAT KINDS OF QUESTIONS WILL WE ASK TO BEST ATTACK IT?
- What is the corner technique? Depth? How and when do they jam? How easily can they be outside released?
- How active are the LBs in coverage? Deep drops or Shallow? Do they wall or spot drop? Do they collision? Do they "cover down" on inside receivers?
- Do the safeties tend to hang tightly on the hash, or do they play wide?
- Are they a pattern-read emphasis team or a "spot drop" team?
- Will they stay in this coverage vs. trips?
- Will the corners flop in "Cowboy" technique vs. a single width side?
- Do they always play with five underneath? Do they ever play with four? six?

COVER 2 "MATCH"

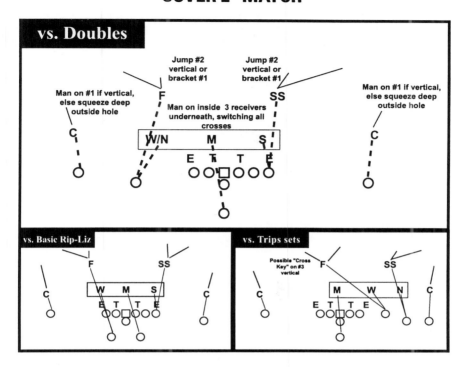

WHAT IS IT? Two-deep coverage that employs a combination of zone and man principles to try to cut down holes left by traditional Cover 2. A "pattern-read" coverage.

HOW IS IT RECOGNIZED? Looks very similar to Cover 2. Corner to wide side often plays with inside leverage, neither corner generally playing a "funnel" position as in normal Cover 2. Safeties never wider than #2 on their side.

WHAT IS THE PHILOSOPHY BEHIND IT? To "cover people, not grass," trying to cut down the voids left by zone coverages while employing the switching techniques that help against crossing routes and rubs. To try to use keys to get people in position to stop most "traditional" route combinations.

WHO PLAYS IT?

WHAT ARE THE THINGS WE MUST DO TO BEAT IT?
- Understand when to "sit" and when to "accelerate" since it can appear to be both man and zone coverage at the same time.
- Separate with decisive breaks and good acceleration away from people.
- Create situations where a corner or LB is in a bad matchup with no help.
- Cause problems for inside defenders in identifying who #1, #2, and #3 are, as well as when to switch.

WHAT KINDS OF QUESTIONS WILL WE ASK TO BEST ATTACK IT?
- Who is their weakest linebacker, and where does he usually get help from?
- Which corner to we want to attack, and how? How do we prevent him from getting help?
- How quickly will the safeties jump #2 on a vertical release?
- With what kind of depth and leverage to the cornerbacks try to play? Which routes are they most trying to stop? At what point do they fully engage #1?
- Will they stay in this vs. trips? Do they cross-key #3 with the free safety?
- Does the bunching and squeezing of receivers cause their interior coverage identification problems?
- Can we gain leverage for certain routes with motion? What kinds of motion?

COVER 2 MAN

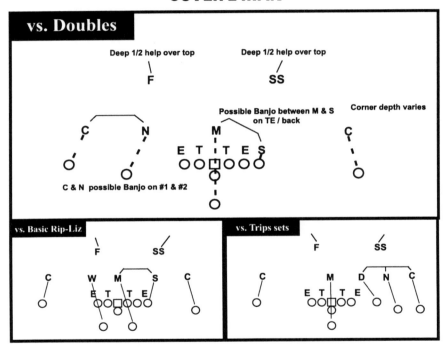

WHAT IS IT? Man-to-man coverage underneath with two deep safeties to help deep on either side. Underneath coverage often with tight, inside leverage, or "trail technique."

HOW IS IT RECOGNIZED? Safeties at normal Cover 2 depth near the hashes with corners playing head up to inside leverage instead of outside.

WHAT IS THE PHILOSOPHY BEHIND IT? Often a long yardage coverage, Cover 2 man enables a defense to play aggressive man technique underneath to eliminate zone holes while having two deep safeties to help deep to prevent deep shots.

WHO PLAYS IT? Walsh, Olivet Nazarene, Saint Xavier

WHAT ARE THE THINGS WE MUST DO TO BEAT IT?
- Use effective releases and violent misdirection moves: attack, then separate.
- Lead receivers away from pressure so that they can run after catch.
- Create and take advantage of good matchups.
- Make use of rubs and picks.
- Understand where safety help is and take people away from those safeties with the right reads and throws.

WHAT KINDS OF QUESTIONS WILL WE ASK TO BEST ATTACK IT?
- What are the Cs' general technique? Can we get underneath and inside them? Will they open their hips if threatened with the Fade? Do they jam? When?
- Do they bump with motion or lock?
- Do they banjo? Who? If they do not, how do they deal with rubs?
- Can we get a LB to move wide with a TE lined up as #1? Can we force a LB to cover a WR by lining him up inside or in the backfield?
- What route(s) are the safeties trying hardest to stop? Do they stay near the hash or prefer to widen and bracket #1? Can they be moved?
- Will they stay in it if we line up in "Bunched" alignments?
- How do they handle flaring actions and backs out of the backfield?
- Do they use a "Cowboy" adjustment vs. Ray & Larry sets?

BASIC COVER 3

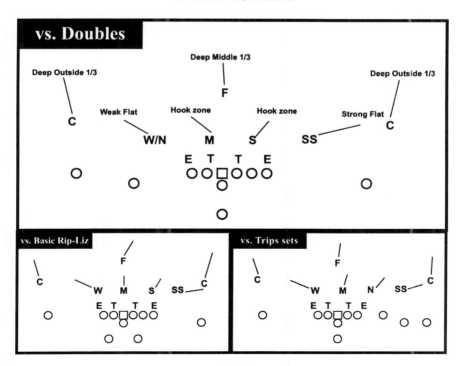

WHAT IS IT? A zone coverage that plays with three deep defenders, each responsible for 1/3 of the deep field. Normally played with four defenders underneath.

HOW IS IT RECOGNIZED? Corners are softer, normally at least seven yards deep and likely outside; a free safety is somewhere deep in the middle of the field. Vs. Rip or Liz, the SS is in a "5 x 5" relationship with the TE instead of the tighter position he has in Cover 1.

WHAT IS THE PHILOSOPHY BEHIND IT? To take away the deep ball, keep receivers in front and tackle them for short gains, forcing the offense to beat them by executing long series of short passes. It also often corresponds with defenses that play eight men in the "box" to stop the run as a first priority.

WHO PLAYS IT? Tri-State, Walsh, Olivet Nazarene, St. Xavier, Westminster, Findlay

WHAT ARE THE THINGS WE MUST DO TO BEAT IT?
- Use smart splits and weaves to widen the seams between zone defenders, then settle into those seams, or windows on good timing in each route.
- Stop receivers in those windows with firm throws away from LB/DB pressure.
- Make tight turns after the catch and split defenders north & south.
- Pound the edges of the field with consistent, timed throws.

WHAT KINDS OF QUESTIONS WILL WE ASK TO BEST ATTACK IT?
- How quickly do the corners get out of their backpedal? Do they settle and squat at any certain depth? What routes are they trying hardest to stop? Will they jump on double moves? Is one of them weaker than the other?
- How active is flat coverage on either side? Which routes will they and will they not "work under?" Do they wall off vertical releases by a #2 over them?
- How active are LBs in coverage? Deep drops or Shallow? Wall or spot drop?
- What's FS's alignment rule—Middle of formation, middle of field or other?
- Does the SS line up to the field or formation strength?
- Are they a pattern-read emphasis team or a 'spot drop' team?
- Can we gain a distinct advantage to one side or another from balanced sets?
- Will the corners flop in "Cowboy" technique vs. a single width side?
- Do they always play with four underneath? Do they ever play with five? When?

COVER 3 "CLOUD"

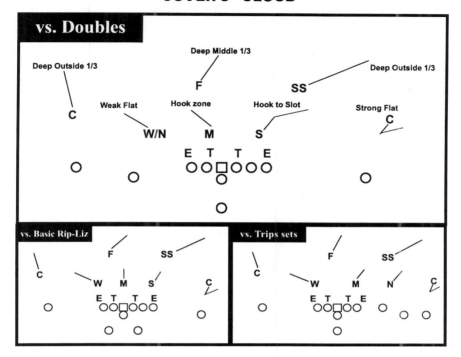

WHAT IS IT? A variation of Cover 3 in which the strong safety and corner exchange jobs, the SS taking deep outside 1/3 and the corner rolling up to cover the flat.

HOW IS IT RECOGNIZED? Often rolled to late out of a Cover 2 shell, with these keys: SS will align wider than normal, and FS will have to cheat toward middle to get to deep middle in time. Safeties many times show rotation just before the snap.

WHAT IS THE PHILOSOPHY BEHIND IT? Maintains three deep secondary while eliminating one soft corner, funneling and constricting routes to the strong side. Can be used as a strong side run support defense, also as a Cover 3 adjustment vs. a tight split by Z.

WHO PLAYS IT? Anderson

WHAT ARE THE THINGS WE MUST DO TO BEAT IT?
- Recognize it through pre-snap and post-snap keys, and make the safeties pay for any late rotation to their areas.
- Use smart splits and weaves to widen the seams between zone defenders, especially on the strongside, then settle into those seams on good timing.
- Stop receivers in those windows with firm throws away from LB/DB pressure.

- Make tight turns after the catch and split defenders north & south.
- Exploit the weakside flat area if they slide the underneath coverage strong; exploit the hole between the strong corner and slot defender if they do not.

WHAT KINDS OF QUESTIONS WILL WE ASK TO BEST ATTACK IT?
- Is the "Cloud" corner someone they are trying to hide? Are they using this to bracket Z? Does he jam? With what leverage and depth does he play?
- Do they slide their backers to try to close down the strongside "Slot" area?
- How active are LBs in coverage? Deep drops or Shallow? Wall or spot drop?
- Do they roll to it from a Cover 2 look? When? Is either S late getting to his 1/3?
- Is it an adjustment defense to tight splits or to the boundary? Are there formations or receiver splits that will chase them out of it?
- Are they a pattern-read emphasis team or a "spot drop" team?
- Do they always play with four underneath? Do they ever play with five? When?

COVER 4

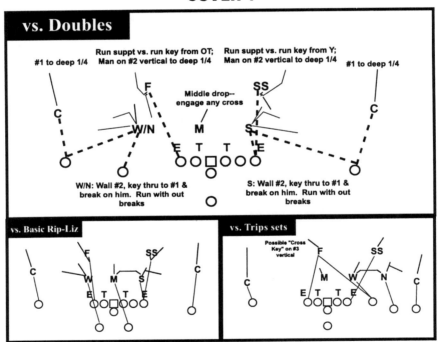

WHAT IS IT? A "four deep" coverage concept that uses safeties in keyed run support and often uses heavy pattern reading techniques by both deep and underneath coverage.

HOW IS IT RECOGNIZED? Similar look as a two deep shell, but corners will often align deeper, and safeties closer together/tighter. Safeties usually "walk up" on the snap.

WHAT IS THE PHILOSOPHY BEHIND IT? To use safety run support as a means of getting nine run defenders in the "box" while minimizing deep ball risk with a "four deep" secondary. Pattern-reading techniques are employed to get in the lanes of many "traditional" patterns.

WHO PLAYS IT? Anderson, Trinity, Saint Ambrose

WHAT ARE THE THINGS WE MUST DO TO BEAT IT?
- Consistently make yards on the outside edges by controlling OLB coverage and maximizing R.A.C. with sharp turns and north-south running.
- Take advantage of over-aggressive safety support with deep shots behind them.
- Receivers understand when to settle and when to continue on routes, with QBs making appropriate throws as this can look like zone and man both.
- Create mismatches on corners and linebackers with formation, and force them into situations where they cannot get help.

WHAT KINDS OF QUESTIONS WILL WE ASK TO BEST ATTACK IT?
- Can Cs and OLBs able to effectively cover quick throws on the outside? How?
- Do they play this with a heavy pattern-read, run support emphasis, or a softer, "deep quarters" emphasis?
- Who are the safeties keying?
- Do they stay in it vs. Trips? If so, how do they handle various releases by #3?
- What are the MLB's responsibilities and keys? Can he be isolated?
- How athletic are the OLBs at reacting to and running with out-breaking routes? How can we create mismatches for them?
- At what point do the safeties engage vertical releases in man coverage?
- How do they like to deal with/help on crossing routes?

"QUARTERS"

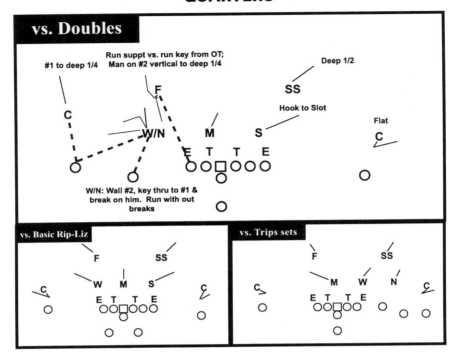

vs. Doubles

Run suppt vs. run key from OT;
#1 to deep 1/4   Man on #2 vertical to deep 1/4

Deep 1/2

SS

Hook to Slot

Flat

C   W/N   M   S   C

E T T E

W/N: Wall #2, key thru to #1 &
break on him. Run with out
breaks

vs. Basic Rip-Liz

F   SS

C   W   M   S   C

E T T E

vs. Trips sets

F   SS

C   M   W   N   C

E T T E

WHAT IS IT? A combination coverage that functions as "Cover 4" on one side, and "Cover 2" on the other.

HOW IS IT RECOGNIZED? Low corner with a high safety on one side, with a safety and a corner on the other whose depths are closer to level. Teams often roll to this from an initial Cover 2 look.

WHAT IS THE PHILOSOPHY BEHIND IT? Can be used in different ways: As a means to bracket an outstanding receiver on one side while keeping three over two help for the other; as a formation adjustment to single width sets; or as a change-up coverage within a Cover 2/4 package.

WHO PLAYS IT? Anderson

WHAT ARE THE THINGS WE MUST DO TO BEAT IT?
* Read coverage on the move and make the right adjustments, including jam escapes, bursts, and proper sit-down points.
* Use checks and "B" tags to provide good routes to both sides.
* Take advantage of matchups and easy throws to the 1/4s side.
* Use combinations and releases that pry the center of the field open to make big yards down the middle.

WHAT KINDS OF QUESTIONS WILL WE ASK TO BEST ATTACK IT?
- What is the technique of the 1/4 side—aggressive pattern read, soft quarters, or man?
- What is the OLB's technique on the 1/4 side? Does he cover the flat well?
- Do they try to disguise to it? From what looks and how late?
- Do they ever put the Cover 2 side to two split receivers? To the wide field?
- Does the Cover 2 side corner jam and funnel? What is his depth? Can he be outside released?
- How quickly does the Cover 2 safety get off the hash?

Quick Passing Game Route Menu vs.
Coverages and Techniques

Throughout the text, we have discussed different ways that various route packages can be used to attack coverages and types of techniques played within those coverages. For this appendix, we have taken five basic coverage families and some basic, distinguishing techniques that can be played within each, and compiled a listing of those quick routes that are the *best* at attacking them. The inherent design of each of the plays listed creates some natural, tactical advantage over the specific coverage and technique being played.

Within our multiple package, this sort of "best of the best" summary is critical to keeping the necessary focus within the scope of a rather large package. We have so many tools available that it is easy to take a coverage we might face on a given week and list dozens of things that *can* work against that coverage. What we need, however, are the things that *best* work against that coverage, narrowed down in such a way that they can be practiced and give our players the absolute maximum opportunity to succeed.

Following our general "menus" against different coverages and techniques, a database of sorts has been provided to allow you to quickly refer to the diagrams throughout the text that illustrate ways we attack those particular defenses.

For the reader who wishes to take a specific, usable amount from this text that can be applied right away, and may only face a few of the coverages mentioned, this appendix can be an invaluable reference in helping him quickly get to the heart of what he needs.

Cover 1

TECHNIQUE	BEST PLAYS
General	93, 94, 96, 98, 90 In, 90 Out
Blitz (no FS)	93, 93 Dupe, 96, 97, 90 In, 90 Wheel
Loose	91, 91 Stutr, 92, 93, 94, 95, 96, 96 Whip, 97, In
Tight	91 Go, 92 Go, 94, 96, 97 Corner, 98, 90 Out
Bump & Run	93 Dupe, 97, 98, 99, 90 Out

COVER 1 DIAGRAM SUMMARY

Diag	Formation	Play	Cover	Techniques	
3: 3-18	Rip 9 F6	Hot 95	1 Blitz	Banjo	Lanes
2: 1-31	Squeeze Ray	Max 96 Whip	1 Blitz	Banjo	
2: 5-20	Strong Rip Z9	Max 190 X In	1 Blitz	Banjo	
2: 5-16	Larry Pair X Trace	Y 90 X In	1 Blitz	Bump	
2: 2-14	Larry H10	Y 94	1 Blitz	Cowboy	
2: 7-25	Strong Ray	Stack 198	1 Blitz	Cowboy	
3: 3-14	Larry Pair X Return	Y 198 Fade	1 Blitz	Cowboy	
1: 7-22	Larry H7	Y 193	1 Blitz	FS mo adj	
2: 3-22	Split Larry H6	95	1 Blitz	FS mo adj	
1: 7-15	Brown Rip Y7	193 H Shoot	1 Blitz	Lock	
2: 1-5	Ray	96	1 Blitz	Tight	
1: 7-38	Brown Larry Z8	Max 193 Dog	1 Blitz		
1: 8-21	Ray 6	Y 99 Swing	1 Blitz		
2: 4-15	Split Rex	97	1 Blitz		
2: 4-16	Larry 11	Colt 197	1 Blitz		
3: 3-16	Rip 9 Z7	193	1 Blitz		
3: 3-17	Black Rip	194	1 Blitz		
2: 5-21	Green Rip 11 X10	90 X In	1 Free	Banjo	
2: 5-22	Rip 10 Z Trace	90 Z Out	1 Free	Banjo	
2: 3-12	Squeeze R 11 Y11	195	1 Free	Bump	
2: 4-20	Ron 11 H9	197	1 Free	Bump	
1: 6-32	Liz H10	91	1 Free	Bumped	
1: 7-29	Squeeze Brown Liz H5	193	1 Free	Bumped	
1: 6-33	Brown Ray H9	192	1 Free	Cowboy	
1: 7-20	Nasty Ray 10 H8	93 Y Sit	1 Free	Cowboy	
1: 7-32	Green Larry 10 H7	Colt 193 Stick	1 Free	Cowboy	
2: 4-30	Weak Ray	97 Corner	1 Free	Cowboy	
3: 1-18	Ray	Y 336 Fade	1 Free	Cowboy	
1: 7-21	Blue Ray In H6	93	1 Free	Lock	Tight
1: 8-10	Flex H Trace	199	1 Free	Lock	Tight
1: 6-30	Lou 9	191	1 Free	Lock	
2: 2-15	Ram H11	Max 194	1 Free	Lock	
2: 3-19	Strong LIz Z8	195 Switch	1 Free	Lock	
2: 5-14	Brown Rip Y9	190 X In	1 Free	Lock	
2: 5-15	Ram H Motion Check	H In	1 Free	Lock	

Diag	Formation	Play	Cover	Techniques	
2: 5-18	Roy 10 Z Trace	90 Z Out	1 Free	Lock	
2: 7-5	Flex H6	90 Fin	1 Free	Lock	
2: 7-8	Rex 6	90 Rub	1 Free	Lock	
2: 1-10	Ram H10	96	1 Free	Loose	SS mo adj
1: 8-9	Larry 7	Y 198	1 Free	Loose	
2: 1-9	Split Roy X8	96	1 Free	Loose	
1: 7-37	Gun Flex	193 Double Dupe	1 Free	Robber	
2: 1-30	Rex Out Z Snug	96 Whip	1 Free	Robber	
2: 7-18	Squeeze Rex 6	Outside 98 H Fade	1 Free	Tight	Banjo
2: 1-6	Rip 8 F11	Y 196	1 Free	Tight	Bumped
2: 1-7	Black Rip H8	96	1 Free	Tight	Lock
2: 1-32	Green Larry 10 X Return	196 Whip	1 Free	Tight	
2: 7-17	Twin X Return	198 Double Trade	1 Free	Tight	
1: 6-14	Weak Rip	91	1 Free		
1: 6-31	Split Roy	92	1 Free		
1: 6-44	Ram	Y 191 Double Stutter	1 Free		
1: 7-23	Lex 7	193	1 Free		
1: 7-27	Quads	Hot 193	1 Free		
1: 7-33	L 8	93 Stick	1 Free		
1: 8-8	Roy	98	1 Free		
1: 8-13	Split Lou	198	1 Free		
1: 8-14	Ram	198	1 Free		
1: 8-25	Green Larry 10 X Return	198	1 Free		
1: 8-26	Squeeze Ray 6	98	1 Free		
2: 1-29	Ray In X Snug	96 Whip	1 Free		
2: 1-33	Twin	96 Double Whip	1 Free		
2: 2-11	Liz 8	Y 94	1 Free		
2: 2-18	Green Liz 10 X11	Y 194	1 Free		
2: 4-17	Larry	197	1 Free		
2: 4-18	Liz 10	97	1 Free		
2: 4-19	Lex 7	197	1 Free		
2: 7-1	Liz 8	90 Drive	1 Free		
2: 7-24	Rex In Z Return	Stack 96	1 Free		
2: 7-27	Bunch Ray 6	Stack 98	1 Free		
3: 3-1	Rip Hip F Return	F 91 Go	1 Free		
3: 3-11	Strong Rip F Shuffle	Y 329 Double Dog	1 Free		
3: 3-22	Weak Rip Wing Z7	Y 192 Go Z Sit	1 Free		
Q-3	Flex	193 Z Slant Back	1 Free		

Cover 2

TECHNIQUE	BEST PLAYS
General	93, 95, 96, 97, 98, 99
Traditional	95, 96, 97, 99
Pattern Read	95, 96, 98, 98 "Late"
Corners Jam & Close	Motion 93, 96, 97 Corner, 98, Squeezed 96/98
Corners "Catch" at 5	93 Dupe, 95, 96, 97
Wide Safeties	95, 97, 99, 90 Wheel
Tight Safeties	96, 98 (normal OR squeezed), 91 Go, 92 Go
Man Under	93 Dupe, 94, 96 Whip
Double Invert	93 Seam, 95 Switch, 97, 99

COVER 2 DIAGRAM SUMMARY

Diag	Formation	Play	Cover	Techniques
2: 3-16	Strong Ray H10	Hot 95 Switch	2	Cowboy
2: 3-17	Ray In	195	2	Cowboy
2: 3-29	Ray Plus Z11	Hot 195 H Thru	2	Cowboy
3: 1-16	Bear 8	Y 324 Quick Smash	2	Invert
1: 7-28	Squeeze Strong Liz Z6	93	2	Jam & Close
1: 7-39	Green Larry 10 X Return	93 Double Dog	2	Jam & Close
2: 4-32	Rip 9	197 Corner	2	Jam & Close
1: 7-25	L 8 Y6	193	2	N run w/ mo
1: 7-35	Rip 9	93 Seam	2	
1: 7-36	Green Larry 10	193 Dupe	2	
1: 8-15	Flex	99	2	
1: 8-16	Larry	Y 198	2	
1: 8-23	Twin	98	2	
1: 8-27	Bunch Rex 6	99	2	
1: 8-32	Green Larry 10 Y Return	98 Y Late	2	
2: 1-13	Flex	96	2	
2: 1-14	Rex Out	96	2	
2: 1-15	Squeeze Rip 9	196	2	
2: 2-7	Ram	94	2	
2: 2-13	Lion X Z10	F 94	2	
2: 3-9	Lex In	195	2	
2: 3-27	Nasty Rip Plus	95 Z Slant	2	
2: 3-33	Tight Ram Z11	Y 195	2	
2: 4-21	Flex	197	2	

Diag	Formation	Play	Cover	Techniques	
2: 4-22	Empty	107	2		
2: 5-25	Empty	Hot 90 Z In	2		
2: 6-17	Weak Rip F10	90 Wheel	2		
2: 6-18	Split Rex H10	90 Wheel	2		
2: 6-23	Green Larry 10 F11	Y 190 Wheel	2		
2: 6-30	Rip Plus H11	Stay 190 Wheel Turn	2		
2: 7-2	Ron Pair H9	190 Drive	2		
2: 7-6	R 9 H7	190 Fin	2		
2: 7-9	Liz 9	190 Rub	2		
2: 7-13	Larry In H Return	Hot 90 Hg-Tw B Short	2		
2: 7-16	Squeeze Ray	98 Trade	2		
3: 1-20	Squeeze Ray 9 H6	Y 324 Fade	2		
3: 2-1	Ray Out	97 B Turn	2		
3: 2-4	L 10	97 B Fade/Seam	2		
3: 2-6	Ron Pair	95 B Stop	2		
3: 2-7	Ron Pair	95 B Stop	2		
3: 2-8	Rip 9	98 B Fade/Seam	2		
3: 2-9	Squeeze Larry 7 H6	198 B Fade/Seam	2		
3: 2-10	Squeeze Lex 7	198 B Slant	2		
3: 2-16	Flex	91 or Counter	2		
3: 2-18	Rex	92 or Isolation	2		
3: 2-22	Ray Hip F7	97 or Stretch	2		
Q-6	Rip 9	197 Y & Z Plant	2		
1: 8-11	Ray 11 X8	98	2 Man	Bumped	
2: 7-19	Squeeze Brown Larry H11	Outside 198 Z Fade	2 Man	Cowboy	Bump
1: 6-42	Rip 9	192 Go	2 Man		
2: 1-28	Ram Z Snug	96 Whip	2 Man		
2: 4-31	Loy 10	97 Double Corner	2 Man		
2: 5-17	Flex H8	90 H In	2 Man		
2: 7-23	Rip 9	Stack 196	2 Man		
3: 1-25	Nasty Brown Rip	306 Turn Switch	2 Invert		
3: 2-5	L 10	97 B Fade/Seam	2 Invert		

Cover 3

TECHNIQUE	BEST PLAYS
General	91, 92, 94, 95, 98, 90 In, 90 Wheel
Inactive Flat/ Flat runs w/ vertical	91 Stutter, 92, 94, 95 Trade, 96, 90 Out
Active Flat	91, 92, 93, 90 In, 90 Wheel
Cloud Rotation	93 Seam, 95, 97

COVER 3 DIAGRAM SUMMARY

Diag	Formation	Play	Cover	Techniques
1: 6-15	Split Larry	192	3	
1: 6-16	Ram	191	3	
1: 6-21	Roy 9	91	3	
1: 6-25	Lex 7	191	3	
1: 6-28	Ram Z	F 192	3	
1: 6-29	Larry Pair	191	3	
1: 6-35	Empty	91	3	
1: 6-41	Ram X	91 Go Y Sit	3	
1: 6-45	Split Larry	192 Stutter	3	
1: 7-14	Black Ray	93	3	
1: 7-24	Rip Plus	Y 193	3	
1: 7-26	Empty	Hot 93	3	
1: 8-17	Ram X	98	3	
1: 8-18	Lex Y9	198	3	
1: 8-22	Blue Loy 7 Y7	Hot 199 Swing	3	
1: 8-24	Twin	198	3	
1: 8-28	Strong Larry F Shuffle	Y 98 Hang	3	
2: 1-19	Flex	196	3	
2: 1-20	Ram X	96	3	
2: 1-21	Strong East	Y 96	3	
2: 2-8	Weak Rip F Shuffle	194	3	
2: 2-16	Weak Ray X9	Max 94	3	
2: 3-8	Rip Plus	95	3	
2: 3-14	Larry Out F10	Hot 95	3	
2: 3-15	Ram H7	Y 195	3	
2: 3-20	Ray 6 H7	195	3	
2: 3-24	Twin X10	95 Trade	3	
2: 3-26	Nasty Rip Plus	95 Z Slant	3	
2: 3-28	Green Larry 10 X6	Hot 95 F Thru	3	
2: 3-34	Strong Rip Tight F Return	X 95	3	
2: 3-35	Split Rip H Left	Hot 95 Switch	3	
2: 3-37	Weak Ray X6	Y 95 Switch	3	
2: 3-40	Blue Flex F6	Hot 95 Switch	3	
2: 3-42	Squeeze Rex 6 H10	95	3	
2: 3-45	Green Larry 10	Hot 95 Switch	3	
2: 3-46	Blue Rip Plus F11	Hot 195 Switch	3	
2: 4-25	Ram Z	Y 197	3	

Diag	Formation	Play	Cover	Techniques
2: 4-28	Ray Plus	Stay 97 Swing	3	
2: 4-34	Split Roy	97 Plant H Swing	3	
2: 4-35	L 8	97 Seam	3	
2: 4-26	L 8	97 Seam	3	
2: 5-23	Flex	90 X & Z In	3	
2: 5-26	Empty	Hot 90 F & H Out	3	
2: 5-27	Split Rex	190 Z In H Swing	3	
2: 5-28	Green Larry Plus H Shuffle	Stay 190 X In Swing	3	
2: 6-16	Brown R H11	190 Wheel	3	
2: 6-20	Liz Minus H11	F 190 Wheel	3	
2: 6-26	Lex Hip H10	Y 90 Wheel Trade	3	
2: 6-32	Weak Rip Wing F10	90 Wheel Turn	3	
2: 6-35	Squeeze Ram H Motion Check	Wheel Turn	3	
2: 7-3	Flex	90 Drive	3	
2: 7-7	Larry 7	190 Fin	3	
2: 7-10	Rex Out H Return	90 Rub	3	
2: 7-11	Tight Ray Out	X 190 Hang-Twist	3	
2: 7-28	Larry 7 H6	192 Turn	3	
3: 1-8	Split Rip	Y 321 Slant	3	
3: 1-11	Ray	Y 310 Dupe Slant	3	
3: 1-13	Bear 9	Y 306 Stop	3	
3: 1-19	Blue Liz Minus Z8	Stay 320 Fade	3	
3: 1-21	Ram X Z Return	F 324 Fade	3	
3: 1-22	L 8	Y 324 Short	3	
3: 1-24	Rip Hip F6	324 Short	3	
3: 2-2	Ray Out	97 B Turn	3	
3: 2-17	Flex	91 or Counter	3	
3: 2-19	Rex	92 or Isolation	3	
3: 2-24	Rip Plus	91 or 95	3	
3: 3-5	Brown L	Y 324 Slant H Shoot	3	
Q-5	Split Liz	194 Panther	3	
Q-7	Green Twin	98 Trade H & X Plant	3	
1: 6-26	Black Ray H10	91 Y Sit	3	Cowboy
1: 6-34	Ray Plus X8	Stay 92	3	Cowboy
2: 2-9	Ram X	F 94	3	Cowboy
2: 3-18	Brown Larry	95 Switch	3	Cowboy
2: 3-43	Larry Plus H Left	Hot 95	3	Cowboy
3: 1-9	Ram X	F 324 Slant	3	Cowboy
3: 1-14	Ram X X11	Max 325 Stop	3	Cowboy
3: 1-3	Ram X	Max 324 Fade	3	Cowboy
1: 6-17	Rip Plus Wing	191	3	Cloud
1: 6-27	Blue R 8	92 Y Sit	3	Cloud
1: 8-30	Rex Out	Hot 98 Sw H Hang B Sl	3	Cloud
1: 8-33	Rip In Z Snug	Badger 98 H Late	3	Cloud
2: 2-17	Rip Plus	Stay 194	3	Cloud
2: 3-10	Liz 9 H Return	195	3	Cloud
2: 3-23	Squeeze Lex 7	195 Trade	3	Cloud
2: 3-41	Squeeze Blue Larry Out X10	95	3	Cloud
2: 3-44	Blue Ray Hip	95 Switch	3	Cloud
2: 6-19	Rex Out F11	Hot 190 Wheel	3	Cloud
2: 6-34	Squeeze R 8 F10	Y 90 Wheel Turn	3	Cloud
2: 7-14	Squeeze Rip 9 F Left	Y 190 Hang-Twist	3	Cloud
3: 2-11	Squeeze Lex 7	198 B Slant	3	Cloud
Q-1	Rip 8	96 X Slant Back	3	Cloud

Cover 4

TECHNIQUE	BEST PLAYS
General	91, 91 Dupe, 92, 94, 95, 96, 98, 90 Wheel
Soft 1/4 1/4 1/4 1/4 Philosophy	91, 91 Dupe, 91 Stutter, 92, 94, 95, 98
Aggressive Pattern Read/"Wall" Philosophy	91, 93 Seam, 95, 96, 96 Whip, Squeeze 96/98

COVER 4 DIAGRAM SUMMARY

Diag	Formation	Play	Cover
1: 6-18	Strong Rip Tight	92 X Sit	4
1: 6-36	Green Larry 10	191 Dupe	4
1: 6-38	Flex	91 Y Slant	4
1: 6-43	Twin	92 Double Go	4
1: 7-18	Rip 8	93	4
1 :8-19	Ray In H Return	98	4
1: 8-20	Larry Out H7	198	4
1: 8-29	Blue Flex X9	Hot 198 Hang	4
1: 8-31	Rip 8	Badger 98 Y Late	4
2: 1-23	Split Lex	196	4
2: 1-24	Black Liz H10	96	4
2: 1-26	Roy H9	96 Whip	4
2: 2-12	Rip 8	Y 194	4
2: 3-11	Weak Rip Wing F10	95	4
2: 3-13	Split Rip	95 Switch	4
2: 3-21	Larry In H Return	95 Switch	4
2: 3-30	Loy Pair	Hot 195 Panther	4
2: 3-36	Brown Rip Y7	195 Switch	4
2: 3-38	Flex Y7	195 Switch	4
2: 4-26	Green Larry In	Colt 197	4
2: 4-27	Split Ray	Flow Y 97	4
2: 4-29	Green Larry 10 F Left	Hot 197 Swing Y Sit	4
2: 4-33	Green Larry Pair X10	197 Plant	4
2: 5-24	Rip 8 F11	Hot 90 F In	4
2: 6-22	R 11 F10	Y 90 Wheel	4
2: 6-25	Ram H Motion Check	Wheel	4
2: 7-4	Larry Out	190 Drive B Turn	4
2: 7-12	Green Larry 10 Z Snug	Hot 90 Hang-Twist	4
2: 7-26	Green Larry 10 X Snug	Stack 198	4
2: 7-29	Flex	92 Double Turn	4
3: 1-10	Ram	Max 324 Slant	4
3: 1-12	Roy	310 Dupe Hitch	4
3: 1-15	Strong Rex	336 Quick Smash	4
3: 1-17	Rip 9	Y 307 Fade	4
3: 1-23	Ray Plus F4	Y 336 Short Z Plant	4
3: 2-20	Rex Out	95 or Veer	4
3: 2-21	Liz 8	98 or Zone	4
3: 3-19	Strong Lou Y9	193 Stick B Stop	4
Q-2	Black Ray X11	195 Sw Z Slant Back	4

TECHNIQUE	BEST PLAYS
General	Refer to Cover 2 & Cover 4 menus, employ "Packaged Sides" to deal with both effectively... 96 & 98 are "universal" throws vs. both

QUARTERS COVERAGE DIAGRAM SUMMARY

Diag	Formation	Play	Cover
2: 2-10	Larry Plus	Stay 194	Quarters
2: 3-39	Zilch H7	Hot 195	Quarters
2: 6-24	Flex F11	Hot 190 Wheel	Quarters
2: 6-31	Brown Liz H11	190 Wheel Turn	Quarters
2: 7-30	Strong Ray F Shuffle	Max 94 Turn	Quarters
3: 1-26	Bunch Liz 8 Y6	324 Turn Trade	Quarters
3: 3-2	Weak Ray Tight	Y 94 H Swing	Quarters
1: 6-19	Larry Minus	Stay 191	Quarters
1: 6-37	L 8 F Left	Y 91 Dupe	Quarters
1: 7-19	Black Larry	Y 193 H Shoot	Quarters
1: 7-34	Larry 7 H6	Stay 193 Seam	Quarters
2: 1-18	Ray Out	96	Quarters
Q-4	Larry Pair X8	98 H Slant Back	Quarters

Misc.

TECHNIQUE	BEST PLAYS
"Cowboy" adjustments to 1, 2, & 3	2 receiver 95, 95 Switch
Zone Blitzes	*Stay on the edges:* 91, 92, 94, 96 *Play action at dropping linemen:* 300 Slant & Slant/Stick, Short, Stop, Fade
Banjos	95 Trade, 96 Whip, 97, 90 In, 90 Out
Spot Drops	91 Dupe, 93, 93 Dupe, 95, 96, 97
Pattern Read Concepts	91, 92, 96 Whip, Trips 98, 98 "Late", 90 In Squeezed: 95 Trade, 96, 98

"COWBOY" TECHNIQUE DIAGRAM SUMMARY

Diag	Formation	Play	Cover	Techniques	
2: 2-14	Larry H10	Y 94	1 Blitz	Cowboy	
2: 7-25	Strong Ray	Stack 198	1 Blitz	Cowboy	
3: 3-14	Larry Pair X Return	Y 198 Fade	1 Blitz	Cowboy	
2: 4-30	Weak Ray	97 Corner	1 Free	Cowboy	
3: 1-18	Ray	Y 336 Fade	1 Free	Cowboy	
1: 6-33	Brown Ray H9	192	1 Free	Cowboy	
1: 7-20	Nasty Ray 10 H8	93 Y Sit	1 Free	Cowboy	
1: 7-32	Green Larry 10 H7	Colt 193 Stick	1 Free	Cowboy	
2: 7-19	Squeeze Brown Larry H11	Outside 198 Z Fade	2 Man	Cowboy	Bump
1: 7-34	Larry 7 H6	Stay 193 Seam	Quarters	Cowboy	
2: 3-16	Strong Ray H10	Hot 95 Switch	2	Cowboy	
2: 3-17	Ray In	195	2	Cowboy	
2: 3-29	Ray Plus Z11	Hot 195 H Thru	2	Cowboy	
2: 2-9	Ram X	F 94	3	Cowboy	
2: 3-18	Brown Larry	95 Switch	3	Cowboy	
2: 3-43	Larry Plus H Left	Hot 95	3	Cowboy	
3: 1-14	Ram X X11	Max 325 Stop	3	Cowboy	
3: 1-9	Ram X	F 324 Slant	3	Cowboy	
3: 3-3	Ram X	Max 324 Fade	3	Cowboy	
1: 6-26	Black Ray H10	91 Y Sit	3	Cowboy	
1: 6-34	Ray Plus X8	Stay 92	3	Cowboy	
3: 3-28	Blue Ray In Z Return	98	2	Cowboy	
3: 3-31	Rip Hip	F 94 Stop	4	Cowboy	

"BANJO" TECHNIQUE DIAGRAM SUMMARY

Diag	Formation	Play	Cover	Techniques	
2: 5-20	Strong Rip Z9	Max 190 X In	1 Blitz	Banjo	
2: 5-21	Green Rip 11 X10	90 X In	1 Free	Banjo	
2: 5-22	Rip 10 Z Trace	90 Z Out	1 Free	Banjo	
2: 7-15	Bunch Ram X	F 90 Hang-Twist Y Option	1	Banjo	Lanes
2: 7-18	Squeeze Rex 6	Outside 98 H Fade	1 Free	Tight	Banjo
3: 3-13	Ray 10	97	1	Banjo	Lanes
3: 3-18	Rip 9 F6	Hot 95	1 Blitz	Banjo	Lanes
2: 1-31	Squeeze Ray	Max 96 Whip	1 Blitz	Banjo	

Keys for Identifying Coverage

In Volume 3 Chapters 7 and 8, we discussed coverage recognition as one of the pre-snap disciplines given both our quarterback and receivers. Knowing the basic form of the coverage they are facing gives them a starting point in "playing with a plan," as we say. While our reads and adjustments tend to be based more on individual defenders rather than actual coverages, having a handle on what the coverage is gives both quarterbacks and receivers a good idea of what to expect from the individual defenders they are keying.

Following is a summary of the basic points we give skill players in identifying coverage. The three factors that are consistent in all of our identification keys are the depth of the defender, the relative positioning or leverage of the defender, and where his eyes are fixed. While teams at higher levels do a better job of disguising their intentions, generally two or three defenders do not lie. One or even two defenders may be able to conceal, to an extent, what they are doing, but it is hard for three players to be in a position completely foreign to where they need to be for their final coverage and still be sound, especially if our quarterback has gotten his hands under center. By having our players check out at least three defenders, we are confident they will at least have a solid working idea of what "family" the final coverage will fall into.

C o v e r 1 (Free)	Corners:	Depth at 7 yds or less, head up to inside leverage on #1, eyes on WR.	
	Free Saf:	Depth of 10 or more yds, aligned no wider than the hash, eyes on QB.	
	Strong Saf:	*#2 wide:*	Depth at 5 yds or less, head up to inside leverage, eyes on #2.
		#2 tight:	Head up to 3 x 3 with #2, no more than 5 yds deep, eyes on #2.
	Weak OLB:	*#2 wide:*	Depth at 5 or less, head up to inside inside leverage, eyes on #2
		#2 tight:	Head up to 3 x 3 with #2, no more than 5 yds deep, eyes on #2.
		No #2:	Tightened hip or rush position
C o v e r 1 (Blitz)	Corners:	Depth at 7 yds or less, head up to inside leverage on #1, eyes on WR.	
	Free Saf:	Depth less than 10 yds, probably wider than the hash, eyes on a receiver.	
	Strong Saf:	*#2 wide:*	Depth at 5 yds or less, head up to inside leverage, eyes on #2.
		#2 tight:	Head up to 3 x 3 with #2, no more than 5 yds deep, eyes on #2.
	Weak OLB:	Tightened hip or rush position.	
C o v e r 2	Corners:	Depth at 5 or less, head up to outside leverage, eyes on QB	
	FS & SS:	Depth of 10 or more yards, eyes on QB, aligned on or outside hash.	
	Weak OLB:	Head up to inside leverage on #2, 4 to 6 yards deep, eyes on QB. Hip position or wider if no #2	
C o v e r 2 (Man)	Corners:	Depth at 5 or less, head up to inside leverage, eyes on WR.	
	FS & SS:	Depth of 10 or more yards, eyes on QB, aligned on or outside hash.	
	Weak OLB:	Head up to inside leverage on #2, 4 to 6 yards deep, eyes on #2. May be in a rush position if no #2.	

Cover 3	Corners:	Depth at 7 or more yards, eyes on QB, head up to outside leverage
	Free saf:	Depth of 10 or more yards, eyes on QB, aligned on or outside hash.
	Strong saf:	5 to 7 yds depth, near head up relationship on any #2 or 5 x 5 off tight #2, eyes on QB.
	Weak OLB:	Head up to inside leverage on #2, 4 to 6 yards deep, eyes on QB. Hip position or wider if no #2
Cover 4	Corners:	Depth at 5-8 yards, eyes on QB, head up to outside technique. Usually deeper than Cover 2.
	FS & SS:	Depth of 8 to 11 yards, closer to LOS and tighter to hash than Cover 2, on to inside the hash. Eyes on tackle/TE to their side.
	Weak OLB:	Head up to inside leverage on #2, 4 to 6 yards deep, eyes on QB. Hip position or wider if no #2.
Quarters	Wk Corner:	Depth at 5 or less, head up to outside leverage, eyes on QB
	SS & SC:	Depth 7-10 yds, head up on #1 & #2 (SS halfway between #1 and a TE at #2). Eyes tell you if they are playing man or zone concept: if on WR, it is man, if on QB, they are playing true "quarters" zones.
	Free saf:	Depth of 10 yards or more, on to outside the hash. Eyes on QB.
	Str OLB:	In a position to cover flat area, at least 5 x 5 off TE/tackle to his side, eyes on QB.

The "Bunch" Principle
in the Quick Passing Game

The concept of "bunching" receivers in close proximity to each other creates a number of positive possibilities for an offensive unit. Among these benefits are natural picks and rubs; quick stretches of zones that create holes against defenses that initially compress with the formation, bad angles by defenders; and increased amounts of open space in which athletes can run after the catch.

The fast-rhythm nature of the quick passing game is well-suited to capitalize on the kinds of benefits that Bunched sets can provide. Among the basic routes that can effectively adapt and function within Bunch environments are the 93 Slant, 95 "Trade," 96 Quick Smash, 96 "Whip," 98 Fade, and 90 In.

Following is a reference guide to the text's examples of the quick passing game in taking advantage of the Bunch concept.

"BUNCH" CONCEPT DIAGRAM SUMMARY

Diag	Formation	Play	Cover
2: 3-12	Squeeze R 11 Y11	195	1 Free
2: 3-23	Squeeze Lex 7	195 Trade	3
2: 3-24	Twin X10	95 Trade	3
2: -41	Squeeze Blue Larry Out X10	95	3
2: 3-42	Squeeze Rex 6 H10	95	3
2: 6-34	Squeeze R 8 F10	Y 90 Wheel Turn	3
2: 6-35	Squeeze Ram H Motion Check	Wheel Turn	3
2: 7-12	Green Larry 10 Z Snug	Hot 90 Hang-Twist	4
2: 7-14	Squeeze Rip 9 F Left	Hot 190 Hang-Tw Y Sit	3
2: 7-15	Bunch Ram X	F 90 Hang-Twt Y Option	1
2: 7-16	Squeeze Ray	98 Trade	2
2: 7-17	Twin X Return	198 Double Trade	1 Free
2: 7-18	Squeeze Rex 6	Outside 98 H Fade	1 Free
2: 7-19	Squeeze Brown Larry H11	Outside 198 Z Fade	2 Man
2: 7-26	Green Larry 10 X Snug	Stack 198	4
2: 7-27	Bunch Ray 6	Stack 98	1 Free
3: 1-20	Squeeze Ray 9 H6	Y 324 Fade	2
3: 1-26	Bunch Liz 8 Y6	324 Turn Trade	Quarters
3: 2-10	Squeeze Lex 7	198 B Slant	2
3: 2-11	Squeeze Lex 7	198 B Slant	3
3: 2-9	Squeeze Larry 7 H6	198 B Fade/Seam	2
3: 3-12	Larry Out X Snug	96 Double Whip	
3: 3-25	Squeeze Rip Out Z7	190 Out B Turn	
3: 3-34	Cluster Rex 6	90 Z In B Slant	
3: 3-8	Squeeze Larry H11	196 Quick Smash	1
1: 6-43	Twin	92 Double Go	4
1: 7-28	Squeeze Strong Liz Z6	93	2
1: 7-29	Squeeze Brown Liz H5	193	1 Free
1: 8-23	Twin	98	2
1: 8-24	Twin	198	3
1: 8-26	Squeeze Ray 6	98	1 Free
1: 8-27	Bunch Rex 6	99	2
2: 1-15	Squeeze Rip 9	196	2
2: 1-28	Ram Z Snug	96 Whip	2 Man
2: 1-29	Ray In X Snug	96 Whip	1 Free
2: 1-30	Rex Out Z Snug	96 Whip	1 Free
2: 1-31	Squeeze Ray	Max 96 Whip	1 Blitz
2: 1-33	Twin	96 Double Whip	1 Free

Advanced Tools:
Backside Outlet Combinations

A number of different backside combinations can be created as "insurance policies" when the side to which the quarterback is looking breaks down. The goal of these backside combinations is not so much to gain large chunks of yardage as it is to provide the quarterback with an available player to whom he can go when the frontside route does not break open cleanly, allowing him to make a completion for positive yardage rather than force something frontside, take a sack, or throw an incompletion. We do not, however, want any of these backside outlet tags to enter the quarterback's thinking until he has gone through his full frontside thought process, which is why we would not put these routes in until our passer is fully functional with the basic routes in the quick passing game. We do not want to confuse the quarterback with too many thought processes too early, and we do not want to give him an excuse to bail out of the frontside read too early.

To correctly serve their purpose, these backside routes must come open on a slower timing than the normal quick passing game. They will not get a look from the quarterback until he has already gone through a complete progression to the other side, so there is no sense in the receivers' routes developing fully until the passer can get back to them. Many of these routes actually function on the timing that would be used on a five-step route, often breaking at deeper depths and/or having the freedom to adjust into openings between defenders.

Related to this, receivers must understand that the quarterback, by the time he gets back to their side of the field, really will not have sufficient time to execute a normal read. It is their job, then, to present themselves in a way that immediately lets the quarterback know whether they are open or not. This information is communicated through eye contact. If the receiver has worked into an opening and has a clear lane through which the quarterback can get him the ball, he looks directly at the quarterback when the quarterback turns to his side. This look communicates instantly to the quarterback that he can deliver the ball. If the receiver is not open, he does not look back in the quarterback's direction. The only read, then, is that the quarterback cannot try to throw to a backside player unless clear eye contact has been made. His rule, capsulized, is "no eyes, no throw." If he gets eye contact from no one, the ball is thrown away. This simple, nonverbal communication speeds the process dramatically and cuts down on mistakes since the burden of decision-making has essentially been removed from the quarterback.

The quarterback uses a normal three-step drop for his initial frontside look. If he does not deliver the ball there, he takes two extra "hippity hop" steps (akin to the last two steps of his normal three-step drop) as he turns his eyes to the backside to gain depth, buy a bit of time, and reestablish good throwing position.

Under what circumstances are these tags useful and under what circumstances are they not ideal? The best time to make use of the backside outlets we will introduce shortly is when teams are playing zone defense on a large scale, dropping seven or even eight into coverage. Eight-man drops generally have the ability to cause problems for basic frontside reads, which is where the backside outlet concept can prove very helpful. Further, heavy zone drops almost always mean an absence of a big pass rush, giving the quarterback the extra time needed to get to the backside.

These tags are also excellent against fast flowing linebackers who key the quarterback's eyes hard in an attempt to disrupt the basic frontside read. In this case, the backside is often completely vacated, or, at worst, the offense will have 2-on-1 "numbers" which can be worked. If we are having consistent problems with the "danger player" in our route progressions, this option is one very good answer.

This type of packaging is not ideal when five or six men are rushing the passer. First of all, the frontside route should be open at some point against these schemes, since fewer men are now in coverage, and more important, the quarterback may not have the time to turn backside and deliver the ball.

The "Slant Back"
The "Slant Back" is an idea we were fortunate to come across through the staff at Valdosta State University. Generally conducted to a single receiver side, the man running the Slant Back originally runs his route exactly as he would a basic Slant, working his way inside the first short defender on his side if he can. Once he is inside this defender, he simply settles in that hole and waits for the quarterback to make eye contact with him. He can either get the ball immediately at that point, or slide back outside away from inside pressure until he gets the ball.

Especially for routes such as the "Turn," which are built on a full-field horizontal stretch, the "Slant Back" may prove to be a higher percentage way to exploit overloads to the frontside than a normal Slant, since the quarterback can get back to it on more relaxed timing and throw to a receiver who is essentially stationary. Illustrations of the "Slant Back" concept follow.

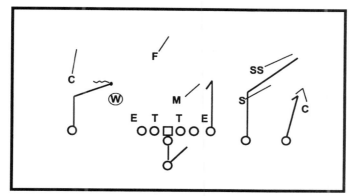

DIAGRAM Q-1
RIP 8 96 X SLANT BACK VS. COVER 3 CLOUD

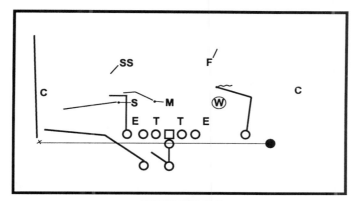

DIAGRAM Q-2
BLACK RAY X11 195 SWITCH Z SLANT BACK VS. COVER 4

Adding the "Under"

With a two-receiver backside, the complementary route used to enhance the Slant Back is an "Under," or a shallow crossing route to a depth of about five yards. The rule is that the man not *told* to run a Slant Back has an Under. This rule gives us the ability to gain the Shallow Cross from either position. The Under is particularly effective against true middle linebackers who have worked to the frontside, because the Under can "replace" him right over the ball. It also gets more directly into the quarterback's line of vision, allowing it to be thrown very quickly when the frontside breaks down.

Ideally, we would like the Under working the next hole inside the hole being worked by the Slant Back. Against zones, the Under has the freedom to slide toward the frontside, opposite the Slant Back, since we do not want him sliding back out into the Slant Back's throwing lane. Against man coverage, the "Drag Principle" dictates that the Under continue to accelerate across to gain separation, which will make him available to the quarterback even sooner than normal.

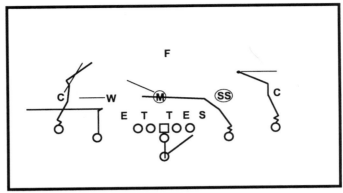

DIAGRAM Q-3
FLEX 193 UNDER Z SLANT BACK VS. COVER 1 FREE

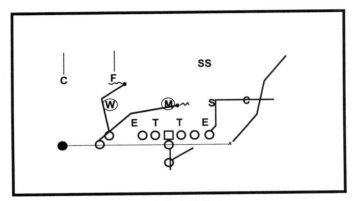

DIAGRAM Q-4
LARRY PAIR X8 98 UNDER H SLANT BACK

"Panther"

"Panther" is a tag that tells the backside #1 receiver to compress his split to six yards or so and run an "Option" route at six to seven yards, and the running back closest to the backside to Swing. In this way, we try to create a 2-on-1 situation on the first short defender backside when the other underneath coverage has taken itself out of the play by flowing frontside.

Both of these routes fit our basic backside outlet criteria well, since the Option route is stationary and adjustable, and the Swing will gain its full width just about the time the quarterback would be ready to deliver it. The Option route understands that he must beat the second short defender inside him since we are working off of the first. The key for the Swing is to get as much width as possible to create a full stretch of the first short defender. Ideally this width would mean that he does not turn up until reaching the numbers.

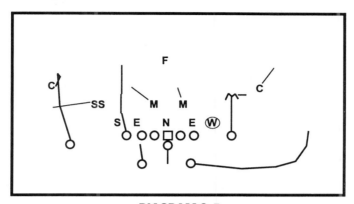

DIAGRAM Q-5
SPLIT LIZ 194 PANTHER

"Plant" Routes

The last of our backside outlet combinations is to assign two receivers "Plant" routes. A "Plant," as we established in Volume 2 Chapter 4, is essentially a Hitch route taken two yards deeper to a breaking point of eight. Both Plant routes will have the ability to slide laterally to get into the voids of a zone after their break. Again, a two-on-one situation is likely to the backside, which should mean that one Plant or the other has a clear lane to the quarterback. Plant routes must keep coming straight back to the quarterback once eye contact has been established— they cannot just stand stationary, or a deep defender will come up and play through them to the ball. Two examples of "Plant" are shown below.

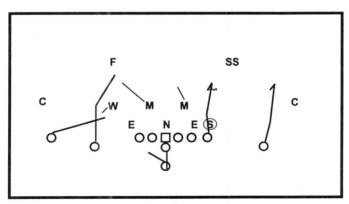

DIAGRAM Q-6
RIP 9 197 Y & Z PLANT VS. COVER 2

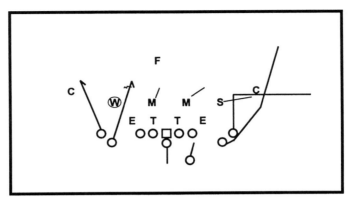

DIAGRAM Q-7
GREEN TWIN 98 TRADE H & X PLANT

Deep Shots

While they require much experience and discretion on the part of the quarterback, placing a deep shot on the backside can have some large-scale benefits. Specifically, they address two situations. Against poorly disciplined secondaries, they can get a man or men free deep up the field when deep defenders stop defending their deep area when they see the quarterback's shoulders and eyes open away from them initially. The other situation in which deep shots are helpful occurs against extremely active, well-trained secondaries who are able to read the quarterback's drop. Often, when these types of secondaries see the quarterback pull up at three steps, they tighten down immediately and prepare to close on the short routes. Having deep routes built into the backside, especially deep routes that have used their route technique to briefly lull those defenders into further believing that they are breaking short, can exploit this activity for big yardage.

To communicate with the quarterback quickly, receivers running deep backside routes indicate that they are open by lifting a hand as they run deep, since they obviously cannot easily establish eye contact. The quarterback now looks for the *arm* rather than the *eyes:* "no arm, no throw." Again, the quarterback is not being forced to read, but merely to find a quick visual cue by one of his own players that tells him whether to throw or not.

Two types of deep backside combinations are illustrated below. The first entails two pure vertical "Go" routes whose technique is similar to the basic routes of 99/199 "Fade/Seam," but is different because it looks to strike a level deeper than the 18-22 yard Fade hole/Seam level. If the quarterback gets back to this route, we want it thrown up and over the top, since the premise is to get behind a safety that has pulled up too tight. The throw should lead the receiver downfield so he does not have to slow for the catch, surrendering some of his separation.

Both deep receivers in this combination should, at about 6 to 8 yards, stutter their footwork and raise up briefly as though they are about to break. This action, along with the quarterback's drop, gives the cornerback and safety on their side the full "sight picture" of a route being thrown on quick timing. All we really need for those defenders to do is stop their feet ever so slightly, and our receivers can blow right by them.

The second deep concept is a deepened form of the "Slant/Stick" combination. This package is specifically geared for Cover 4 and Cover 2 Invert, since those coverages often result in the safeties playing lower and essentially covering the receiver over them man to man. The inside man, deepening his Stick from 4 yards to 7-8 yards (making it in essence a "Plant") wants to engage the safety on his side and pull him up to open the middle for the man outside him. If his man does not bite up, he will become a stationary eye contact outlet for the quarterback.

The outside man runs a Slant or a Seam Post that breaks at 8 to 9 yards, making sure he gains separation from the cornerback while maintaining a "skinny" angle that enables him to stay outside the safety.

The quarterback, upon getting back to the backside looks for the hand of the outside receiver first, then the eyes of the inside receiver, throwing it away if he gets neither.

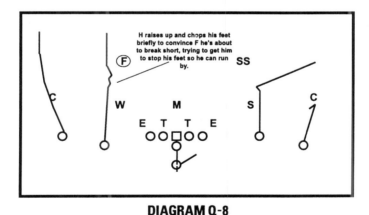

DIAGRAM Q-8
FLEX 96 B GO

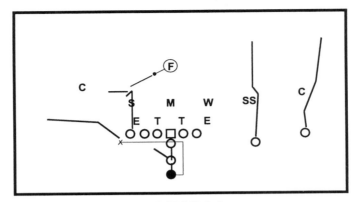

DIAGRAM Q-9
RAY H7 195 B GO
FS who jumps Turn gets out of position for verticals

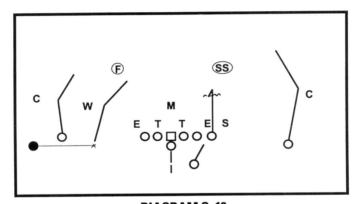

DIAGRAM Q-10
GREEN LARRY 10 X8 193 DUPE B DEEP STICK
Two sides work hand in hand: if safeties stay <u>deep</u>, the
Dupe Slants will be 2 on 1 vs. W; if safeties pull up <u>tight</u>
when they see a three-step drop, the Stick will hold the
SS down and Z will run free deep down the middle.

Positional Skills Lists
for the Quick Passing Game

Among the most valuable of Bill Walsh's many contributions to offensive football has been the development of specific skills lists by position. Every skill that must be mastered by players at a certain position is listed one-by-one. Developing and using these breakdowns are critical for a number of reasons:

1) It maximizes the effectiveness with which practices can be planned on a long-term basis. Each skill must obviously be *practiced* for some amount of time for it to be polished. By seeing a detailed breakdown of exactly what must be practiced, you can be certain that you have allotted sufficient practice time for each phase of that position's overall play. This plan is important to making sure that your team is "fundamentally sound" coming out of pre-season camp.

2) Having a completely broken down skills list enables you to clearly see those skills that build on other skills and how they do so. This knowledge helps make the most of your teaching by enabling you to best build these skills in a logical progression, rather than in a scattershot manner.

3) The skills list gives definitive focus to your drill work; it helps you set up and maximize your drilling since you have a quantified understanding of the skill or skills you want to be working on during drill period. This focus helps the players since learning and development are drastically improved when they have a clear understanding of what skills they are trying to improve. If you have a drill in which you can not identify one or more of the skills that is being specifically addressed, you do not want to waste practice time with that drill.

4) Once the season begins, you can continue developing individual play by focusing on different areas of your skills list as you set up your schedule for individual work that week. The areas you focus on may be related to weaknesses your players need to improve, or skills that will be particularly important to defeating your next opponent (e.g., you are playing a team which plays heavy doses of bump & run man coverage, so receivers get extra time allotted to work on release moves).

Following are the specific skills lists for quarterbacks, receivers, and running backs in the quick passing game. Tese lists are not comprehensive list, rather an abridged version that focuses only on those elements they would use within our 90/190 series.

Quarterbacks

Ball Handling
- Stance
- Center exchange
- Reach step: 2 step drop right
- Reach step: 2 step drop left
- Reach step: 3 step drop

Drops/Actions
- 2 step drop right
- 2 step drop left
- 3 step drop on fast rhythm
- 3 step drop and hold
- 306/307 action
- 310/311 action
- 320/321 action
- 324/325 action
- 336/337 action

Pocket Presence
- Step up/avoid rush
- Keeping focus downfield under heat
  —"feel" the rush
- Scramble
- Army throw off back foot
- Safe hook slide
- Throwing the ball away

Identification (Pre-snap)
- Coverage identification
- Identifying read player
- Identifying danger player
- Checks:
  —Run/Quick
  —Quick/Quick
  —"B" tag combinations
  —Blitz checks

- Uncovered recognition and throws:
  —Orange
  —Black

Basic Reads (Post-snap)
- Hi-low off cornerback (96, 98)
- Seam Read (91, 92,94)
- First short defender inside C (95, 97, 90 In)
- Flat coverage read (93, 90 Out, 90 Wheel)
- Vertical reads (99)
  —Off FS (Cover 1/3)
  —Off hash saf (Cover 2/4)
- Sight adjustment

Throwing Motion
- Pre-throwing, relaxed position
- Stride/weight transfer
- Hip reset to target
- Front arm push-pull
- Follow-through
- Hands on ball
- High release point/wrist snap/ trajectory

Individual Routes/Ball Placement (left & right)
-Hitch
-Seam
-Slant
-Shoot
-Stop
-Turn
-Quick Smash
-Whip

-Squeezed/Wing Hitch
-Short
-Fade
-End zone Fade
-Break Out
-In combination
-Out combination
-Plant

Situational Management
-4 minute offense
-2 minute offense

Receivers

Mental Checklists/Recognition
- Six second rule
- Coverage recognition
- Uncovered recognition, courses
- Sight adjustment
- Scramble rules

Blocking
- Blocking after catches by other receivers
- Uncovered blocks

Route Running
- Stance and starts
- Weave mechanics
  - Attacking defender's technique
  - Eyes/arms/weight distribution
  - Phony acceleration and bursts
- Body control through breaks
- Releases vs. jam
  - At L.O.S.
  - Variable depths
- Bunched releases/traffic rules

Individual Routes (both left & right)
- Hitch
- Seam
- Slant
- Shoot
- Stop

- Turn
- Quick Smash
- Whip
- Squeezed/Wing Hitch
- Short
- Fade
- End zone Fade
- Break Out
- In combination
- Out combination
- Plant
- Hitch/Fade Read (conversion)
- Quick Out/Fade Read (conversion)

Catching
- Hand position:
  - High throws in front
  - Low throws in front
  - Over the shoulder
- Sideline catches
- End zone catches

Run After Catch
- Drag principle
- Catch, tuck, turn vs. zones
- Sideline turn up
- Underneath reversal on out breaks
- Feeling defender pressure for turn on stationary routes

Running Backs (from backfield positions)

Mental Checklists/Recognition
- Calls and adjustments vs. fronts
- Blitz recognition
- Overload recognition
- Secondary blitz pickup (sight adjust situations)

Blocking
- One-on-one blocks vs. ends
- One-on-one blocks with stunting LBs
- One-on-one blocks with secondary blitzers
- "Eraser" situations when relieved of responsibility

Pass Actions
- 306/307
- 310/311
- 320/321
- 324/325
- 336/337

Route Running
- Swing
- Wheel from motion
- Shoot from backfield
- Thru
- Wheel/Fade conversion

Run After Catch
- Getting the sideline
- Underneath reversal on Shoot
- Zone north and south split

"More for Less":
Ideas for Condensing Quick Route Packages

The text to this point has presented twelve quick route packages. Obviously, most offenses would have a difficult time devoting enough attention to the quick passing game to incorporate all of these within the course of a season. At the same time, each of the ideas within these different route packages has definite value and a great deal of use against different types of defenses and techniques.

In this appendix, we will explore some different ideas for structuring these routes that would, through the use of "tags," enable a coach to incorporate a great number of these ideas while having fewer base routes than the twelve depicted in this book.

Integrating the Slant and the Short

By reworking the default rules for the "Slant" package as presented in this text, the "Short" concept can easily be incorporated within that package as a tag. This reworking would entail changing the rule of the #2 receiver to a Slant. The quarterback's read, then, becomes the first short defender inside the cornerback: if he stays inside #2, either by walling inside-out, or collapsing from outside-in, the ball is thrown to the outside Slant; should the read player widen past #2, the ball is thrown inside. This read stays consistent when the "Short" route is given to #1 as a tag.

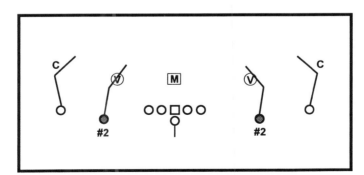

DIAGRAM S-1
BASIC SLANT PACKAGE WITH SLANT AS THE DEFAULT RULE
FOR #2: READ PLAYER IS THE FIRST SHORT DEFENDER INSIDE C

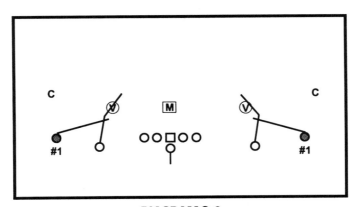

DIAGRAM S-2
ALTERNATE SLANT PACKAGE WITH A "SHORT" TAG FOR #1:
READ REMAINS THE SAME FOR THE QB.

The traditional Slant/Shoot combination, then, would be adapted as a tag for #2, as could all the other #2 variations illustrated in Volume 1 Chapter 7 (e.g., Stick and Seam). An additional benefit of this packaging concept is that a three receiver Slant can be gained simply by giving #3 a "Shoot" as the default definition without creating, as we did in Volume 1 Chapter 7, new learning for a "trips rule."

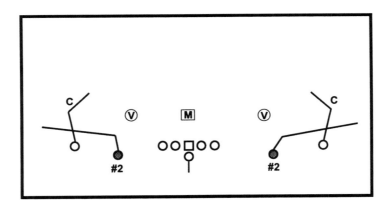

DIAGRAM S-3
ALTERNATIVE SLANT PACKAGE WITH A "SHOOT" TAG FOR #2
TO GAIN THE TRADITIONAL SLANT/SHOOT COMBINATION

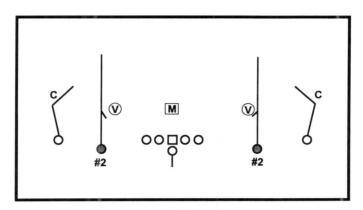

DIAGRAM S-4
ALTERNATIVE SLANT PACKAGE WITH "STICK" AND "SEAM"
TAGS FOR #2

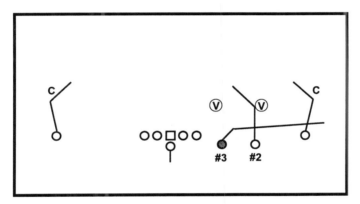

DIAGRAM S-5
ALTERNATIVE SLANT PACKAGE WITH A "SHOOT" AS A DE-
FAULT DEFINITION FOR #3 WITHOUT A SEPARATE "TRIPS RULE"

Incorporating the "In" Route into the Slant Package

The Slant can be further diversified by creating a tag for #2 to become a "picker" for the Slant, essentially providing an "In" route combination as described in Volume 2 Chapter 5. An example of a descriptive word that could fill that bill would be something like "Scrape." "Scrape" would tell the #2 receiver to act as a picker for the Slant, the Slant knowing he will weave to the outside a bit wider than normal to turn the cornerback's hips, and will work to time his break in such a manner that he comes underneath the "scraping" #2. While gaining the In concept in this manner takes away some of the flexibility of the full-blown package shown in Volume 2 Chapter 5, it is a simple and effective way to really free up the basic Slant (especially vs. man coverages of any type) without adding much new learning at all.

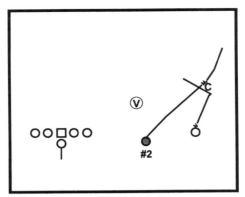

DIAGRAM S-6
CREATING AN "IN" CONCEPT WITH A "SCRAPE" TAG
OFF THE BASIC SLANT COMBINATION

Integrating the "Out" into the "Fade/Break Out" Package

In a similar fashion, the "Out" as described in Volume 2 Chapter 5 can be made a part
of the 98/198 Fade/Break Out package by telling a receiver outside of the Break Out
to pick, running through the outside leg of the defender over the Out. An example of
a word that could do this is "Wall." The "Wall" tag could be applied to the #1 receiver
of a two receiver side, or to the #2 receiver on a three receiver side.

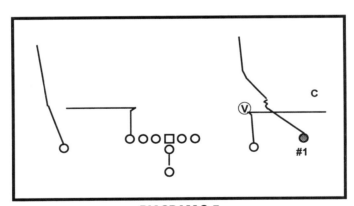

DIAGRAM S-7
98 "WALL" ON A TWO RECEIVER SIDE TO GAIN AN
"OUT" PICKING CONCEPT

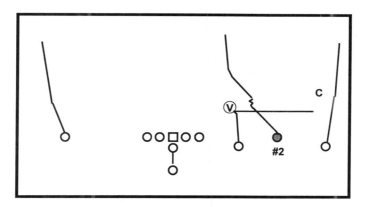

DIAGRAM S-8
98 "WALL" TO A THREE RECEIVER SIDE: #2 WALLS FOR #3

Creating a Fully Integrated "Seam Read" Package

Another approach that would be extremely "quarterback friendly" would be to integrate all of the "Seam Read" route concepts into a single package, and tag the outside receiver with the desired route. By packaging in this manner, the 91/191 Hitch, 92/192 Quick Out, 94/194 Stop, and 99/199 Fade/Seam can all be incorporated together without the quarterback's thought process changing at all. One of the routes mentioned would serve as the "default" for outside receivers—perhaps the Hitch because it is the easiest to complete—and the other three would become "tags" off this Seam Read package.

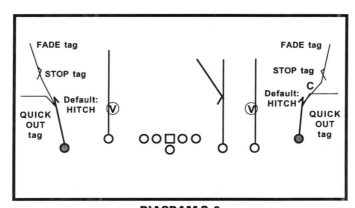

DIAGRAM S-9
SEAM READ PACKAGE WITH "HITCH" AS THE DEFAULT RULE FOR
#1, WITH "QUICK OUT," "STOP," AND "FADE" AS TAGS

Using Read Concepts to integrate the Hitch & Quick Smash and the Fade/Out & Fade/Seam

In cases where the receivers are advanced enough to read coverage on the move or opponents' defenses do not disguise and pre-snap coverage identification is plausible and reliable, receivers can be given different route options within a given package, that would allow for the use of fewer route packages.

One example of this concept would be to fully integrate a single "Hitch" package (rather than having both 91/191 Hitch and 96/196 Quick Smash) by telling the #2 receiver to run a Seam vs. Cover 3 (since it controls Cover 3 flat coverage with a true "seam read) and a Quick Smash vs. Cover 2 and Cover 1 (allowing you to control the cornerback with a high/low read).

Another example would be the creation of a consolidated "Fade" package by giving #2 a similar read: Break Out vs. Cover 2 or Cover 1 (again, to gain a high/low on a Cover 2 cornerback or a good man-beater vs. Cover 1), Seam vs. Cover 3 (create a two-on-one situation vs. the free safety).

By "reading" and teaching "route conversion" in this manner, four route ideas can effectively be utilized within two blocks of learning. This route conversion also enables you to always have a play on that is best suited to attacking the coverage it faces.

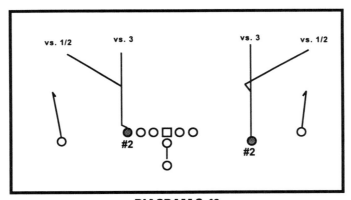

DIAGRAM S-10
INTEGRATING 91/191 HITCH AND 96/196 QUICK SMASH
WITH A "READ" OR "CONVERSION" ROUTE FOR #2

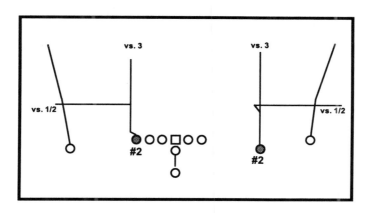

DIAGRAM S-11
INTEGRATING 98/198 FADE/OUT AND 99/199 FADE/SEAM
WITH A "READ" OR "CONVERSION" ROUTE FOR #2

Footwork "Grey Areas":
Alternative Drops for Various Routes

Depending on your protection, the idiosyncrasies of your quarterback, the quickness of your receivers, and the techniques of your opponents, some of the drops prescribed for certain route packages in this text may not always be ideal. We have always been willing to make those types of adjustments with our quarterback's feet that best allow him and our receivers to get their jobs done. The job of a quarterback's drop is to get him set up in the pocket in a good, sound throwing position in the correct timing to get the ball off. If, for personnel reasons, the drop that we "traditionally" associate with a given route is not getting this job done, it only makes sense to use a drop that does.

Specifically, a handful of the routes presented throughout the book may be better suited, in some circumstances, to deeper drops than we have established here. Some compelling factors that might cause a coach to use deeper drops within the quick passing game include the following:

1) Aggressive, three-step protection schemes do not hold up for the time it takes a particular "quick" route to develop.

2) Along the same lines, receivers are not able to get to their assigned depths and affect the defense properly within the time frame normally allotted a three-step action by the quarterback.

3) The drop does not allow the quarterback to throw in any kind of rhythm because receivers are not yet available upon the completion of his two- or three-step drop. As a result, defenders are able to break more quickly on routes because his eyes take them to his receiver, and/or his mechanics break down because the extra wait in the pocket breaks his continuity, causes him to stand up and lock his knees, etc.

4) Advanced training on the part of opposing defensive backs allows them to key the quarterback's shortened set-up and break up quickly on quick routes.

Specifically, the deepening of drops could mean changing some routes from a three-step drop to a "quick five"-step drop (In others, it may mean switching from a two-step drop to a standard three-step). Without going into much depth, a "quick five"-drop can be taught in a couple basic ways, either by telling the quarterback to simply "take the five quickest steps you can," or, as we would be apt to do, take "a reach step, two crossover steps, and 'hippity-hop.'" Regardless of which basis you use to teach, you are not looking for much more than six to seven yards' depth out of the drop, and are emphasizing being in throwing position immediately upon the drop's completion, delivering on time without benefit of a hitch step.

Obviously, this change of drop may, in many cases, entail an adjustment of receiver depth. A table summarizing our basic quick route packages, the drops we have assigned them as default, possible alternative drops, and potential receiver adjustments follows.

Alternative Drops

Route	Base Drop	Alt. Drop	Receiver adjustments
91 HITCH 91 DUPE	2 steps	3 steps > 5 quick >	None Hitches deepen to 8-9
92 QK OUT	2 steps	3 steps	None
93 SLANT 93 DUPE	2 steps	3 steps	None
93 STICK 93 DOG	3 steps	5 quick	Stick & Slant 1 step deeper Dog: Push 1 step deeper on initial weave
94 STOP	3 steps	5 quick	None
95 TURN (Most forms)	2 steps	3 steps	None
95 SLANT	3 steps	5 quick	All routes go one step deeper
96 QK SMASH 96 WHIP	3 steps	5 quick	Both routes go one step deeper
97 SHORT 97 SEAM	2 steps	3 steps	None
97 CORNER 97 PLANT	3 steps	5 quick	Corner: Corner pushes 1 step deeper
98 FADE/OUT 98 HANG	3 steps	5 quick	None
99 FADE/SM 99 SWING	3 steps	5 quick	None
90 IN 90 OUT	3 steps	5 steps	In or Out can hesitate a bit more

GLOSSARY

Alert—A term used to tell a designated receiver that he automatically runs a "Split" route if the middle of the field is left open as a reaction to pre-snap motion.

"B" Tag—A specific tag to a given route package that tells backside receivers to execute the rules of a different route package from the one being run on the frontside (see Chapter 2).

Backed Up—Refers to the game situation in which the offense is "backed up" inside its own 15 yard line.

Backside—Side of the field away from the play call. Most often, it is the side opposite the one to which the quarterback initially looks in his read, and it is generally synonymous with the weak side of the formation.

Banjo—Defensive technique in which defenders in man coverage exchange responsibilities based on the initial releases of the receivers; i.e., the inside most defender covers the receiver who releases furthest inside.

Boundary—The side of the field to which the offense has the least amount of lateral operating room.

Box—
1. An area spanning from the line of scrimmage to seven yards' depth vertically and from approximately tight end to tight end horizontally; used as a parameter by the offense to count the number of defensive players who can easily defend the run and/or rush the passer.
2. An individual route in which a receiver is given freedom to get open anywhere inside this area.

Break Out—An individual route used within the 98-198 "Fade" package in which the receiver pushes straight upfield for 5-6 yards, exerts "pressure" on his man to the inside, then breaks outside at a flat angle.

Bubble—Refers to the impeded, roundabout path a defender has to take in running around traffic to cover his assigned receiver.

Bump, or Bump and Run—Refers to a coverage technique in which the defender attempts to jam and collision a receiver to destroy the timing of his route.

Bumped Man Coverage—A man-to-man defense in which defenders switch assignments when a receiver motions based on the relative position of the receiver; i.e., the outside most defender changes responsibilities when a new receiver becomes the outside most receiver instead of "locking" on the receiver he originally lined up over.

Bracket—Refers to a situation in which two defenders are naturally able to double team a receiver inside and out because of having been released from other responsibilities.

Bunch—
1. Concept of pass offense that entails compressing receivers in close proximity to each other to create certain advantages in attacking defenses.
2. Formation term that places all receivers on a side in close proximity starting 7-8 yards outside the tackle/tight end.

Burst—Action of a pass receiver who, just before making a final, shorter break, drops his head and drives his arms quickly to convince a defender that he intends to go deep, thereby driving the defender backwards and away from the receiver's final break.

Cloud—Defensive term used to designate that the cornerback rotates up and has responsibility for the flat area.

Cluster—Term which groups all receivers to a side in close proximity to each other, beginning 11-12 yards outside the tackle/tight end on their side.

Corner Route—Refers in general to individual routes that take receivers at an angle to the deep outside portion of a defense, or in some cases to the corner of the end zone. "Dog" and "Quick Smash" are the two fundamental routes from this text that fit this category.

Cowboy—Term used to refer to a defensive technique in which both cornerbacks play on the same side of the ball to maximize their matchups against certain formations.

Cut—Refers to the route or pattern of an individual receiver.

Danger Player—The defender in a given route who, in the case of an extreme or unusual drop, has the potential of disrupting the quarterback's basic read.

Dog—An individual cut in which a receiver releases exactly as though he is running a Slant, then plants on his inside foot and drives back out to the Corner.

Double—Offensive term that designates that backside receivers mirror the assignments of their counterparts on the frontside.

Doubles—General formation term that refers to a two receiver side or a formation that has two receivers on both sides.

Double Move Route—Type of route in which a receiver distinctly fakes a certain route, attempting to create a full reaction on the part of a defender, then drives off of his initial move to another route, often a deep route. Examples include Go and Dog.

Drag Principle—Basic concept of the passing game that tells receivers they must settle in a void between defenders vs. zone coverages, and continue accelerating for separation vs. man coverages.

Dump—Refers to the receiver within a pattern that is designated as the player to whom the quarterback throws if his initial read breaks down.

Dupe—Tag that tells an inside receiver to "duplicate" the route of the #1 receiver in a pattern.

Escape—See *Release Move*

Fade—Refers to a "Cut" in which a receiver sprints deep and outside to a landmark 6 yards from the sideline and 20-25 yards deep.

Field—See *Wide Field*

Flat—
1. Refers to the short, outside area of defensive coverage.
2. Refers to a "Cut" or individual pattern executed by a receiver in which he works upfield 4-5 yards before breaking "Flat" into the short, outside area of a defense.

Formation Integrity—Refers to the idea of, within a game or from game to game, demonstrating the ability to both run and pass from a given formation as opposed to only doing one or the other.

Free—Designation given a pure man-to-man coverage scheme with a free safety responsible for the deep middle 1/3 of the field.

Frontside—Side of the field, as designated by the play call, given as a reference point to determine route assignments and direct protection. Most often, it is the side to which the quarterback initially looks in his read. Can be, but is not necessarily synonymous with the strong side of the formation.

Funnel Corner—A low cornerback who works to "funnel" a receiver to the inside, attempting to prevent any sort of outside release. Usually associated with Cover 2 or "Quarters" coverage. Within this technique, the cornerback may or may not use a hard "jam."

Get Open—A route, often run by the #3 receiver, in which the player has the freedom to "Get Open" anywhere above the box. His options include running straight up the seam, hooking between linebackers, and bending his route deep down the middle of the field.

Hard Corner—Term used to describe a defensive cornerback who aligns and/or plays closer than six yards from the receiver he is over.

Hash Player or Hash Safety—Term used to refer to a defender who often aligns on the hashmark and is responsible for a deep 1/2 of the field, generally in a 2-deep defensive scheme.

High-Low—A type of read in which a certain defender is isolated against a short receiver and a deeper receiver. If the defender works for depth, the quarterback throws to the shorter of the two receivers; if he does not he throws to the deeper receiver.

Hitch—Refers to a "Cut" or individual pattern executed by a receiver in which he drives straight at the defender over him for 5-6 yards stops, turning to the inside. In its basic form, it converts to a Fade against a hard corner.

Hitch/Fade Read—The process a receiver uses in running a Hitch of deciding whether to execute a basic Hitch or convert to a Fade. As a general rule, he converts to a Fade if he sees the cornerback's feet within five yards of him as he releases.

Hitch Run It—Variation of the Hitch used in the 96-196 "Quick Smash" route package in which a receiver runs the Hitch regardless of coverage as opposed to converting, at certain times, to the Fade.

Hot—
1. Basic passing game principle in which a quick throw is made to a receiver on a short pattern because a defender not accounted for in the protection rushes.
2. A variation of basic 90-190 protection in which a frontside linebacker is left unaccounted for in order to get five receivers into the pattern.

In—
1. An individual, in-breaking route in which the receiver breaks at 5 to 6 yards off the hip of another player and adjusts his angle based on his feel for coverage.
2. A route package that combines an In route with a Picker as well as complementary Box and Hitch routes.

Invert—A variation of Cover 2 in which the safeties lock down tighter, reading the end man on their side for run support or coverage while the cornerbacks essentially play loose man coverage.

Jam and Close Corner—A technique used by Cover 2 funnel cornerbacks in which they work hard to engage the receiver in a prolonged jam, "closing" him down as they do in an attempt to constrict the offense's routes into a tighter area.

Joker—A special term referring to a combination rush/drop player who plays from the edge of the defense in nickel packages, often operating from a "3-3" alignment.

Landmark—A specific spot on the field to which a receiver is to run his route.

Lanes—Refers to a goal line coverage technique similar to a Banjo in which defenders cover vertical lanes of the field, using man-to-man techniques within those lanes, switching receivers when a receiver leaves their lane.

Level corner—Refers to a Cover 2 cornerback who stays in the flat area regardless of the pattern he sees from the offense; i.e., under no circumstances does he gain depth toward the deep outside hole in the defense.

Locked Man Coverage—Form of man-to-man coverage in which defenders remain assigned to whichever receiver they aligned on initially, regardless of offensive motion or alignment change.

Low corner—Term for a cornerback who plays from a position less than five yards off the receiver on his side; can refer to a corner playing Covers 1, 2, or Quarters.

Low Swim—Release move in which a receiver cups and turns the wrist/forearm of a jam defender with the hand opposite the side of the direction to which he is releasing.

Mesh—The point at which two receivers cross closely.

Misdirection Route—A type of individual cut in which a player releases and fakes as though he is running a certain route, and then breaks opposite that route.

Misdirection Steps—Quick steps used at the line of scrimmage against a low cornerback to escape the jam and turn the cornerback away from the direction of the final release.

Near-stack—Refers to a bunched alignment that, through a receiver's motion into it, has become almost indistinguishable at the snap in terms of who the outside, inside and middle receivers in the alignment are.

Nod—A brief change of direction by a receiver designed to gain separation from a defender; it is done without losing speed.

Out—
1. Individual route similar to a Break Out that is specifically designed to work off the hip of a pick.
2. Route package that pairs and Out and a Picker with complementary Box and Hitch routes.

Outlet—Refers to a receiver to whom the quarterback can go if his initial reads do not get open; often this is a stationary receiver, preferably coming into as opposed to going away from the passer's line of vision. Generally it is this man's responsibility to determine whether he is open and communicate this to the quarterback. Also see *Dump*.

Outside—Structural tag that moves the routes of #2 and #3 "outside" to the #1 and #2 positions.

Packaged Side—Side of a route that has been set up or tagged to attack a specific defense.

Pattern—An overall distribution of individual cuts designed to work together in attacking defenses.

Pattern Read—Defensive technique in which zone defenders react specific ways to specific releases and routes by the offense, often employing man-to-man principles within a zone instead of just dropping to predetermined spots on the field.

Phony Acceleration—Technique by a receiver in which he uses exaggerated arm drive to convince a defender that he is gaining speed when he is not.

Pick—See *Rub*.

Picker—A route runner specifically designed in the "In" and "Out" route packages to create an impediment for the man covering the primary receiver.

Plant—An individual route that is essentially a cross between a traditional "Hook" and a "Hitch," broken to the inside at 8 to 9 yards in the same "pivoting" fashion as a Hitch; also a tag used in the 97-197 "Short" route package.

Play Action—Pass action in which a run is quickly faked prior to the quarterback setting up for a pass in order to hinder the coverage ability of one or more defenders (See Chapter 16).

Quick Out—
1. Individual route in which a receiver pushes to a depth of 4 yards and executes a Speed Turn, levelling at 6 yards. Often converts to a Fade against a low corner.
2. Route package that incorporates a Quick Out with a Seam and a Get Open route.

Quick Out/Fade Read—The process a receiver uses in running a Quick Out of deciding whether to execute a basic Quick Out or convert to a Fade. As a general rule, he converts to a Fade if he sees the cornerback's feet within five yards of him as he releases.

Quick/Quick Check—A packaged call in which the quarterback is given the option between two quick passes, choosing and checking to the one at the line of scrimmage that is best suited to the coverage he sees.

Quick Smash—
1. An individual route in which a receiver breaks to the corner at six yards, attempting to split the difference between the cornerback and safety on his side.
2. Route package that pairs a Quick Smash by an inside receiver with a Hitch Run It by an outside receiver.

R.A.C.—Refers to a receiver's yardage or opportunities to make yardage on the Run After the Catch.

Read Go—Individual route used in the 95-195 "Turn" package that functions primarily as a "clear out," but has the option to break down along the sideline if a low cornerback collapses hard to the inside to take away other parts of the package.

Read Player—The defender in a given route that the quarterback reads in order to know where to throw the ball.

Return—Refers to a type of receiver motion in which he sprints hard in motion one direction, passing the center, and then returns in motion the other direction before the snap.

Red Zone—Term used to describe the area of the field from the defense's 25-yard line to the defense's goal line.

Release Move—Any of four basic techniques that a receiver can use to avoid being collisioned/engaged by a jam defender so that he can release into his pattern unimpeded (see *Low Swim, Swim, Rip,* and *Slam and Spin*).

Rip—Release move in which a receiver uses the arm opposite his final release direction to "rip" up, under and through the armpit of his defender to the side to which he wants to release.

Robber—Refers to a coverage technique in which a player (usually a safety) who is expected to be in deep coverage moves to a short or intermediate area late in an attempt to disrupt normal offensive reads and "rob" certain pass routes.

Route—Refers to either an individual route by a receiver, or a series of routes within a package that work together.

Route Package—An overall passing attack concept that begins with a basic distribution of routes and can be varied by tags. In our system, packages are generally numbered 1-9 (e.g., "Short" package is "7").

Rub—Offensive term used to describe two receivers running routes in close proximity of each other in hopes of defenders colliding or being otherwise impeded.

Run/Quick Check—Packaged call in which the quarterback is given a running play and a quick pass to choose from; he makes his decision and check at the line of scrimmage, usually based on the number of defensive players in the box.

Seam—

1. Refers to an individual route in which an inside receiver releases straight up the field, looking to catch the ball in a crease between short and deep coverage. In certain situations, this route has the freedom to break into the deep middle.

2. General term that refers to open holes between zone defenders.

Seam Read—Basic read off a flat defender in which the quarterback throws the Seam route if the flat defender widens quickly, or throws some type of quick, outside route if the flat defender does not widen.

Separation—General offensive term that refers to a receiver creating distance between himself and the defender over him through good technique and/or acceleration to increase his chances of being open and getting the ball.

Shoot—Refers to a "Cut" or individual pattern executed by a receiver in which he sprints to the flat area at a depth of two to three yards.

Short—

1. A route in which an outside receiver breaks quickly underneath the defense, gaining depth to a level of 3 to 4 yards.

2. Route package that complements a Short route by outside players with Slants by interior receivers.

Short Side—See *Boundary.*

Sight Adjust—Refers to cases in which a receiver must break off his normal route quickly into an opening left by a blitzer that had originally been "counted" as a coverage player and is unaccounted for by protection.

Sit—An individual "cut" in which a tight end or wing receiver works to get in a hole between linebackers directly over the ball at a depth of 4 to 6 yards.

Six-Second Rule—Pre-snap discipline used by receivers in which they go through a specific mental checklist between the break of the huddle and the snap to get properly aligned, recognize coverage, and properly prepare mentally for the upcoming play.

Skinny—Descriptive technique term used to tell a inside-breaking receiver not to bring his route very far into the interior area of the defense; a "skinny" angle would be 60-70 degrees as opposed to 45 degrees.

Sky—Defensive term used to designate that the strong safety rotates up and has responsibility for the flat area.

Slam and Spin—A release move in which the receiver initiates contact in an attempt to "bounce" off a jamming defender, gaining enough temporary separation that he can release cleanly into his route.

Slant—
1. Refers to a "Cut" or individual pattern executed by a receiver in which he pushes up the field for five to six yards before making a distinct, angled break in.
2. A route package in which Slant cuts are paired with Shoot routes.

Slant Return—Individual route used on the backside of routes as an outlet in which a receiver runs a Slant, stops in between zone defenders, and waits for the quarterback to make eye contact with him so that he can continue to work to stay open until he gets the ball.

Snug—Offensive term used to bring a designated receiver in short motion toward the formation.

Soft Corner—Term used to describe a defensive cornerback who aligns and/or plays deeper than six yards from the receiver he's over.

Speed Turn—Refers to a type of break in which a receiver "rolls" into his break before flattening to the outside as opposed to breaking down, planting, and attempting to make a "square" break.

Split—
1. The distance a wide receiver aligns outside of the offensive tackle or tight end on his side.
2. An offensive term used to designate that both backs (H and F) align between the offensive guard and tackle to their designated side at a depth of four to five yards behind the center.
3. Specific pass route in which a receiver is told to "split" the defense and get open anywhere beyond 20 yards deep on the other side of the guard on his side.

Spot Drop—Refers to a general coverage technique/philosophy by underneath defenders in which they attempt to blanket the field by dropping to predetermined "spots" on the field and reacting from there.

Squat Corner—See *Low Corner* and *Level Corner*.

Squeeze—Offensive term used to set a group of receivers in tight proximity of each other approximately 4-5 yards outside the offensive tackle.

Stem—Refers to the initial upfield release of a receiver before he makes his break; he should be trained to make this portion of the route look identical every time.

Stick—An individual route in which a receiver plants and snaps his head inside at a depth of 4 yards with the option to work back to the outside later if he gets pressure from the inside out by a linebacker.

Switch—
1. An exchange of assignments by pass defenders when offensive receivers cross, often within a "Banjo" technique.
2. Offensive term used to tell #2 and #3 receivers to trade route assignments.
3. Offensive term used to describe a route in which two vertical receivers exchange route paths using crossed releases.

Stop—
1. An individual route in which a receiver gives every appearance of running a Fade until planting and working back outside at a depth of 10-11 yards. Ball is thrown on time.
2. A route package that pairs the Stop cut with a Seam route, providing the quarterback with a basic "Seam Read."

Stutter—General term applied to certain triple move routes in which they run the basic route twice, one on top of another (See Volume 1 Chapter 6).

Swim—Release move in which a receiver pushes in a defender's elbow to the side he wants to release and "swims" to get his other arm up and over the defender as he goes by.

Swing—An individual backfield route in which a back gets fast width while losing a bit of depth before turning up through the original position of the #1 receiver on his side. Often used either to control flat coverage or to provide an outlet.

Tag—Word or words added to the end of a play call to change one or more people's routes within a route package

Trace—Refers to a motion technique in which a receiver motions toward the center as though he's going across the formation, then turns and "traces" his steps back to his original position prior to the snap.

Trade—Structural tag that tells the #1 and #2 receivers to exchange route responsibilities.

Trail Technique—Technique used by man-to-man defenders in which they play tightly inside the receiver, "trailing" him by one-half to one full step wherever he breaks.

Triangle—
1. A defensive technique played by three players in which the outside defender has the first receiver to release outside, the middle defender has the first receiver to release deep, and the inside defender has the first receiver to release inside.
2. A type of route design in which three receivers' patterns are spaced so that they form a "triangle" that is difficult to defend.

Triple Move Route—A general category of individual cuts in which a receiver fakes running a route, then fakes another double move route off that original route before making a final break. See *Stutter* illustrations in Volume 1 Chapter 6.

Trips—Any formation with three receivers on a side.

Turn—
1. Refers to a "Cut" or individual pattern executed by an inside receiver in which he releases upfield for 6 yards and then breaks outside, accelerating away from man coverage, or "turning" into the first available hole in a zone coverage.
2. The "5" route package in the quick passing game that is built off a read of the first short defender inside the cornerback, generally thrown to either a Turn route or a Shoot route frontside.

Twist—Offensive term that tells the #2 and #3 receivers that they are to cross each other's releases, after which they execute their normal assignments.

Uncovered Receiver—A receiver who, prior to the snap has no defender in close enough proximity of him to prevent him from catching the ball quickly and making at least four yards.

Under—Tag given to a backside receiver telling him to run a Shallow Cross pattern.

Weave—Refers to the initial angle of release taken by a receiver.

Wheel—

1. A route executed by a man in motion in which he simply turns and faces the quarterback if the defender over him is soft, or Fades if the defender over him is tight.

2. A quick route package that combines frontside and backside Slants with a Wheel and a Split route.

Whip—Route in which a receiver angles inside as if he is going to cross at a depth of 5 to 6 yards, then plants and accelerates back the opposite way without gaining any additional depth; also a "tag" that may be used with the 91-191 "Hitch" or 96-196 "Quick Smash" route packages.

Wide Field—Refers to the side of the field that, because of ball placement, has the most lateral space in which to operate.

Wrap—Offensive term that tells the #1 and #2 receiver that they are to cross each other's initial release and change normal assignments.

Zone Blitz—Defensive technique in which extra rushers are brought while zone defense is played by defenders behind or a combination of linebackers and secondary people rush with defensive linemen dropping into the areas they vacated to cover after feigning a rush to "use up" offensive blocks.

Andrew Coverdale spent the past football season as the Quarterbacks and Tight Ends Coach at Taylor University. Prior to working at Taylor, he coached for three years at the high school level. While at Northwestern High School in Kokomo, Indiana, he was promoted to Offensive Coordinator and gave clinic presentations on the Tigers' "Bunch" Passing Package. At Noblesville High School, he coached receivers, during which time a player under his direction broke the school record for receptions and earned AAAAA all-state honors.

Coverdale has previously coauthored, *The Bunch Attack*. He has contributed in articles in both the Indians and Wisconsin quarterly coaches' manuals, and works as a receiver's instructor at the Bishop-Dullaghan Passing Clinic. He may be contacted via e-mail at: andy_coverdale@mail.nobl.k12.in.us or aecover@sprynet.com

Dan Robinson spent the past two seasons as the Offensive Coordinator at Taylor University, after being a high school head coach for 13 years at Northwestern High School. Prior to his duties at Northwestern, he was the Offensive Coordinator at East Central High School for nine years.

During his tenure at Northwestern, the Tigers became known for their pro passing attack and explosive offense, which helped produce two undefeated regular seasons, four Mid-Indiana Conference titles, and a trip to the Indiana AAA State Championship Game. The Tigers were among the state's top ten passing teams several times during his tenure, leading the state in 1983. Six quarterbacks under Coach Robinson's tutelage earned all-state honors.

He has worked various summer camps for many years, including the Bishop-Dullaghan Passing Clinic, where he wrote the camp's receiver manual. He has also lectured at clinics throughout Indiana and the Midwest on different aspects of Northwestern and Taylor's offense, and published several articles on different aspects of offensive football. Robinson has also coauthored *The Bunch Attack* with Coach Coverdale. He may be contacted via e-mail at: robinsond@nwsc.k12.in.us